MW00562922

"Beyer and Jones are great storytellers, and here to the greatest story of all. The result i of us hear the grand story afresh and learn it saves and changes lives."

—BILL T. ARNOLD
Asbury Theological Seminary

"*Scripture's Grand Story through the Old Testament* is a fascinating overview of each book of the Old Testament. As readers desire to understand the masterpiece of God's work, this Bible tool will present an outstanding review of each book. Beyer and Jones share their insights in an organized and prolific way."

—MARK A. SMITH
Columbia International University

"In our era of well-documented and widely bemoaned biblical illiteracy, Beyer and Jones have determined not merely, as it were, to curse the darkness but instead to light a candle. The Old Testament's structure and literary diversity are illuminated clearly and cogently so that those unfamiliar with or intimidated by the Bible can elicit its meaning, embrace its central character, and enter into his global mission."

—RALPH E. ENLOW JR.
International Alliance for Christian Education

"This is an exceptional resource and tool for your everyday relationship with Jesus. As you journey through this book, you will come to a greater understanding of Scripture and your place in God's story."

—BRAD COOPER
NewSpring Church

"Beyer and Jones . . . summarize the contents of the Old Testament book by book and outline its storyline. They provide an easily accessible overview that helps Bible reading become understandable and spiritually profitable . . . With Beyer and Jones's help, the student of the Old Testament will read with increased confidence and understanding."

—JOHN CRUTCHFIELD
Columbia International University

"*Scripture's Grand Story through the Old Testament* provides a creative overview of the Old Testament. This work reveals how each book points to Jesus as the central figure in the grand story in an easy-to-follow manner. Many will use these in discipleship circles with new believers, and it could serve as a main text in undergraduate courses . . . This work will be a blessing to churches and college alike."

—ANDRE ROGERS
Columbia Metro Baptist Association

Scripture's Grand Story through the Old Testament

Scripture's Grand Story through the Old Testament

Bryan Beyer
and
Bill Jones

WIPF & STOCK · Eugene, Oregon

SCRIPTURE'S GRAND STORY THROUGH THE OLD TESTAMENT

Copyright © 2022 Bryan Beyer and Bill Jones. All rights reserved. Except for brief quotations in critical publications or reviews, no part of this book may be reproduced in any manner without prior written permission from the publisher. Write: Permissions, Wipf and Stock Publishers, 199 W. 8th Ave., Suite 3, Eugene, OR 97401.

Wipf & Stock
An Imprint of Wipf and Stock Publishers
199 W. 8th Ave., Suite 3
Eugene, OR 97401

www.wipfandstock.com

PAPERBACK ISBN: 978-1-6667-0245-3
HARDCOVER ISBN: 978-1-6667-0246-0
EBOOK ISBN: 978-1-6667-0247-7

01/10/22

All Scripture quotations, unless otherwise indicated, are taken from the Holy Bible, New International Version,® NIV.® Copyright © 1973, 1978, 1984, 2011 by Biblica, Inc.® Used by permission of Zondervan (www.zondervan.com). All rights reserved worldwide. The NIV and New International Version are trademarks registered in the United States Patent and Trademark Office by Biblica, Inc.®

To Yvonne Beyer and Debby Jones, two women of noble character
(Prov 31:10)

So I stand here and testify to small and great alike. I am saying nothing beyond what the prophets and Moses said would happen—that the Messiah would suffer and, as the first to rise from the dead, would bring the message of light to his own people and to the Gentiles.

THE APOSTLE PAUL, ACTS 26:22–23

Contents

Acknowledgments | ix

List of Abbreviations | xi

Introduction: The Bible's Grand Story | 1

Part One: The Torah ("Instruction") | 13

    1   Genesis | 15

    2   Exodus | 28

    3   Leviticus | 35

    4   Numbers | 42

    5   Deuteronomy | 53

Part Two: The Historical Books | 63

    6   Joshua | 65

    7   Judges, Ruth | 74

    8   1–2 Samuel | 87

    9   1–2 Kings | 101

    10   1–2 Chronicles | 110

    11   Ezra, Nehemiah, and Esther | 121

Part Three: The Poetical Books | 133

    12   Job | 135

    13   Psalms | 141

    14   Proverbs | 149

    15   Ecclesiastes | 153

    16   Song of Solomon | 157

Part Four: The Prophetic Books | 161

    17   Isaiah | 163

    18   Jeremiah and Lamentations | 169

    19   Ezekiel | 177

    20   Daniel | 183

    21   Hosea, Joel, and Amos | 191

    22   Obadiah, Jonah, and Micah | 201

    23   Nahum, Habakkuk, and Zephaniah | 213

    24   Haggai, Zechariah, and Malachi | 221

Epilogue: "Brethren, What Shall We Do?" | 233

Bibliography | 235

Subject Index | 237

Scripture Index | 257

Acknowledgments

As UNIVERSITY LEADERS, WE know the value of teamwork, and the publication of *Scripture's Grand Story through the Old Testament* provides another example of a great team effort. The authors accept responsibility for any errors in the final work, but we want to thank the many who have helped bring this project to fruition.

We express our gratitude to the Wipf and Stock team for their capable assistance. Matthew Wimer and George Callihan initially engaged us in the project, and Kara Barlow and Emily Callihan assisted in many logistical aspects. We also appreciate the roles Rebecca Abbott and Rachel Saunders played in copyediting and finalizing the manuscript.

We are grateful to serve at Columbia International University, an institution whose purpose is to educate students from a biblical worldview to impact the nations with the message of Christ. Indeed, many at CIU have assisted us as we worked on this book. Nicole Brooker transcribed much of the manuscript and proofread and commented on the initial draft. Tuesday Wilson and Chris Carlson completed the rest of the transcription and offered additional insights. Dr. Sandra Young, director of CIU's English major and division chair of CIU's liberal arts division, reviewed the revised manuscript despite a pressing schedule and offered valuable counsel. Special thanks to all of you!

Acknowledgments

We are deeply grateful for our wives, Yvonne Beyer and Debby Jones, and it is our joy to dedicate this book to them.

Finally, we express overwhelming gratitude to our Lord, who has chosen to include us in the incredible story he is still writing.

Bryan Beyer and Bill Jones

List of Abbreviations

Bible Books

Old Testament

Gen	Genesis	Job	Job
Exod	Exodus	Ps/Pss	Psalms
Lev	Leviticus	Prov	Proverbs
Num	Numbers	Eccl	Ecclesiastes
Deut	Deuteronomy	Song	Song of Songs
Josh	Joshua	Isa	Isaiah
Judg	Judges	Jer	Jeremiah
Ruth	Ruth	Lam	Lamentations
1–2 Sam	1–2 Samuel	Ezek	Ezekiel
1–2 Kgs	1–2 Kings	Dan	Daniel
1–2 Chr	1–2 Chronicles	Hos	Hosea
Ezra	Ezra	Joel	Joel
Neh	Nehemiah	Amos	Amos
Esth	Esther	Obad	Obadiah

Jonah	Jonah	Zeph	Zephaniah
Mic	Micah	Hag	Haggai
Nah	Nahum	Zech	Zechariah
Hab	Habakkuk	Mal	Malachi

New Testament

Matt	Matthew	1–2 Thess	1–2 Thessalonians
Mark	Mark	1–2 Tim	1–2 Timothy
Luke	Luke	Titus	Titus
John	John	Phlm	Philemon
Acts	Acts	Heb	Hebrews
Rom	Romans	Jas	James
1–2 Cor	1–2 Corinthians	1–2 Pet	1–2 Peter
Gal	Galatians	1–2–3 John	1–2–3 John
Eph	Ephesians	Jude	Jude
Phil	Philippians	Rev	Revelation
Col	Colossians		

Introduction

The Bible's Grand Story

The Power of Stories

WHAT COMES TO YOUR mind when you hear the word *story*? Throughout the ages, certain stories have impacted many generations. For some, these are children's stories; they may be fairy tales or they may be real life stories, but they have retained their relevance over time. Over the centuries, certain stories or novels have continued to sell well. The message in those stories transcends time and culture. Consequently, people use them to teach important life lessons.

Stories Evoke Childhood Memories

Many of us remember our parents reading stories when we were children. Perhaps our bedtime ritual included hearing a story to help us fall asleep. To be sure, some children might have requested a story to forestall bedtime, but in many cases, story time provides a time for parents and children to connect at the end of the day.

Sometimes the stories we heard as children were true. Perhaps our parents read us stories from the Bible. Others chose history books to provide historical accounts of days gone by. Perhaps at the end of each story, question and answer time would follow. Some parents used these times as teaching moments, making sure the children understood the implications of the story they heard.

However, sometimes the stories we heard were not true. That is, they were true to life, but the events in them did not actually occur. Nonetheless, such stories often had a powerful moral to them. Stories such as *Aesop's Fables* remain popular over the generations, because the stories they relate contain teachings that help people live better lives.

Stories Can Profoundly Impact Our Lives

Why do we remember the stories that profoundly impact us? First, people remember stories because they relate truth in a way that's easy to remember. Stories tie details together, and in doing so they help the hearer remember important items. The details of the story may parallel details in people's lives, so as they listen, they can relate to them.

Second, many stories are true to life, even if they are not technically true. During his earthly ministry, Jesus used many parables—short stories with a teaching point. People who listened to Jesus's stories could relate to his stories even though Jesus wasn't describing a particular individual or group of individuals. Jesus used their shared experiences to drive home life issues.

The Power of Great Story Tellers

We all know great storytellers, whether they be teachers, pastors, family members, or friends. What do these storytellers have in common? How do they so captivate their listeners?

First, great storytellers tell their stories passionately. They are deeply interested in what they are sharing, and everyone in the room catches their enthusiasm. Storytellers find it easy to share their stories' impact because their stories impacted them first.

Second, great storytellers know how to highlight key details. Listeners can anticipate when important details are coming from the storyteller's heightened sense of excitement. Great storytellers also know how to bring a story together to its grand conclusion.

Most of us have childhood memories of stories we heard. These memories affirm the power of stories on our lives. We also know great storytellers who have helped us grasp important lessons through their stories. But there is one story that started at the beginning of time and will continue through the ages. That story has the potential to impact our lives and change them forever. It is a story that both has been written and continues to be written. That story is found in the Bible.

The Bible Contains the Greatest Story

The Bible's subject matter makes it the greatest story ever told. First, it tells us about the God of history, who is writing his story. (Catch the wordplay?) Second, it tells us about life, and it itself is life. Third, it tells us about Jesus, the Son of God, who secured our salvation two thousand years ago.

It Tells Us about the God of History, Who Is Writing His Story

Some people might think of the Bible as a history book, and indeed the Bible contains many facts of history. It tells us about Abraham and Sarah, an elderly couple from whom the Jewish people came. It records many details about Israel's exit from Egypt and its entry into Canaan. During the course of Israel's history, the nation had many good kings and many bad kings. In many of the Bible's historical and prophetic books, the writers describe their successes and failures.

The Bible also tells us about the God of history. The Scriptures are clear that God is in control of history, raising up nations, bringing down nations, and leading the events of history to the end he has determined. Some religions of the world view history as cyclical—going around and around and around forever. However, the Bible says history is linear; that is, history is going somewhere. The biblical writers credit to God the great events of history.

Third, according to the Bible, history is *his* story. That is, when the Scriptures record events of history, they are concerned mostly about highlighting the key events in the great story God is writing in this world. An old song proclaims, "He's got the whole world in his hands." This is the testimony of the God of history and his story.

It Tells Us about Life, and It Itself Is Life

The Bible also contains the greatest story ever told in that it tells us about life. The Bible records how after the creation of man, God breathed into him the breath of life, and man became a living being. God also gave his people commandments so that they would know what he expected of them and what kind of life pleased God. God designed life, and to live according to his principles was to embrace life in its fullness.

This fullness of life is what the Bible describes in Deuteronomy 32:47. There, Moses assured the people of Israel that the word of God was no idle word. Rather, it was their life. God's word did not represent the most important teachings of life; instead, it itself was life.

It Tells Us about Jesus, the Son of God

Third, the Bible contains the greatest story ever told in that it tells us about Jesus. We will talk more about this in the pages ahead, but the entry of Jesus, God's Son, on the pages of history two thousand years ago marked a decisive turning point in the story God was writing.

The Bible contains the greatest story ever told, because it tells us about history and about the God of history. It tells us about life and how it itself is life. It also tells us about Jesus the Son of God. If the Bible has such a wonderful story to tell, why don't more people read it?

Why Don't More People Read the Bible?

The English language has seemingly countless numbers of Bible translations. Why, then, don't more people read the Bible? Let's look at some of the common reasons people give.

"I got bogged down in all the 'begats'"

Some people will say, "I started reading the Bible once, but I got bogged down in all the 'begats.'" What they usually mean is that they began by reading the book of Genesis—the first book of the Bible—and as they read, they soon found its terminology unfamiliar to them. When they began to read family trees, they lost the connection somehow and used that as a reason to put down the book. Rather than skipping ahead to something that looked more interesting, they simply stopped reading.

"I just couldn't relate to all those picky laws in Leviticus"

Others stop reading because they come to books such as Leviticus where they find "nitpicky laws" that just don't seem to relate to us today. Indeed, many items in the law of Moses sound quite foreign to us. They either contain commands to do things we would never think of doing or prohibitions against things we would never think of doing.

Much of our confusion lies in the fact that the Bible wasn't written to us. It was written *for* us, but it wasn't first and foremost *to* us. It was written to another people—Israel—in another time, so we have to understand what was going on historically and culturally for some of it to make sense. Nonetheless, many today find it harder to relate to some of the stipulations in the law of Moses, and for that reason they stop reading the Bible.

"The prophets all seem to say the same thing—God's mad at his people"

Others who have tried to read the Bible come away with the notion that all the prophets say the same thing. They all bring bad news about how upset God is with his people! To be sure, the prophets do proclaim God's judgment against his people for violating the covenant he made with them. At the same time, the prophets tell us much more about God's coming salvation and about the blessing he will bring his people when they turn back to him. Usually when one understands the prophets' role in biblical history and takes the time to read them a bit more carefully, the distinctives begin to appear. Nonetheless, the judgmental tone of some of the prophetic passages discourages some readers.

"All those names and places are really hard to pronounce"

Some people try reading the Bible and stop because they get stuck on the difficult pronunciation of unfamiliar names and places. At first this may not seem like a good reason to stop reading the Bible, but perhaps when we do not immediately identify with the names we read or with the places about which we read, that creates a distance between us and the stories of the Bible. Many of us have not been to Jerusalem, Nazareth, or Megiddo; where are they in Israel? Where is Dan in relationship to Beersheba? How far is Bethlehem from Jerusalem? Or sometimes in a Sunday school class, people are called upon to read and are embarrassed because they don't know how to pronounce a particular name. It's understandable.

In sum, people provide a lot of reasons why they started reading the Bible at one time and then put it down, never to pick it up again. Many of the Bible's distinctives appear foreign to modern readers, and indeed, the Bible is different from many books. However, it is precisely these distinctives that make the Bible so important to study and understand. Let's turn to that topic now.

How Is the Bible Unique?

In the prior section, we looked at many reasons people give for not reading the Bible. Indeed, behind some of those reasons lies the fact that the Bible is unique. At the same time, its uniqueness makes the Bible all the more important to read and understand. Let's look at various issues in turn.

It's Sixty-Six Books, Yet It's One Book

The Bible contains sixty-six books and at the same time is just one book. Some of the portions we call books are in fact quite short; we might more accurately refer to some of them as letters or brief messages. For the sake of convention, however, we'll use the term books.

The Bible contains thirty-nine books in the Old Testament and twenty-seven books in the New Testament. To a large extent, the Old Testament records the formation of the nation of Israel and the great story God is writing in his people and through his people. But the Old Testament ends an incomplete story; it remains for the New Testament to announce the fulfillment of that to which the Old Testament pointed. The thirty-nine books of the Old Testament and the twenty-seven books of the New Testament add up to sixty-six books that tell one story.

It Was Written over 1,500 Years, but with One Theme: Jesus

The Bible is also unique in that it was written over 1,500 years and yet contains one central theme. God's Son, the Lord Jesus Christ, receives the lead role in God's story. In the Old Testament, the term messiah refers to an anointed one who would come and establish God's kingdom. During that Old Testament period, prophets, priests, and kings all sometimes were designated by this term; however, Jesus came as the ultimate Anointed One, the ultimate Messiah of God.

Understanding the central role of Jesus in God's story is important, because we then see how each book of the Bible highlights Jesus's place in the story God is writing as it unfolded. Let's look at each step in the development of this theme.

Promised in the Old Testament (Genesis–Malachi)

First, the Messiah was promised in the Old Testament (Genesis–Malachi). As early as the book of Genesis, God announced the coming of One who would destroy evil forever. God's promise to Abraham announced that through him and his descendant, all the world would receive God's blessing. The prophets likewise looked ahead to a day when God would establish his Messiah as ruler of the world. Even as the Old Testament ended, the prophet Malachi warned of the coming day of God's judgment, followed by the day of God's salvation.

Presented in the Gospels (Matthew, Mark, Luke, John)

Second, the coming of Jesus the Messiah is then presented in the Gospels (Matthew, Mark, Luke, John). Each of the four writers has a slightly different perspective, but they all point to Jesus as the fulfillment of the Old Testament prophetic message. In him, God's kingdom has come to earth. The Gospels also record Jesus's death and resurrection—an event that secured the salvation of all who place their faith in him.

Proclaimed in the Book of Acts

Third, Jesus's place in the story God is writing is proclaimed in the book of Acts. Before Jesus left earth, he commanded his disciples to be his witnesses in Jerusalem, Judea, Samaria, and the uttermost parts of the earth. The book of Acts records how the gospel went forth as the disciples could not keep quiet about what they had seen and heard regarding their risen Lord Jesus.

Introduction

Propounded in the Epistles (Romans–Jude)

Jesus's lead role in God's story is also propounded in the Epistles (Romans–Jude). The Epistles are letters written by individuals to churches or to other individuals. These letters encourage, admonish, reprove, and exhort Jesus's followers to follow him faithfully and confidently. They provide further instruction on how God's people should live in light of Jesus's first coming and in light of his second coming.

Praised in the Book of Revelation

Finally, Jesus's place in God's story is praised in the book of Revelation. The final book of the Bible records how one day, human history as we know it will come to an end when the Lord Jesus returns to establish his everlasting kingdom. On that day, all the world will know him as King of kings and Lord of lords. The Bible was written over a period of 1,500 years, but it has one central theme: Jesus.

It Was Written by Forty Human Authors, but Has One Divine Author

The Bible is also unique in that although it is written by forty different human authors, it has one divine Author. The Scriptures themselves talk about how God interacted with the writers of Scripture so as to allow their personalities to come through in what they wrote. At the same time, God the Holy Spirit guided the process so that the finished product accurately conveyed what God wanted written. Consequently, the Bible is not merely the word of man, but it is the word of God. It has forty human authors, but it has one divine Author, who ties everything together.

It Contains Many Stories, but It Is One Great Story

The Bible is also unique in that it contains many stories, and at the same time is one great story. Throughout its pages, the Bible highlights many exciting events and accounts of those who followed God's directives. It also records the failures of many to obey God, and we can learn from the sad consequences they experienced as well. Some of the stories are quite powerful and could stand on their own as classics. At the same time, all these stories form mere subplots in the grand narrative of the one great story.

It Places a Call on Our Lives to Read It and to Live It

Finally, the Bible is unique in that it places a call on our lives to read it and to live it. Throughout history, many books have been written, and many have deeply impacted both their generation and future generations. At the same time, no book has impacted life as much as the Bible. Since it is the word of God, it commands us to read it, but also to live it out.

First, since the Bible is God's story, we should want to read it so we can master the word of God. The Old Testament records the account of the priest and scribe Ezra, who desired to study the word of God carefully so that he could live it out and be an example while teaching others. The writer of Psalm 119 crafted one hundred seventy-six verses that extolled the virtues of God's word and the blessing of living by it. We should want to read God's word so that we can master it. With all the translations and helps available, we can do this if we set our minds to it.

Second, since the Bible is God's story, we should want to read it so the word of God can master us. Jesus said that he came so that we might have abundant life. This abundant life comes from knowing God. If we read the word of God and master it and become an expert on its content, that's good. At the same time, we want the word of God to master us. We want it to so lay hold of our lives that we are never the same. As we live the life God describes in his word, we become the people he intended for us to be.

Who Should Read This Book?

We have designed this book especially for three categories of people. If one of these categories fits your situation, we believe this book will help you.

First, we have designed this book for people with little biblical knowledge. Perhaps this is your first book on the subject, and you're looking for something that will help you gain a basic framework for understanding the Bible. If this is you, we believe you will find this book helpful. If you are looking for something even more basic, consider *Putting Together the Puzzle of the Old Testament* and *Putting Together the Puzzle of the New Testament*, both by Bill Jones.

Second, others may have already read the books mentioned above or have a basic knowledge of the Bible. You might be looking for that next step in a more detailed Bible study. Perhaps you understand the basic skeleton of Scripture, but you are looking for a tool to help you put some meat on the bones. If so, this book can help you do that.

Third, other readers may be familiar with some of the Bible stories. Many people who have spent their lives in the church may find themselves in this category, because they have studied various Bible passages but without seeing how they all relate together. Such readers are looking for an essential framework to the knowledge they already have; in contrast to the second category of readers above, you're looking to provide a skeleton for the meat. If that's your situation, we believe this book will help you.

We want our readers to become more familiar with the big story of Scripture so that as they read it, they will be able to understand it and embrace it more fully. If we help you do that, we will have succeeded.

What's the Primary Goal of This Book?

In this book, we are focusing on the first major section of God's story: the Old Testament. We had two primary goals as we set out to write this book: to make the Scripture's message understandable, and to help you understand your place in God's story.

We Want to Make the Bible Understandable

First, we want to make the Bible understandable. Let us say up front that many parts of the Bible are already understandable; nevertheless, we hope to assist readers in understanding the overall story and how it fits together. But once you have such a framework for Bible study, we want you to read the Bible through, cover to cover. We hope that once you are armed with essential tools, you will be able to study the Bible for yourself, because ultimately, it is the Bible, not books about the Bible, that changes lives.

We have written this book to help break down any barriers that might stand between you and the Bible. We want people to feel comfortable picking up the Bible and reading it.

Introduction

We Want You to Understand Your Place in God's Story

We have also written this book because we want you to better understand your place in the story God is writing. Earlier in the chapter, we talked about the amazing story he has written in Scripture. Indeed, the Bible contains the greatest story ever told, but the story is not finished. God is still writing it!

The apostle Peter told us that God's word reveals all we need for life and godliness (2 Pet 1:3). That means that all we really need to follow Jesus and to live life as God designed it is the instruction we find in his word.

The most amazing part of all to God's story is that he wants to include us in that story. Sometimes people say, "I believe it is important to include God in my plans," but God does not really want that. Rather, he wants to include us in *his* plan—in the great story he is writing. The Almighty God, King of the universe, has included you in his plan, and he wants you to lay hold of your part and go for it, because you will find your fulfillment in fulfilling your role in his story.

As we said earlier, as we allow the word of God to master us, we lay hold of the life for which God created us. That's when life really begins. Are you ready to begin the journey?

Part One

The Torah ("Instruction")

*Also sometimes called
the Law,
the Pentateuch ("five scrolls"), or
the Five Books of Moses (Israel's great leader)*

Books Covered

Genesis
Exodus
Leviticus
Numbers
Deuteronomy

1

Genesis

THE FIRST FIVE BOOKS of the Bible—Genesis, Exodus, Leviticus, Numbers, and Deuteronomy—are also sometimes called the Pentateuch or Torah. Pentateuch comes from two Greek words and means "five scrolls," a term that highlights the original format for these books. The word Torah literally means "teaching" or "instruction," and sometimes translators render it "law." The Bible affirms in many places that Moses, Israel's great leader, was responsible for the composition of these five books. We'll learn more about Moses in the chapter on Exodus.

The book of Genesis divides into two major parts, though the parts are not equal in length. Genesis 1–11 highlights what many Bible scholars have called the *primeval history*, a period of time in which key events lay a foundation for the rest of God's story.[1] The second part of Genesis, Genesis 12–50, has often been called the *patriarchal narrative* and describes the founders of the Jewish faith as God began to carve out a people for his name.[2] Genesis 1–11 contains four key events: creation (chs. 1–2), the fall (chs. 3–5), the flood (chs. 6–9), and the tower of Babel (chs. 10–11).

---

1. Jones, *Puzzle of the Old Testament*, 8, refers to this as the Nothing Era.
2. Jones, *Puzzle of the Old Testament*, 8, describes this as the Something Era.

Primeval History (Gen 1–11)

Creation (Gen 1–2)

Many ancient Near Eastern societies wrote their own creation accounts.[3] In general, however, all of those creation accounts described many gods who together brought the world and humanity into existence. Genesis 1, however, records the deliberate actions of an all-knowing God—one God—who both spoke the universe into existence and then created the matter from which he would form everything. Genesis 1 lays out a careful sequence God established to put everything in its place. Scholars have interpreted these verses of Genesis in different ways. Some view the six days of creation as literal six-day periods. Others interpret them as periods of time. Regardless of what interpretation we take on this issue, what remains clear in Genesis 1 is that the creation of the world is the creation brought about by one God, not many, and that our God is a God of order, not of chaos.

Genesis 1:1—2:4 records the big picture of God creating the world and placing humanity in it. Genesis 2 provides somewhat of a zoom lens approach, where the text zooms in on particular details of the creation of man and woman as parents of the human race. The Lord formed man from the ground and woman from man. At the end of Genesis 2, Adam and Eve, humanity's first couple, stood together in a perfect world.

God had given humanity the responsibility to till the garden of Eden in which he had placed them. In the midst of that garden lay the tree of the knowledge of good and evil, a tree from which God commanded them not to eat. If they did, they would be doomed to die. What happened with regard to that tree is described in the next section.

The Fall (Gen 3–5)

Genesis 3 records the sad fall of humanity into sin. The text records a dialogue between Eve and a deceptive serpent whom Scripture later identifies as Satan. The serpent subtly twisted God's words, assuring Adam and Eve they would become like God, knowing good and evil. The text records the fateful moment when, after contemplating the desirability of the fruit, they partook of it together (Gen 3:6). Both Adam and Eve now knew good and

---

3. For a sampling of these texts, see Arnold and Beyer, eds., *Readings from Ancient Near East*, 13–66.

evil firsthand and experientially knew evil for the ugly thing it was. The text records how God banished Adam and Eve from the garden of Eden, an action that really involved a measure of grace, so that they would not lay hold of the tree of life and live forever (Gen 3:22). He also spoke words of consequence to the woman and man but words of judgment to the serpent. One day, the seed of the woman would crush the serpent forever (Gen 3:16). Perhaps Adam and Eve wondered if the serpent's destruction would mean that one day, God would let them return to Eden. Indeed, the rest of the Bible points to a great day when God will give his people a new world in which to live. However, the end of the story reveals he has something much greater than the garden of Eden to give us.

Adam and Eve began life apart from the garden of Eden in chapter 4, which records the birth of their two sons Cain and Abel. The sad truth of sin's ugliness is highlighted when sin led to murder in one generation, as Cain became jealous of Abel and killed him. Cain then fled the area, leaving Adam and Eve bereaved of both their sons in one day. However, God's grace began anew for Adam and Eve with the birth of a new son they named Seth.

God had told Adam and Eve that sin would lead to death, and Genesis 5 records how it did. The family tree mentions the lives of many individuals, ending each individual's record with the words "and he died" (Gen 5:5, 8, 11, etc.). The end of chapter 5, however, breaks the chain by mentioning the birth of Noah, who would figure prominently in Genesis 6–9.

The Flood (Gen 6–9)

Genesis 1–11 records how God repeatedly answered humanity's sin with grace. God created people, but when they fell into sin, God promised them a Savior (Gen 3:16). Genesis 6 records God's sorrow at making humanity when he saw the extent to which sin had pervaded the earth. Nonetheless, Noah found grace in God's eyes, and God determined he would continue writing the great story he had begun in Genesis 1. He instructed Noah to build an ark, a large ship, on which Noah would take his family and representatives of the animal kingdom.

Genesis 7 and 8 record the destruction of the earth through this great deluge. The "floodgates of the sky were opened" as "the fountains of the great deep burst forth" (Gen 7:11). The text gives the impression that water was falling from above and churning up from below. All life perished except for the life God preserved on the ark.

Genesis 9 records the exit of Noah's family and all of the animals from the ark after spending a year and ten days there (Gen 8:15–22). Noah gratefully offered a sacrifice to God, and in response, God established the rainbow as his covenant in the sky. It was a reminder that he would never again destroy the earth by flood (Gen 9:11–17). The narrative about Noah tragically ends with an unfortunate account of drunkenness and shame (Gen 9:20–29). It serves as a reminder that God can use sinful people to accomplish his perfect purpose.

The Tower of Babel (Gen 10–11)

The biblical writers often provide us the big picture first and then fill in key details. This happened in Genesis 1, where the first verse tells us the big picture: "In the beginning God created the heavens and the earth" (Gen 1:1). The rest of Genesis 1 then describes the six days of creation in more detail. Chapter 2 provides a zoom lens in which we focus on the creation of man and woman in the garden. Chapter 10 records the big picture of how the families of Noah's sons Shem, Ham, and Japheth spread across the earth. The detail to which the text highlights the various people groups—some known to us, others unknown to us—highlights God's heart for the nations. The people he created turned their backs on him, but he continued to reach out to them. Genesis 10 thus reminds believers of the task left ahead to impact the nations with the message of Christ. It highlights the various people groups according to their ancestry and languages.

After describing the big picture of the development of people groups in chapter 10, Moses then focused on where languages originated. How was it that people who came from one ancestor ended up speaking many different languages and dialects? The answer lies in Genesis 11:1–9.

As Noah and his family left the ark, God commanded them to fill the earth (Gen 9:1, 7). This command was a reiteration of God's command at the beginning of creation (Gen 1:28). However, a large population settled in Shinar (part of modern southern Iraq) and determined they would establish a civilization there. Further, they would build a tower to the heavens that they might make a name for themselves. Thus, their sin seems twofold: they wanted to stay in one place in defiance of God's command to fill the earth, and they wanted to make a name for themselves when they should have been glorifying the God of heaven. By confusing the people's languages, God ensured the project would cease, and in fact, it did. The people learned the hard way that God's commands were not to be taken lightly as they scattered across the face of the earth.

Nonetheless, God's amazing story continued. Moses, the author, reintroduced the genealogical line he had temporarily ceased in chapter 5. Interestingly, the words "and he died," so obviously present in chapter 5's list, do not appear here. This does not mean the people recorded in Genesis 11 did not die, but rather, that God was doing a new work on behalf of the living.

In Genesis 11:26-30, the Bible mentions a man named Terah and his sons Abram, Nahor, and Haran. It also mentions Abram's barren wife Sarai (later renamed Sarah) and the reader is immediately confronted with the question, "Why does the text note that Sarai was unable to conceive children?" We will find out soon enough. At any rate, the text records how Terah and his family intended to travel as far as Canaan but instead settled in Haran in upper Syria.

Genesis 11:32 records that Terah died in Haran. It was the end of Terah's life, but it was not the end of God's purpose through Terah's line. God would now continue his incredible story through Terah's firstborn son Abram, later known as Abraham.

The Patriarchal Period (Gen 12–50)

Genesis 12–50 records the patriarchal period. The word patriarchs literally means "founding fathers" and denotes those who laid a foundation for the nation of Israel. The book of Genesis focuses especially on the lives of four of those patriarchs: Abraham, Isaac, Jacob, and Joseph.

The Story of Abraham (Gen 12–25)

God told Abraham to leave his land and journey to a land God would show him (Gen 12:1). In other words, Abraham did something quite countercultural: he left his homeland. Furthermore, he left it for a new land he did not yet know.

God told Abraham he would make him a great nation, a promise Abraham must have pondered seriously. One needed people to comprise a nation, and Sarah his wife was barren. God further promised his blessing on Abraham and his house, a promise he would repeat in later generations: "In you, all the families of the earth will be blessed" (Gen 12:3). Thus, the incredible story God is writing took a dramatic turn about 2100

BC. Abraham and Sarah went out, not knowing where they were going but determined to follow where God led. Genesis 12:3 again points us to Jesus, because Jesus came from Abraham's line. Are you willing to follow God even if you don't know what your next steps are?

Genesis 3:16 promised that one day, Jesus, the seed of the woman, would crush the serpent's head and destroy sin forever. Genesis 12:3 described the blessing that would one day come to people everywhere because of Abraham. The apostle Paul, later writing in the book of Galatians, considered this an early statement of the gospel, for through Jesus, Abraham's descendant, great blessing came to the world (Gal 3:8).

Abraham's travels (Gen 12:4—14:24) feature many spiritual ups and downs as Abraham pursued God's directive and promise. He arrived at a place called Shechem in Canaan's heartland, and God told him he was now in the land God would give to Abraham's descendants (Gen 12:6–7). Abraham journeyed southward to Egypt, where he became concerned the Egyptians would kill him and take Sarah as their own. Note the irony: Abraham had the faith to go hundreds of miles, not knowing where he was going, but was concerned God might forget him in Egypt. Of course, God intervened and protected both Abraham and Sarah.

The biblical text does not hesitate to highlight Abraham's weaknesses as well as his strengths. Our lives also contain moments where we trust God in the face of amazing circumstances, only to let our faith guard down when we face another challenge. It is a testimony to God's grace that he continues to use us in his story.

God blessed Abraham and his extended family so much that Abraham and his nephew Lot needed to separate in order to sustain their flocks in the land (Gen 13:5–17). Lot chose the Jordan valley, an area rich in agriculture, but also rich in temptation in evil cities such as Sodom and Gomorrah. Abraham remained in the heartland of Canaan and journeyed southward. On one occasion, battles in the region resulted in Lot's capture, but Abraham rescued Lot and received God's blessing through Melchizedek, a high priest of that region (Gen 14:18–20).

Abraham's testing (Gen 15–24) continued over a period of twenty-five years. When Abraham first struggled to believe, God told him he would have more descendants than the stars of the sky (Gen 15:5). That was an awesome promise with which to test Abraham, when at that point, Abraham would have likely appreciated even *one* descendant! Nonetheless, Abraham, in an astounding act of faith, chose to believe God even though he was advanced in years and his wife was barren. God counted Abraham's faith as righteousness for him (Gen 15:6). It was a defining moment in the grand story God was writing, and the apostle Paul would highlight it two thousand years later when he wrote his letter to the Romans (Rom 4:3, 16–22).

God had promised Abraham that one who would come from his own body would be his heir (Gen 15:4). Consequently, perhaps Abraham and Sarah reasoned that God would give them a son through Sarah's maidservant Hagar. Many ancient cultures practiced this custom, and maybe Abraham and Sarah decided this was how God might fulfill the promise. Ishmael was born, and Genesis 16:16 mentions that Abraham was eighty-six years old at Ishmael's birth.

The Bible's very next verse (Gen 17:1) skips ahead thirteen years to when Abraham was ninety-nine years of age. Up until this point, he might have thought Ishmael, whose name means "God has heard," was the fulfillment of God's promise to him. However, God told Abraham that Sarah herself would bear him a son. It was a promise so astounding that Abraham laughed (Gen 17:17), and one chapter later when God's messengers appeared to confirm that promise, Sarah laughed (Gen 18:12–15). In response, God told Abraham he should name his son Isaac, which means "laughter." Every time Abraham and Sarah called their son, it would remind them that they had laughed at God's promise. Indeed, Isaac's birth brought them great laughter as they celebrated their son. God was writing an amazing story, and he was writing it through them! Isaac was born to Abraham when Abraham was one hundred years of age and Sarah was ninety. Nothing would be impossible for God.

Do you suppose Abraham loved his son Isaac? We don't even have to ask. How incomprehensible, then, that God later tested Abraham by asking him to take his son and offer him as a burnt offering (Gen 22:1–2)! Abraham set out to the place God had directed, taking along Isaac his son. The old man no doubt struggled with every step he took; yet, he clung to God's promise that somehow, God would work all this out. After all, how could he become the father of many nations if God cut off his heir? Abraham believed that God would somehow provide a lamb for the burnt offering (Gen 22:8), and in fact, God did so with a ram caught in a thicket. God's angel intervened at the last minute, and the knife intended to kill Isaac cut the ropes that bound him on the altar. Abraham had passed the supreme test; he had learned to trust God completely, even with the life of his son Isaac.

The story of Abraham's supreme test finds its ultimate parallel in the New Testament. There, God placed his Son Jesus on a different kind of altar—a Roman cross—and through his Son's sacrifice on that cross, God secured the salvation of all in every generation who would place their faith in him. God stopped Abraham short of sacrificing Isaac, but God sacrificed Jesus for us.

Meanwhile, the grand story God was writing through Abraham continued as Isaac took a wife (Gen 24). The Lord led Abraham to send his servant back to Haran where Abraham's extended family resided; there he secured a wife for Isaac. God clearly guided the circumstances, so Rebekah was the obvious choice (Gen 24:12-19). The story God was writing and had continued writing through Abraham now continued through Abraham's son Isaac.

The Story of Isaac (Gen 25-26)

Genesis 25–26 focuses on the life of Isaac. Abraham's death is described in verses 1–11, followed by the family lines of Ishmael (Gen 25:12–18) and Isaac (Gen 25:19–34). Genealogical records (family trees) often seem foreign to us in our culture, but in many parts of the world, knowing one's ancestry comprises an important part of one's identity. The account confirms that God continued to have a plan in the story he was writing for Ishmael and his descendants, but the main story line would feature Isaac and his descendants. The birth of Isaac's sons is special in God's story, because the text records how Isaac and Rebekah had twin boys after having hoped for twenty years to have children. Esau was born first, but God had revealed to Rebekah that Jacob would be the primary man in God's story (Gen 25:22–23). Indeed, God calls each of us to align ourselves with his purpose.

Somewhat surprisingly, after the long wait we experienced for Isaac's birth in the book of Genesis, his life as a whole is relatively ordinary. Genesis 26 describes his settling in the southern region of Canaan, where God appeared to him and reiterated the promise he had made to his father Abraham (Gen 26:3–4). Nonetheless, Isaac was faithful in his calling. Throughout history, people of God serve him in various ways. God chooses the role they will play in the story he is writing and asks only for their faithfulness. In the end, every piece of the story is necessary, because every story matters to God.

Genesis

The Story of Jacob (Gen 27–36)

The Bible describes Jacob's life in much more detail than it describes the life of his father Isaac. His life comprises five areas: Jacob's treachery (Gen 27), Jacob's task (Gen 28–31), Jacob's transformation (Gen 32), Jacob's troubles (Gen 33–34), and Jacob's travels (Gen 35–36).

Genesis 25 recorded the rivalry between the two brothers Jacob and Esau that began while they were in Rebekah's womb (Gen 25:19–34). God revealed to Rebekah that the older brother (Esau) would serve the younger (Jacob), but Genesis 27 records how Rebekah and Jacob decided to act deceitfully to ensure Jacob received the blessing. Isaac thought he was approaching death and asked Esau to prepare him some game to eat that he might bless Esau before Isaac died. However, Rebekah, who favored Jacob, concocted a scheme where Jacob could go in and steal Esau's blessing from their father. The plan worked, and Jacob received the blessing Isaac intended for Esau. Of course, God had indicated that the blessing was to be Jacob's all along, so Jacob had not needed to take matters into his own hands (Gen 25:23; 27:33). At Isaac's urging, Jacob left to visit his uncle Laban's family in Haran (Gen 28:2). Isaac told Jacob to take a wife from there, but Jacob's departure also may have saved his life. Esau planned to kill him as soon as Isaac died (Gen 27:41).

As Jacob journeyed toward Haran, alone and afraid, God revealed himself to him in a dream (Gen 28:10–22). God reaffirmed the covenant he had made with Jacob's grandfather Abraham and Jacob's father Isaac. He would see Jacob through and would protect him everywhere he went. Jacob responded by pledging his own allegiance to the God of his ancestors.

Genesis 29–30 records the birth of Jacob's children. Jacob married his uncle Laban's two daughters Leah and Rachel,[4] and a wifely rivalry began between the two sisters. Through these two women and their two maidservants, Jacob ended up fathering twelve sons[5] and a daughter. God blessed Jacob's time in Haran, but jealousy between Jacob and Laban's sons eventually led Jacob to depart. Jacob and Laban made a covenant of peace, and the two of them parted, apparently forever (Gen 31:44–55).

Jacob's transformation occurs in Genesis 32. As he prepared for a meeting with his brother Esau whom he had not seen in twenty years, Jacob

4. Genesis 29:15–27 records how Jacob the deceiver was himself deceived by Laban into marrying Leah first.

5. Israel's twelve tribes descended from these twelve sons.

no doubt feared for his life. The text records that as Jacob remained alone by the river Jabbok, a man or being began wrestling with him. Jacob, sensing the divine source of the individual, insisted he would not let the angel go until he blessed him (Gen 32:26). In response, Jacob received a new name, Israel, which means "he has striven with God." The wrestling match between Jacob and the angel likely paralleled the emotional wrestling match going on in Jacob's own soul. Yet, Jacob's determination to receive God's blessing became one of his defining moments, and he received a new name, indicating his closer relationship with God.

Genesis 33–34 describes more of Jacob's troubles. First, as he anticipated his meeting with his brother Esau, he feared Esau might seek revenge. However, his fears were unfounded, and he and Esau reconciled at least to some extent (Gen 33:1–17). Esau invited Jacob to come and live with him, but at the conclusion of their meeting, the two parted.

Jacob settled in the area of Shechem, in Canaan's heartland. Unfortunately, one of the leaders of Shechem raped Dinah, Jacob's daughter. When Jacob's sons heard of it, they were horrified, and two of his sons, Simeon and Levi, led an attack upon the city and killed every male (Gen 34:24–29).

Jacob's adventure continued in Genesis 35–36. God appeared to him and sent him back to Bethel, the first place God appeared to Jacob when he fled from Esau (Gen 35:1; see 28:15). Jacob moved his family and all he had back to Bethel, where God again met him and reinstituted his blessing (Gen 35:9–15). Two deaths also occurred in chapter 35: Rebekah's nurse died and was buried, and Rachel also died giving birth to Jacob's twelfth son Benjamin. Chapter 36 closes this section by highlighting Esau's descendants, the Edomites, and the kings who reigned in Edom. It is Moses's way of tying off or finishing his discussion of these people, though the Edomites would appear in later books of the Bible.

The Story of Joseph (Gen 37–50)

The Joseph account (Gen 37–50) comprises the climax of the book of Genesis. Four sections highlight the Joseph story: Joseph's interaction with parents and family (Gen 37–38), Joseph's interaction with Potiphar (Gen 39), Joseph's interaction with prisoners (Gen 40), and Joseph's interaction with Pharaoh and the royal court (Gen 41–50).

Genesis 37 frames the Joseph story by telling us how Joseph was his father Jacob's favorite son. Jacob favored Joseph and gave him a nice coat of a quality he had not given to his other sons (Gen 37:3–4). Furthermore, Joseph shared his dreams with his family, dreams that suggested Joseph one day would rule over them. His brothers hated him even more for this, and one day, they received their opportunity to exact their revenge. Jacob sent Joseph to check on the welfare of his brothers, and when they saw him coming, they concocted a plan to throw him into a pit. They then sold him to a caravan on its way to Egypt, took his coat that was the object of their hatred, smeared it with goat blood, and let their father draw his own conclusions of what had happened to Joseph. Jacob was naturally horrified by news of Joseph's death, but Joseph actually was on his way to Egypt, where he was sold to a man named Potiphar (37:35–36).

Genesis 38 records a parenthetical story from the life of Judah, Jacob's fourth son. On the one hand, the story comprises almost a parenthetical thought in the flow of Genesis. On the other hand, the birth of Judah's son Perez through Judah's daughter-in-law Tamar again highlights the fact that God uses imperfect people in the story he is writing. Perez became an ancestor of the Lord Jesus Christ (Matt 1:3).

Genesis 39 records how Joseph became a slave to Potiphar, who was an official of Pharaoh, king of Egypt. The text stresses "the LORD was with Joseph" (Gen 39:2), a fact that led to Joseph's promotion over Potiphar's entire house. However, Potiphar's wife desired Joseph sexually, and when he refused her, she accused him of attacking her. Joseph found himself falsely accused of sexual assault and thrown into prison, though he had done nothing wrong.

Nevertheless, the text again reminds us that "the LORD was with Joseph" (Gen 39:21), and consequently, Joseph soon found himself second in command in the prison and in charge of the other prisoners. One day, Joseph found two of the king's prisoners dejected over troubling dreams they had experienced the night before. Joseph gave an interpretation of each of the dreams, and the interpretations proved true. The chief butler was restored to his place in Pharaoh's court, while the chief baker was hanged. However, the chief baker forgot about Joseph and made no more mention of him to Pharaoh (Gen 40:20–23).

After two years, Pharaoh experienced troubling dreams. He summoned his wise men for counsel, but no one could explain them. At that point, the chief butler stepped forward and recalled a Hebrew slave with whom he had been imprisoned who could interpret dreams. Pharaoh summoned Joseph, and Joseph was able to interpret the king's dreams.

Joseph said the king's two dreams were in effect one dream; both predicted seven years of plenty followed by seven years of incredible famine. Joseph suggested Pharaoh appoint a man to oversee the administration and storing of food during the years of plenty so the people would not starve during the years of famine. Pharaoh commended the wisdom he saw in Joseph and appointed him in charge of this project (Gen 41:37–40). Again, we see how the Lord was with Joseph in all that he did.

In the course of time, Jacob and his remaining sons became hungry, because the famine had spread to Canaan (Gen 42:1–2). Jacob sent his sons—minus Benjamin, Joseph's brother and Jacob's youngest son—to Egypt to buy food. The brothers had no idea they would encounter Joseph when they arrived in Egypt. Furthermore, they did not recognize him, no doubt due to Joseph's clean-shaven appearance[6]—and after all, he was the last person they expected to see. Joseph questioned them and accused them of being spies, a charge they flatly denied. However, when they told him of their younger brother Benjamin, Joseph insisted they bring Benjamin down to meet him, or they would receive no further rations from him. Furthermore, he held Simeon hostage until they returned (Gen 42:24).

In the course of time, Jacob's family ran out of food and discussed returning to Egypt to buy more (Gen 43:1–2). Against his will, Jacob let Benjamin go along with his brothers. The brothers again met Joseph, who ordered a great feast for them. The next day, they departed with more provisions. However, Joseph had hidden his silver cup in Benjamin's sack.

Scarcely had the brothers departed when Joseph's soldiers overtook them and accused them of stealing Joseph's silver cup. The brothers denied it, offering to serve as Joseph's slaves if the cup was found in their possession. Imagine their dismay when Benjamin's bag contained the cup!

The brothers pleaded with Joseph, who responded that only the guilty one needed to remain as his slave. At that point, Judah stepped forward and recounted the entire family history for Joseph, a story Joseph well knew (Gen 44:18–34). Perhaps for the first time in his life, Joseph realized the hurt of brothers who were also Jacob's sons, but not by Rachel and never could be. When Judah offered to stay in place of his younger brother, Joseph lost all control and broke into weeping. He revealed his identity to his brothers, who at first were terrified. However, Joseph told them not to fear,

---

6. Egyptian officials, including Pharaoh the king, were typically clean shaven. Assyrian officials, on the other hand, often sported long beards.

for God had led him to Egypt, even through circumstances they meant for evil (Gen 45:4–8).

Joseph sent his brothers back to Canaan to retrieve their father Jacob. Joseph would provide for his family in Egypt. The rest of the book of Genesis records Jacob's arrival in Egypt, Jacob's blessing of his family before he died, Jacob's death, and Joseph's death.

Concluding Thoughts from Genesis

As we come to the end of the Joseph story, we come to the end of the book of Genesis. The grand story God is writing through his people found some resolution. At the end of the book, Jacob's family is back together in Egypt. However, Egypt is not the promised land; Canaan is. Thus, tension remains in the narrative. If Canaan is the promised land, why are God's people now in Egypt? For the answer to that question, we need to follow the story into the book of Exodus.

In summary, the book of Genesis contains two main divisions: Genesis 1–11, the primeval history, and Genesis 12–50, the patriarchal period. Genesis 1–11 recounts creation, the fall of humanity into sin, the great flood, and the tower of Babel incident. Genesis 12–50 records the lives of Abraham, Isaac, Jacob, and Joseph and their families. God made Abraham a great promise (Gen 12:1–3), a promise he would reiterate to future generations in the book of Genesis and to future generations throughout Scripture. Ultimately, God would fulfill this great promise in Jesus, a descendant of Judah, son of Abraham, and Son of God.

2

Exodus

THE GREAT STORY GOD began writing in the book of Genesis continues in the book of Exodus. The book of Exodus, like Genesis, was written by Moses. The book's name implies that someone is leaving somewhere, and indeed, the book of Exodus records the dramatic exodus of God's people from Egypt after over four centuries of slavery.[1]

Exodus focuses on three major concerns of God: his people, his law, and his tabernacle. The book also centers on the worship of God—the people who worship him, how they worship him, and where they worship him. The book begins with the Hebrews (God's people Israel) enslaved in Egypt and ends with them a free people at the foot of Mount Sinai in the Arabian Peninsula.

The book of Exodus contains three major sections. First, in Exodus 1–18, God delivers his people from bondage and leads them into the wilderness. Second, in Exodus 19–24, God declares his covenant to the Israelites so they would know better how to worship him. Third, in Exodus 25–40, God designs his tabernacle, a sacred space where God's people can gather to worship him.

---

1. Jones, *Puzzle of the Old Testament,* 8, designates this period as the Exiting Era.

God Delivers His People (Exod 1–18)

The book of Exodus begins by highlighting how the Hebrews went from being a favored people to an enslaved people in Egypt. A new king arose who had no memory of Joseph (Exod 1:8), and the Hebrews became a threat to the Egyptians, who enslaved them out of fear the Hebrews might conquer them. The Hebrews served their Egyptian masters for over four centuries. Meanwhile, Pharaoh and his officials took measures to reduce the Hebrew population; they determined to kill every Hebrew newborn male. Moses was born during this period of persecution, and through events only God could orchestrate, Moses's life was spared, and he ended up being raised in Pharaoh's court (Exod 2:1–10). In the course of time, Moses killed an Egyptian and fled to the land of Midian to escape Pharaoh's wrath. Perhaps Moses thought his time in Egypt was finished, but the story God was writing would lead him back there.

While in Midian, Moses married a woman named Zipporah and pastured the flocks of his father-in-law Jethro for about forty years. One day, God appeared to Moses in a burning bush that was filled with flames but was not consumed (Exod 3:2–5). Moses learned he was God's choice to bring the Hebrews out of Egypt (Exod 3:10). Moses's protests went unheeded, for when God calls, he equips.

In Exodus 5–12, God warned Pharaoh that plagues would come upon Egypt. Many scholars have observed in the ten plagues an overall pattern. First, the plagues came according to God's plan. God instructed Moses to "go to Pharaoh and speak to him" (Exod 5:1). Second, the plagues involved God's proclamation: "Let my people go that they might serve me in the wilderness" (Exod 5:1). God clearly revealed his intent to Pharaoh, although Pharaoh was unwilling to hear it. Third, the ten plagues are God's plagues. Each one focused on a particular Egyptian deity, demonstrating God's power over the gods of Egypt.[2] Fourth, the plagues of Egypt revealed God's purpose. God wanted Pharaoh to know "there is no one like the LORD" (see Exod 7:5, 17; 8:10, 22; 9:14–16, 29; 10:2). Exodus 12 records the final plague, a plague that struck the firstborn throughout Egypt. God's angel would pass through the land and strike down the firstborn from every family. Only those who put the blood of a lamb on the doorposts and lintels of their homes would be spared (Exod 12:7, 13). The plague struck Egypt, and

---

2. Walton, *Chronological Charts of Old Testament*, 85.

as God had said, only those with the blood of the lamb on the doorposts of their homes escaped death.

In subsequent generations, this night was known as Passover, and commemorated the night when God passed over the Hebrews' homes and struck down all the firstborn of Egypt. Ultimately, this event foreshadowed the coming of the final Passover Lamb, the Lord Jesus Christ (1 Cor 5:7). The death of God's perfect Passover Lamb Jesus did not merely bring about the deliverance of the firstborn. Rather, it secured the salvation of all throughout history who would place their faith in him. The Passover stands as the Old Testament central event of salvation, and the New Testament announces its ultimate fulfillment in Jesus Christ.

Exodus 13–18 records the two-month journey as the Hebrews left Egypt and headed towards Mount Sinai. These chapters describe several significant events. First, as the Hebrews left Egypt, the Egyptians changed their minds and decided to pursue them. God, however, intervened, miraculously parting the waters of the sea so the Hebrews could cross on dry land and then closing the waters on the Egyptian armies who pursued his people (Exod 14:21–31).

Second, as God's people journeyed through the wilderness, God began to demonstrate his marvelous provision through something called manna (Exod 16:13–35). Manna was a sweet, bread-like substance, and God provided it for the people each day as a way to teach them to trust him daily.

Third, Moses learned a lesson on leadership from Jethro, his father-in-law, who observed that Moses was wearing himself out trying to deal personally with every problem the Hebrews faced (Exod 18:13–26). Moses delegated some of his responsibilities to others, and all benefited.

God Declares His Covenant (Exod 19–24)

Exodus 19–24 comprises the heart of the book of Exodus. Here God described his relationship with his people and the responsibilities he expected them to fulfill.

God highlighted his relationship with his people in Exodus 19:5–6: "If you obey me fully and keep my covenant, then out of all nations you will be my treasured possession. Although the whole earth is mine, you will be for me a kingdom of priests and a holy nation." These verses closely parallel 1 Peter 2:9, where Peter describes the New Testament people of God as a chosen race and a royal priesthood as well. God outlined his expectations for his people in Exodus 20–23. The Ten Commandments (Exod 20) formed the foundation not only for the law of Moses but for much of Judeo-Christian society today. Indeed, many have pointed out that these Ten Commandments summarize the full range of God's expectations for his people.

The first four commandments focus on our relationship with God:

1. "You shall have no other gods before me." (We are to worship God alone.)

2. "You shall not make for yourself an image." (We must not try to represent God in any form.)

3. "You shall not misuse the name of the LORD your God." (God expects us to use his name reverently.)

4. "Remember the Sabbath day by keeping it holy." (Humanity follows God's pattern by ceasing from work activity.)

The next six commands focus on our relationship with one another:

5. "Honor your father and your mother." (God desires healthy family relationships.)

6. "You shall not murder." (Only God can take life; human life is precious.)

7. "You shall not commit adultery." (God expects integrity in our marriage relationships.)

8. "You shall not steal." (We must respect the property of others.)

9. "You shall not give false testimony against your neighbor." (God expects integrity in all of our words.)

10. "You shall not covet . . . anything that belongs to your neighbor." (We are to be content with what God has given us.)

God prefaced the Ten Commandments with the words "I am the LORD your God, who brought you out of the land of Egypt, out of the land of slavery" (Exod 20:2). This verse provides a context for the Ten Commandments. God did not give us the Ten Commandments so that by keeping them, we may establish a relationship with him. Rather, he intended his commandments for his redeemed people. He gave us his commands so that we would know better how he would live if he lived among us. Indeed, the New Testament highlights how Jesus did live by God's commands during his earthly life.

Exodus 21–22 consists largely of civil laws, designed to guide Israel as a nation. Exodus 23 describes details regarding Israel's annual feasts. God established these commemorative times so the people would have specific opportunities to reflect during the year on who they were in terms of their relationship with God. The Feast of Unleavened Bread followed the commemoration of Passover and reminded the people how God had set them free from slavery to serve him. The Feast of the Harvest took place in the spring, around May, and was known as the Feast of Weeks. It culminated at Pentecost, a celebration of the spring harvest. The Feast of Ingathering, also called the Feast of Booths or the Feast of Tabernacles, celebrated the gathering of the fall harvest. It also commemorated a time when the people of God lived in booths or temporary shelters as they traveled through the wilderness. It reminded them of their dependence on God.

Many Bible scholars have connected the feasts with Jesus. We already mentioned the Feast of Passover earlier in the chapter, and the Feast of Unleavened Bread further connects Passover with the Lord's Supper in the New Testament. Jesus took the elements of the Passover meal and gave them new meaning, describing how they were fulfilled in him (Luke 22:19–20). At Pentecost, the celebration of the Feast of Weeks and the wheat harvest, the Holy Spirit fell on the early church, and a harvest of three thousand people occurred that day (Acts 2:41). It was as if the Spirit of God said, "I'll show you a real harvest—a harvest of people!" Finally, at the Feast of Tabernacles, a festival celebrating God's provision, Jesus stood in Jerusalem and announced that he was the ultimate provision of the blessed life God offered them (John 7:37–38).

Exodus 24 records the people's response to all God communicated to them. They affirmed, "Everything the LORD has said we will do" (Exod 24:3). They committed themselves anew to following the Lord who had brought them out of Egypt and was leading them to the land he had promised to their ancestors.

God Designs His Tabernacle (Exod 25–40)

Exodus 25–40 comprises the third major section of the book of Exodus and describes God's design for his tabernacle. The tabernacle was a tent structure. The Hebrew word *mishkan* literally means "dwelling place." In Exodus 25:8, God said, "Have them make a sanctuary for me, and I will dwell among them." The construction of the tabernacle required approximately ten months (Exod 19:1; 40:2).

Exodus 25–31 provides the blueprint for the tabernacle. God prescribed how his people would worship him, and he instructed Moses to construct it exactly according to his pattern (Exod 25:9). The tabernacle complex included an outer court, and the tent of meeting that sat within the court included a holy place and a most holy place (Exod 26:33; 27:9). God also gave specific details for the various pieces of furniture to be placed inside the tent of meeting or on the tabernacle complex. Exodus 31 records the names of two individuals who led the project: Bezalel and Oholiab (Exod 31:1–6). The text affirms how God had given these men and others the skill to work with their hands and produce the structure God commanded. Such passages as this remind us that true ministry is, at its core, service to God. Some of us might serve as professional ministers within a church or church-based ministry or organization, while others serve as ministering professionals in the marketplace. Nonetheless, all we do in the name of Jesus our Lord is ministry and is valuable for God's kingdom work.

Exodus 32–34 describes a sad situation that occurred in between God providing a blueprint for the tabernacle (Exod 25–31) and the people building the tabernacle (Exod 35–39). When Moses delayed coming down from the mountain, the people decided they would make for themselves a golden calf and worship it (Exod 32:8). God's judgment came against the people for their sin, but he graciously pardoned them when Moses interceded (Exod 32:11–14). Exodus 34 records God's renewal of the covenant for his people.

Exodus 35–39 records the tabernacle's construction. The words are quite similar to the instructions provided for the tabernacle in Exodus 25–31. Those who constructed the tabernacle did all the work exactly in accordance with the instructions God had given to Moses. The emphasis is on how God's people are to worship him in the way God prescribes. Many nations worshiped gods they had created in their own image; the Israelites were to worship God as he prescribed, to come to him on his terms.

The book of Exodus closes with God's blessing on the tabernacle (Exod 40). Moses ensured everything was in its place, and once it was, "the glory of the LORD filled the tabernacle" (Exod 40:34). Not even Moses, the great man of God, could enter the tabernacle, because the glory of the Lord filled it. Imagine how exciting and awesome it would be if one day, we were not able to enter one of our church buildings because the glory of God filled it!

God's glory filling the tabernacle represented his stamp of approval on the work the Hebrews had done. He was pleased to dwell among them, for they had prepared the tabernacle in accordance with the design he gave them.

Concluding Thoughts from Exodus

As the book of Exodus ends, the text highlights how God continued to lead his people on the journey toward the promised land. He led them with a pillar of cloud by day and pillar of fire by night, and they waited on his leading.

The book of Exodus describes God's deliverance of his people from slavery in Egypt, his declaration of his covenant with them at Mount Sinai, and his design for his tabernacle. God desired that the nations see his glory through his miraculous work in Egypt. He foreshadowed the ultimate day of redemption by delivering his people, who placed the blood of a lamb on the doorposts of their homes in Egypt. He gave his people his commands, so they would better know how to embrace the life to which he had called them. He did not give them his laws so they could earn a relationship with him; rather, he gave them his laws as an expression of how to live life as he intended. Finally, God designated proper worship. God is a holy, awesome God, and we approach him on his terms.

3

Leviticus

In 1986, my (Bryan's) second year at what is now Columbia International University, I received an offer from a publisher to participate in a study Bible project. As a young scholar, I was eager to write on virtually anything, so I accepted the publisher's offer to produce the study notes for the book of Leviticus. I probably wouldn't do that today, but I was eager to publish something then!

However, as I continued my study, I began to appreciate this book that many find so intimidating. I realized that concepts such as the holiness of God, the sinfulness of humanity, the need for blood atonement, and many more key biblical concepts find their roots and basic expression in this book. Indeed, probably the reason the New Testament never stops to define holiness is because the writers assume we have read Leviticus and understand what God's holiness is all about.

Leviticus is a "stand still" book. While the Hebrews waited at the foot of Mount Sinai, God formalized their worship by articulating regulations concerning his offerings, his priests, his laws, and his covenant. As you read the book, you should imagine yourself at the foot of Sinai waiting for Moses to come down with God's commands. Keeping God's commands did not make his people holy; rather, God's holy people were to live by the commands as an expression of who God was and is.

The book of Leviticus divides into two major sections. Chapters 1–10 discuss the concept of sacrifice and the proper worship of God. Chapters 11—27 describe sanctification: walking with God step-by-step.

Sacrifice: Worship of God (Lev 1-10)

Instruction about Offerings (Lev 1-7)

Leviticus 1–7 describes five different kinds of offerings God commanded the Hebrews to bring to him. Each type of offering came with specific instructions his people were to follow when they brought that particular offering. As with the details regarding the construction of the tabernacle (Exod 25–31), the Israelites were to worship the Lord in the manner he prescribed. They must approach him on his terms, not on their own. (See the discussion at the end of the chapter on Exodus.) What follows is a brief synopsis of the offerings and their general purpose.[1]

The burnt offering (Lev 1) was typically offered for general dedication to the Lord. The animal could come from the cattle, flock, or from birds, depending on the wealth of the worshiper. The entire sacrifice was consumed, and the ashes were taken outside the camp.

The grain offering (also called cereal offering or meal offering, Lev 2) consisted of various types of grain. It typically was associated with some part of the agricultural season, particularly the time when a crop's first fruits appeared. The priest burned a token portion of the offering on the altar, and the rest belonged to the priest and his family.

The fellowship offering (or peace offering, Lev 3) was also to come from the herd or from the flock. A worshiper might bring a peace offering because of an unexpected blessing or because of general thankfulness. In this case, a slight blemish of the animal was allowed but was never preferred.

Worshipers brought a sin offering (Lev 4) when they became aware of a sin they had committed. The law of Moses prescribed various levels of sin offering depending on whether the sinful party was an individual, the congregation as a whole, a leader, or a poor person.

A guilt offering (Lev 5:14–19) often was required when some sort of desecration of God's holy things had occurred or, like the sin offering, when a sin had been committed. Guilt in the Bible is always a condition, never a

---

1. For more detail on these sacrifices, see Arnold and Beyer, *Encountering the Old Testament*, 94–95.

feeling. It is similar to our court system today when a jury says, "We find the defendant guilty." Guilt is a legal term and requires restitution. As with the peace offering and sin offering, a token portion was burned on the altar, and the priest and his family received the rest of the sacrificial animal.

Consecration of the Priests (Lev 8–10)

As the spiritual leaders of the God's people, the priests bore a sober responsibility. The basic meaning behind the word priest is "mediator." That is, the priests represented God to the people and the people to God. Leviticus 8–10 describes the consecration of the priests as they were anointed first with anointing oil (Lev 8) and then atoned for with the blood of an animal (Lev 9). Tragically, Leviticus 10 describes the sinful actions of Nadab and Abihu, two sons of Aaron who offered fire before the Lord in an unprescribed manner. They died for their sin when fire came out from before the altar and slew them. God was teaching his people an important lesson. The worship of a holy God is serious business, and people must worship him in the way he prescribes.

Sanctification: Walk with God (Lev 11–27)

Leviticus 11–27 contains more commands and guidelines for God's people. God gave them his commands so that they could be a holy and separate people for him. He wanted them to be holy, just as he was (Lev 19:2). As they followed his commands and teachings, they would find the joy of living their lives according to the great story God was writing.

Food (Lev 11)

Leviticus 11 contains laws concerning clean and unclean animals and what God intended for the Israelites to eat or not eat. Some interpreters believe that at least some of the guidelines had to do with reasons of health. For example, eating the meat of animals that were scavengers or animals of prey might more naturally lead to disease if the animal eaten had consumed a sickly animal. Some have also pointed out that sea creatures such as shrimp and lobster are generally not as healthy.[2]

---

2. For a helpful summary chart, see Walton, *Chronological Charts of Old Testament*, 23.

Motherhood (Lev 12)

Leviticus 12 prescribed an offering a new mother might bring after giving birth. As with other sacrifices, the sacrifice commanded was in proportion to the mother's wealth. This command gives us insight into the account of Jesus's dedication in the Gospel of Luke, where Joseph and Mary brought two birds, indicating their lesser wealth (Luke 2:22–24). God did not seem concerned that his only Son was born to parents with a lower income.

Potentially Unhealthy Conditions (Lev 13–15)

Leviticus 13–15 describes procedures people should follow when dealing with various potentially unhealthy conditions. Chapters 13 and 14 deal especially with leprosy or perhaps mildew or rot when it occurred on people, in fabrics, or in homes. Again, the goal was cleanliness and healthiness. One could not allow conditions that threatened the public health to continue in the community, even if it meant the affected person needed to be put outside the camp for the good of the group or that a home needed to be demolished for the sake of containing the spread of rot or mildew. Leviticus 15 described normal and abnormal discharges from the body and the procedures the people should follow. In general, the concern was for purity and health.

Yom Kippur, the Day of Atonement (Lev 16–17)

The day of atonement (Lev 16–17), known in Hebrew as *yom kippur*, was a very significant day of the year. The people set aside the day to worship God and seek him. It was also the day when the priest led the worshipers in confessing their sins for the past year. One of the highlights of the ceremony was the selection of two goats, one for a sin offering and one to serve as a scapegoat. Aaron (and so later priests) laid his hands upon the scapegoat and confessed over it all the sins of Israel. After this, a man led the goat away into the wilderness to a place from where it could not find its way back. This action symbolized that God had removed the people's sins far from them. The other goat was sacrificed as a sin offering, which also reminded the people of the great weight of sin. Sin was always serious to God.

The writer of Hebrews discussed the day of atonement and its parallel with the perfect sacrifice the Lord Jesus Christ provided. He pointed out that year after year, the high priest continued to offer sacrifices that could never take away sin, but Jesus, by his perfect sacrifice once and for all, secured eternal redemption (Heb 9:14). Jesus fulfills the day of atonement in that he serves as the sacrifice, as the scapegoat who takes away sin, and as our great high priest who intercedes to God for us (Heb 7:25).

Immorality and Morality (Lev 18–20)

Leviticus 18–20 further highlights God's expectations for holy living. Chapters 18 and 20 focus on prohibitions and sins that separated the people from God. Chapter 18 focused on many kinds of immorality; many offenses were sexual in nature, though some were spiritual. God wanted his people to honor him with pure lives of worship and with pure lives in marriage. Chapter 20 highlighted the many sins that could lead to capital punishment. Christians may differ on whether capital punishment should be applied today. Regardless, the fact that sins such as murder, adultery, and rape could lead to the death penalty reveals how seriously God takes these areas of life. Sandwiched between chapters 18 and 20, Leviticus 19 contains many positive examples of holiness, such as honesty in business dealings and respect for one's elders. A key verse is Leviticus 19:2: "Be holy because I, the LORD your God, am holy." God calls his children to be like him.

Priests (Lev 21–22)

Leviticus 21–22 describes God's requirements for priests. Priests, like the sacrifices they offered, were to be men without blemish. They were to hail from the tribe of Levi through Aaron. That is, any man from the tribe of Levi could serve as a Levite, assisting in worship at the tabernacle or later the temple. However, only Aaron's sons could serve as priests (Exod 28:1).

Festivals (Lev 23)

Leviticus 23 highlights the seven feasts God prescribed for the nation of Israel. Again, as in the book of Exodus and earlier in Leviticus, God established specific guidelines as to how the people were to worship him. Whether they were celebrating the Sabbath, Passover, Feast of Weeks, Feast of Booths, or one of the other festivals, they were to do so as God had prescribed. Doing so galvanized their identity as a people. They were part of the grand story God was writing, and the feasts provided opportunity to reflect on that amazing fact.

Sabbath and Jubilee Years (Lev 25)

God also built commemorations of the Hebrews' freedom into the agricultural cycle. Leviticus 25 described cycles of seven years in which during the seventh year, the Israelites were to let their ground lie untilled. By allowing the land to rest, they provided a visible reminder of God resting on the seventh day and on their own responsibility to rest each sabbath. The land as well needed its "year of sabbath rest" (Lev 25:4). However, at the end of seven sabbath years (forty-nine years), God commanded that the fiftieth year be a year of jubilee, in which debts were canceled and land reverted to its original owner (Lev 25:10–17). We do not know to what extent the nation of Israel ever actually practiced this; however, the year of jubilee demonstrated God's concern that his people be able to stop their everyday lives periodically and celebrate all he had done for them. The year also provided for the economy to somewhat stabilize itself and bring people back toward some level of economic balance.

The Covenant's Potential Blessings and Judgments (Lev 26)

Leviticus 26 highlights God's relationship with his people as the book moves toward its end. God affirmed the incredible promises he was offering his people if they would confirm the covenant by living it out (Lev 26:1–13). They would see the Lord bless every aspect of their lives. On the other hand, Leviticus 26:14–39 outlined the penalties for breaking the covenant. God would bring his judgment and discipline on them if they disobeyed. Nonetheless, God promised to hear his people even in the midst of terrible judgment (Lev 26:40–46). He would restore them to their land and remember the covenant he had made with their ancestors.

Vows (Lev 27)

Leviticus 27 closes the book with a series of guidelines regarding the keeping of one's vows. God expected people to take their commitments seriously, and if people broke their vows, it was a serious matter. Centuries later, in the Sermon on the Mount, Jesus would encourage his followers not to swear oaths or to take vows, but simply to keep the words they said (Matt 5:33–37).

Concluding Thoughts from Leviticus

Perhaps you know people who have said, "I tried to read the Bible once, but I got bogged down in Leviticus." Maybe you yourself have said that. Indeed, the book of Leviticus contains many ideas and concepts that are quite foreign to us today as Jesus followers. Yet, the book of Leviticus has much to teach us about God, about ourselves, about the holiness God expects, about the ugliness of our sin, and about the need of the shedding of blood to make atonement for our sins.

As you read the book of Leviticus, ask the Lord to show you insights into how the ancient customs of Israel parallel in some way experiences you yourself are living. Ask the Lord to help you apply his word, whether Leviticus or another book, for his honor, as he continues to write his story in you and through you.[3]

3. For an interesting article on how Christians can apply Leviticus today, see Harrell, "Thirty-Day Leviticus Challenge."

4

Numbers

THE BOOK OF NUMBERS gets its name in our English Bible because twice in the book, Moses numbered the people, and detailed lists appear. However, the book is about much more than merely numbering the people of Israel. In the Jewish tradition, the book is called "In the Wilderness," a name that also fits the book.[1]

The book of Numbers provides a transition between the first generation that departed from Egypt to the second generation that was preparing to enter into the promised pand. In the book, the people depart Mount Sinai for the promised land. However, due to unbelief in God's protection and provision, the Hebrews refused to enter the land. Their rebellion led to forty years of wandering in the wilderness until the entire unbelieving generation died. The book closes with God's people camped on the plains of Moab, with only the Jordan River separating them from the land God had promised to them centuries earlier.

This transition from the first generation of people who left Egypt to the second generation occurs naturally in the book. Numbers 1–21 focuses primarily on the first generation, whereas Numbers 22–36 focuses primarily on the second generation.

---

1. Jones, *Puzzle of the Old Testament,* 8, calls Numbers part of the Exiting Era.

First Generation (Num 1–21)

Census 1 (Num 1–2)

Numbers 1–2 records the first numbering of the people. Most English translations list the total population as 603,550 men (Num 2:32), which would put the total estimated population around two million. It is likely we misunderstand the intent of the Hebrew language at this point. Such a population would have easily filled to overflowing the space they occupied in Egypt and the wilderness through which they traveled. Their numbers would have dwarfed many of the ancient populations, including the Egyptian armies. We probably should understand the words translated "thousand" or "hundred" as originally referring to tribal clans or units of somewhat smaller number. It is important to understand we are not suggesting the Bible is wrong, only that we are misunderstanding Moses's intentions in recording the numbers of the census. The words may not have represented exactly what we have rendered them today.[2]

However we understand the numbers in the census, it is clear the text wants us to see the blessing God had brought to his people. He had led them into Egypt as a small group of around seventy (Exod 1:5), but now they represented a great multitude.

Preparations Made: Levites Assigned New Responsibilities (Num 3–9)

Numbers 3–9 records preparations God gave the Levites, the descendants from the tribe of Levi. The Levites had the role of God's professional ministers among God's people. Today many people associate the terms minister or ministry only with people of this category. However, ministry at its core is serving God, whatever our profession. Many have found it helpful to use the terms "professional minister" and "ministering professional" to designate these categories of ministry.

Numbers 3–4 describe many of the Levites' duties divided up according to family line. One of the most significant events in these chapters is God's substitution of the Levites for the firstborn. The firstborn held a

---

2. For further detail, see Arnold and Beyer, *Encountering the Old Testament*, 104.

special place in God's redemptive story, because they were spared by the blood of the Passover lambs (Exod 12:12–13). The book of Numbers records how God substituted the Levites for the firstborn as his tribe of ministers to lead the people.

Numbers 5–9 records various acts of dedication. Faithful women whose husbands suspected them of unfaithfulness could take their case to the Lord and be exonerated (Num 5:11–31). Men or women could dedicate themselves for life or for a period of time to serving God in some special way (Num 6:1–21). Numbers 7 records how the leaders brought their offerings to the tabernacle as the tabernacle was dedicated (Num 7:1–89). Numbers 8 records the consecration of the Levites to their sacred service (Num 8:5–26). Finally, Numbers 9:15–23 highlights God's leading. God guided them by a pillar of cloud by day and a pillar of fire by night. If the cloud or flame hovered over the tabernacle, the people stayed in their places. When the cloud or flame moved out, the people followed. (Exod 40:36–38 first mentioned this phenomenon.) Central to this entire dedication section is a priestly blessing the Lord instructed Moses to give to Aaron to bless the Israelites (Num 6:22–27). God desired to bless and protect his people, to make his face shine upon them always, and to look upon them with his favor, so they would experience his peace, his *shalom*.

Path Traveled: From Mount Sinai to Kadesh (Num 10–12)

Numbers 10–12 records the path traveled as the people began to make their way from Mount Sinai, where they had received God's laws, to Kadesh, a strategic stopping point in their journey. The Hebrews' journey was marred by two spiritual failures. First, the people began to complain and grumble over God's provision (Num 11:1–9). Moses interceded for the people to the Lord; yet, they were becoming quite a burden to him (Num 11:10–14). In response, the Lord anointed seventy elders to help Moses bear the burden (Num 11:16–30).

A second failure occurred when Miriam and Aaron criticized Moses and became jealous of his leadership (Num 12:1–16). The Lord struck Miriam with leprosy but healed her when Moses and Aaron pleaded for mercy. God's judgment of Miriam and Aaron teaches us an important lesson about competing in ministry. To be sure, the apostle Paul encouraged us to seek the greater spiritual gifts for maximum spiritual effectiveness (1 Cor 12:31).

At the same time, we also must be content with the ministry God has given us. Spiritual one-upmanship has no place in God's story.

Plans Established: The People Reject God's Plan at Kadesh (Num 13–14)

Numbers 13–14 recounts a tragic turning point in the story of God's people. They arrived at Kadesh-Barnea, at the southern border of the promised land. At God's command, Moses sent in twelve spies, one from each tribe, to spy out the land to determine the best strategy for conquest (Num 13:1–16). However, ten of the twelve spies brought back a bad report, arguing that the land was too difficult, the people were too gigantic, and the obstacles too great. They could never take the land! Only Joshua and Caleb believed God's promise that the land belonged to Israel (Num 13:30; 14:6–9). Note that Joshua and Caleb saw all the same challenges and all the same obstacles the other ten spies saw. However, these two faithful men put their faith in a big God rather than choosing to fear the obstacles. Their faith and courage provide us a great spiritual example.

The people's decision to follow the majority report led to disaster (Num 14:10–38). As they began to consider going back to Egypt, God's glory appeared and the Lord handed down his judgment. Because of Moses's intercession, God would pardon the people's sin, but they would face serious consequences: the entire generation of Israelites would die in the wilderness. They had seen his glory time after time, but even so, they still didn't believe God could bring them into the land.

About 1,500 years later, the writer of Hebrews recounted this story as he encouraged new believers to press on to spiritual maturity. The people of God in Numbers 13 stood right at the verge of inheriting the promises God had made. Similarly, many of the people in the book of Hebrews were young Christians who were not pressing on to Christian maturity. Some were considering going back to their old ways. The writer of Hebrews reminded them that the only correct move was forward to Christian maturity and used Israel's tragic example to warn them of the dire consequences of unbelief (Heb 3:12–19; 6:1–2).

The Hebrews tried to turn back to God and embrace his plan, but it was too late; the hardness of their heart was clear. They received God's forgiveness, but they would experience the sad consequences of their unbelief and rebellion. The entire unbelieving generation would die in the wilderness without experiencing the fulfillment of God's promise to Abraham.

Penalty Suffered: Wandering in the Wilderness (Num 15–21)

Numbers 15–21 describes the wilderness wanderings and much of the suffering that first generation experienced for their sin. Some of the challenges likely occurred because the people were bitter about their own spiritual failure and took out their frustration on Moses.

More Priesthood Issues: God's Choice of Aaron's Line (Num 16–19)

In Numbers 16–17, a man named Korah and his family were not content to serve as Levites; they wanted the priesthood as well. However, God had reserved that for Levites who were of the line of Aaron, and he made that clear in a miraculous way by causing Aaron's staff to sprout (Num 17:1–11). The Lord provided further instructions regarding the priesthood and the priests and Levites (Num 18–19). It was essential that those who mediated between God and his people stayed clean and set apart for him. Even today, God desires his believers, who are likewise called priests (1 Pet. 2:9), to live faithfully and in a holy manner.

Moses and Aaron Disobey God's Command (Num 20)

As the people continued their journey, they became thirsty, and God gave Moses instructions for providing water for his people. Moses and Aaron were to assemble the people before a rock cliff and speak to the rock, that it might yield water. However, as they once again faced the people's grumbling and complaining, Moses and Aaron did not follow God's command to the letter but instead struck the rock. In response, God told them that because they had not treated him as holy, they would not enter the land he had promised to give his people (Num 20:12). The penalty sounds severe in light of all Moses and Aaron had had to endure. At the same time, we must remember that God holds leaders especially accountable, for their failures can have disastrous ripple effects among those they lead. Aaron's death on Mount Hor sounds a somber tone in the story (Num 20:22–29).

Fiery Serpents of Judgment (Num 21:4–9)

Numbers 21 records two significant events. First, the people's recurring complaint about God's lack of provision (in their eyes) led to the Lord judging them by sending fiery serpents among them. However, God in his mercy ordered Moses to erect a bronze serpent in the middle of the camp, and anyone bitten who had the faith to go and look at the bronze serpent would live. Jesus later used that historical event as a reference to his own suffering. People who were bitten by the fiery serpents but looked upon the serpent on a pole would live; likewise, people who had been bitten by the spiritual snake bite of sin could look upon Jesus as he hung upon the cross and experience eternal life through faith in him (John 3:14–15).

Victories over Sihon and Og East of the Jordan River (Num 21:21–35)

Second, Numbers 21:21–35 records significant victories the people of God accomplished east of the Jordan River. They conquered Sihon, king of the Amorites, and Og, king of Bashan, to the north. These victories prepared the way for an Israelite settlement east of the Jordan River (Num 32).

Second Generation (Num 22–36)

Penalty Suffered: Plague for Baal Worship (Num 22–25)

As the focus of the book of Numbers transitions to the second generation of God's people, Numbers 22–25 records the account of Balak, king of Moab, who saw the threat the Hebrews posed and summoned Balaam, a professional prophet from Mesopotamia (modern Iraq), to come and curse God's people. Balaam initially refused to come, but when Balak implied he would grant him a large honorarium, Balaam decided to come. However, through a sobering and perhaps somewhat humorous encounter and dialogue Balaam had with his own donkey, God redirected Balaam, and Balaam ended up blessing Israel three times. Tragically, the Hebrews soon begin to practice idolatry and sexual immorality, sins that Balaam somehow instigated (Num 31:16).

Census 2 (Num 26)

Numbers 26 records a second census that was taken, and again, the numbers roughly reflect the numbers of the first census in Numbers 1–2. (See footnote 2 regarding the issue of census numbers in the book of Numbers.)

Preparations Made for Joshua to Succeed Moses (Num 27–32)

Numbers 27–32 record the many preparations made as the leadership transition from Moses to Joshua neared. Moses followed the Lord's directive and laid his hands on Joshua to commission him for the task that lay ahead (Num 27:18–23). The Lord also reminded his people regarding regulations for offerings and the carrying out of vows (Num 29–30). War with the Midianites was again necessary both to bring judgment on the Midianites and to keep God's people pure (Num 31:1–18).

Numbers 32 records a crucial request made by the tribes of Reuben, Gad, and the half tribe of Manasseh. These tribes requested to settle on the east side of the Jordan instead of in the land of Canaan as God had originally designated. Moses consulted the Lord and granted the tribes permission, with the caveat that they help their brothers conquer Canaan. This the tribes promised to do.

Path Reviewed: From Egypt to the Plains of Moab Opposite Jericho (Num 33)

Numbers 33 reviews the wilderness travels of God's people. On the one hand, we are grateful Moses took the time to outline the itinerary with such precision. Unfortunately, we do not know exactly where most of these sites were. Most likely many of them lay in the wilderness or desert regions south of Israel. Nonetheless, the itinerary again reminds us of God's faithful provision for the Hebrews every step of their journey, just as he provides for us every step of our spiritual journeys.

Plans Established: How to Divide the Promised Land (Num 34–36)

Final decisions on how to divide the promised land comprise the focus of Numbers 34–36. The Lord outlined the boundaries for the land he would give to Israel (Num 34:1–15) and assigned leaders to assist in the land's distribution (Num 34:16–29).

Numbers 35 records instructions for establishing cities of refuge. The cities of refuge were places where people who accidentally brought about the death of another person could flee. They would remain in one of these cities of refuge until the death of the high priest, at which point they were free to go home. Such a requirement emphasized that human life was precious and that the person who had brought about the accidental death owed some kind of restitution. Nonetheless, there was also the recognition that offenders should not have to pay with their lives for accidentally killing someone. The book of Joshua records the completion of this assignment (Josh 20:1–9).

The book of Numbers ends with the discussion in chapter 36 of the inheritance of Zelophehad's daughters. In a culture where inheritances typically passed from fathers to sons, Zelophehad had only daughters, who were concerned their family would lose its inheritance when they married. Moses provided instructions to ensure that would not happen. Such an account may at first seem strange to us, because it seems like a very small matter in the grand story God is writing. Nonetheless, it demonstrates the specific care God took with individual families as they traveled through the wilderness. He was concerned about his people as a whole, but he was also concerned about individuals.

Concluding Thoughts from Numbers

As we come to the end of the book of Numbers, a few clarifications are in order. First, the chart below illustrates the who, where, and when details of the book. It illustrates when the focus shifts from the first generation of Hebrews who left Egypt to the second, highlights the places they traveled, and provides chronological notes.

Chapter	Who?	Where?	When?
1	First Generation	Mount Sinai (Num 1:1)	Year 2 (Num 1:1)
2	First Generation	Mount Sinai	Year 2

Part One: The Torah ("Instruction")

Chapter	Who?	Where?	When?
3	First Generation	Mount Sinai	Year 2
4	First Generation	Mount Sinai	Year 2
5	First Generation	Mount Sinai	Year 2
6	First Generation	Mount Sinai	Year 2
7	First Generation	Mount Sinai	Year 2
8	First Generation	Mount Sinai	Year 2
9	First Generation	Mount Sinai	Year 2
10	First Generation	Marching (Num 10:11–12)	Year 2 (Num 10:11–12)
11	First Generation	Marching	Year 2
12	First Generation	Marching	Year 2
13	First Generation	Kadesh (Num 13:26)	Year 2
14	First Generation	Kadesh	Year 2
15	First Generation	Wandering (Num 14:22–25)	Years 2–40 (Num 15:1, 23)
16	First Generation	Wandering	Years 2–40
17	First Generation	Wandering	Years 2–40
18	First Generation	Wandering	Years 2–40
19	First Generation	Wandering	Years 2–40
20	First Generation	Wandering	Year 40 (Num 20:28; 33:38)

Chapter	Who?	Where?	When?
21	Transition (Num 21:12, Deut 2:14)	Wandering	Year 40
22	Second Generation	Plains of Moab (Num 22:1)	Year 40
23	Second Generation	Plains of Moab	Year 40
24	Second Generation	Plains of Moab	Year 40
25	Second Generation	Plains of Moab	Year 40
26	Second Generation	Plains of Moab	Year 40
27	Second Generation	Plains of Moab	Year 40
28	Second Generation	Plains of Moab	Year 40
29	Second Generation	Plains of Moab	Year 40
30	Second Generation	Plains of Moab	Year 40
31	Second Generation	Plains of Moab	Year 40
32	Second Generation	Plains of Moab	Year 40
33	Second Generation	Plains of Moab	Year 40
34	Second Generation	Plains of Moab	Year 40
35	Second Generation	Plains of Moab	Year 40
36	Second Generation	Plains of Moab	Year 40

Second, the book of Numbers highlights God's continued protection and provision of His people. He remained faithful, even when they failed him. Under his blessing, they grew to great numbers, and as they became a people and he led them through the wilderness, he provided for them. Their ultimate failure at Kadesh-Barnea (Num 13–14) stands as a tragic turning point in the narrative. God forgave them, but those who failed to embrace God's promise ultimately did not get to experience the blessing of entering the promised land.

Finally, with respect to the place of Jesus in the grand narrative in the book of Numbers, we need to make two points. First, the writer of Hebrews drew heavily on the sad situation in Numbers 13–14 when he wrote his letter. As he reflected upon how God's people came to the southern edge of the promised land but did not have the faith to go in and embrace it, he encouraged the people to whom he wrote to press ahead into spiritual maturity and not to sit stagnant at the beginning of their Christian faith. He wanted to see growth in their lives so that he could be assured of their spiritual birth in Jesus (Heb. 5:11—6:2). For Christians today, the two passages together sound a clear warning: we must ask God to give us the grace to press on to all he has for us, never settling for less than his best. Sometimes today Christians will say, "I believe it is important to include God in my plans," but God doesn't want that. Rather, he wants to include us in *his* plan!

Second, the account of the bronze serpent in Numbers 21 parallels the cross of Jesus. A sinful people bitten by fiery serpents could look upon the bronze serpent on a pole in the middle of the camp and live. Likewise, in a world snakebitten by sin, all those who look to the cross of Jesus in faith receive his salvation (John 3:14–15).

5

Deuteronomy

DEUTERONOMY IS THE LAST of the five books Moses wrote. When we covered the book of Leviticus, we referred to it as a "stand still" book, because God's people were at the foot of Mount Sinai waiting for Moses to receive God's laws. As Deuteronomy begins, we find the Hebrews again standing still as they camped on the plains of Moab across the Jordan River from the promised land. Before they possessed the land, Moses used five sermons to remind them of the covenant God had confirmed with them at Mount Sinai. Indeed, the book of Deuteronomy is all about covenant.[1]

The word Deuteronomy literally means "second law." Fittingly, as we read the book, we find many concepts the law of Moses has already discussed. We should keep in mind the purpose of Deuteronomy was to help people review the key aspects of God's covenant with them prior to entering the promised land.

Covenant Relationship with the People (Deut 1–4)

In Deuteronomy 1–4, Moses essentially did two things. First, he reviewed the Hebrews' journey from Mount Sinai to the plains of Moab (Deut 1–3). Second, he recalled the covenant between God and the people and encouraged them to follow it (Deut 4).

1. Jones, *Puzzle of the Old Testament*, 8, puts Deuteronomy in the Exiting Era.

The journey from Mount Sinai to the promised land was potentially a journey of eleven days; however, the people's sin had turned it into a forty-year journey (Deut 1:2; see Num 13–14). Moses nonetheless encouraged the people; God's laws were for their good and brought great blessing. Indeed, no other nation had such a great God, and no other nation had such wonderful laws and commands by which to live (Deut 4:5–8).

Covenant Responsibility for the People (Deut 5–26)

As we said earlier, Deuteronomy provides a helpful summary of what the people had already received from Sinai. Much of what we are going to read in this section parallels passages in Exodus 20–23.

Moses Pronounces the Ten Commandments (Deut 5)

The Ten Commandments appear in Deuteronomy for the second time; they appeared earlier in Exodus 20:1–17. Indeed, these commandments form the foundation for life. Many scholars have pointed out that all commands fall under these ten; any sin we commit is a violation of at least one of them. As we saw in Exodus, God does not intend for his laws to confine us or restrict us. Rather, he gives us his laws so we will know the best way to live.

Moses Provides One General Motivation: Obey God from a Heart of Love (Deut 6–11)

The book of Deuteronomy stresses how God's people should obey him from a heart of love, not merely out of a sense of duty or fear. A few of Moses's most important admonitions appear below.

Love the Lord with all you are (Deut 6:4–9)

Deuteronomy 6:4–9 comprises what Jewish people call the *Shema* (sheh-MAH), the Hebrew word translated "hear" or "listen." The Shema challenges God's people to recognize that he alone is God. Second, it challenges them to love him with all their heart, soul, and might. Third, it challenges them to teach God's principles to the next generation. Fourth, it challenges them to live all of life in light of God's word.

God's people are his because of his gracious covenant (Deut 7:7–8)

Moses reminded the people that God did not choose them because they were very numerous; rather, he chose them because he loved them and remembered his covenant with their ancestors. God's grace forms a foundation for all of life. Everything we are flows from our relationship with him.

Both times of plenty and times of want can point us to God (Deut 8)

Moses reminded the people how God had humbled them through the wilderness. Through difficult times of hunger and thirst, they learned deep spiritual lessons about God's provision. Moses also warned the people that in times of plenty, they would face temptation to forget the Lord their God, who had given them everything they had.

Remember your great disappointments (Deut 9)

Moses reminded the people of the rebellious attitude they had displayed throughout the wilderness journey. He did not do this to rub their noses in their sin. Rather, he wanted them to remember that if they ever took their eyes off God, they would be right back in the mess they were in earlier. One of Satan's favorite strategies today is to remind us of our past failures. He tries to convince us God can never use us because of our past failures. The Scriptures, however, affirm that by God's grace, we have been delivered from our past lives to serve him today (1 Cor 15:9–10).

We should serve the Lord fully (Deut 10–11)

Moses reminded the people that life was not about rules but about a relationship—a relationship with the living God, who had called them to be his people. God had established a relationship with his people by grace through faith, just as he does today with his people.

Moses Proclaims Many Specific Mandates (Deut 12–26)

Deuteronomy 12–26 proclaims many specific mandates and statutes that God wanted Moses to deliver to Israel. These mandates and statutes fall under three essential categories: religion (Deut 12–16), rulers (Deut 17–21), and relationships (Deut 22–26).

Religion (Deut 12–16)

THE TABERNACLE (DEUT 12)

Deuteronomy 12 provides a summary of God's prescriptions for the tabernacle. (See Exod 25–31 for the original instructions). It was God who determined how the people should worship him.

IDOLATRY (DEUT 13)

Deuteronomy 13 reminded the people that they needed to worship the Lord alone. False prophets or leaders might arise who would challenge them to go in another spiritual direction, but the law of Moses firmly warned them not to do so. They needed to maintain their primary allegiance to the Lord, no matter the cost.

DIET (DEUT 14)

Deuteronomy 14 is essentially a restatement of Leviticus 11, which prescribed God's commands regarding clean and unclean animals. The people were to honor the Lord with what they ate and how they ate. While Christians don't face the same dietary restrictions today, we are under the command of Scripture to glorify God by what we eat and how we eat (1 Cor 10:31).

SABBATH YEAR (DEUT 15)

Leviticus 25 had instructed the people to let the ground lie fallow and celebrate a "sabbath rest" every seven years, just as they experienced a weekly sabbath rest. Deuteronomy 15 now reminded them of this. Giving the land a year to rest, of course, was an act of faith, because the people had to trust God to provide for them even in the year they didn't work the land.

Deuteronomy

Feasts (Deut 16)

Deuteronomy 16 summarized Moses's earlier commands in Leviticus 23 and elsewhere. A central theme that linked all of the feasts together was the goal of helping God's people focus on and remember who they were because of their relationship with God. They were to find their ultimate identity in him, just as we do today.

Rulers (Deut 17–21)

Deuteronomy 17–21 has much to say about the responsibilities of rulers of various levels. Rulers needed to be above reproach, setting a good example as they led the people. As leaders, they bore a special responsibility for the Lord.

Judges and Kings (Deut 17)

Deuteronomy 17 highlights the responsibility God placed on judges and kings. We may think of such offices as primarily legal or political, but each of these offices also contained a strong spiritual component. Judges and kings were to judge and rule according to the law of Moses.

Priests and Prophets (Deut 18)

The priests bore a special responsibility as mediators between the people and God. So did the prophets, who often spoke as God's mouthpiece. Both priest and prophet were to provide godly examples for the people at all times, just as spiritual leaders should today.

Protectors of Justice (Deut 19–21)

Deuteronomy 19–21 provides general instructions for rulers as they faced various situations. They were to establish cities of refuge for people who accidentally brought about the death of another. They were to ensure that courtroom proceedings proceeded in an honest and appropriate manner. They were to fight their battles with the understanding that God went with them. They also were to maintain fairness as they administered various cases and to work for the general good of society.

Relationships (Deut 22–26)

Deuteronomy 22–26 dealt with three areas of human relationships: sexual (Deut 22–23), marital (Deut 24–25), and financial (Deut 26).

SEXUAL (DEUT 22–23)

The Bible tells us that God created sexuality, including male and female relationships, for our good. The laws of Deuteronomy 22–23 called people to purity in their sexual relationships. They were not to violate God's design; they must keep sexual relations within the marital union of one man and one woman. Furthermore, they were not to use their sexuality as an expression of worship as the Canaanites around them did.

MARITAL (DEUT 24–25)

Deuteronomy 24 allowed men to divorce their wives for certain reasons. At the same time, God's word recognized the seriousness of divorce and stipulated that if a divorced woman got married again, she could never go back to her first husband. Women also were people created in God's image; they were not to be passed around as sexual playthings.

The law of Moses also provided for the security of women who became widows. They normally would marry the nearest relative in her dead husband's family. (Bible scholars refer to this as levirate marriage.) While this practice may sound strange to us, we must remember that ancient Hebrew society featured close relationships among people and extended families, and people depended on one another for existence. Further, this practice recognized a different perspective from today: people often would commit themselves to each other in marriage and then fall in love. In our culture, we tend to put falling in love ahead of the commitment. Levirate marriage in the Bible recognized that once a woman became part of an extended family, she became part of the family for life. Some cultures today still maintain this practice.

FINANCIAL (DEUT 26)

Deuteronomy 26 reminded the people that they were to honor the Lord with their giving. Moses reminded them to bring the first fruits of their harvest every year to the Lord, because it was the Lord who had provided the blessing of the seasons. Further, they should bring an additional tithe every three years, so that the less fortunate in their society might eat and be satisfied. It is important to remember that God does not ask us to give because he wants something from us as much as he wants something for us. He wants us to know the joy of providing for others, just as he knows the joy of providing for us. The Hebrews brought blessing to their society by giving their tithes and offerings and sharing what they had with others; likewise, we can help advance God's kingdom today by doing the same. And no matter how much we give, we can never outgive God.

Covenant Reminders to the People (Deut 27–28)

In Deuteronomy 27, Moses exhorted the people to ratify the covenant upon entering the promised land. They were to journey to the central region of Shechem, located between Mount Ebal and Mount Gerizim, and there affirm the stipulations of the covenant.

Second, Moses explained the blessings and curses that would accompany the people's obedience or disobedience (Deut 28). If the people demonstrated their faith through obeying God's commands, they would see the Lord bless every aspect of their lives. On the other hand, if they disobeyed the Lord, they would see every aspect of their life come to ruin. The strong warnings of this chapter look ahead to a time when God would scatter his people because of their sin.[2] The words of Deuteronomy 27–28 recall Leviticus 26, where Moses earlier had laid out the blessings of obedience and the curses of disobedience.

Covenant Recommitment by the People (Deut 29–30)

Moses called the people to renew the covenant that day (Deut 29). He wanted them to recognize that God's relationship with his people was not only something he had made with their ancestors, but he had made this covenant with them, too! The same is true today in the way God works with his people; each generation needs to make its own personal commitment to follow him.

---

2. See Jones, "Scattered Era," in *Puzzle of the Old Testament*, 139–62.

Moses also challenged the people to return fully to the covenant (Deut 30). There may come a time when they would wander from God, and if they did, they needed to recognize the consequences that could follow. Moses told the people he set the awesome responsibility before them—the choice of life or death, the choice of blessing or curse. He encouraged them to choose life. Indeed, their relationship with God was more than the most important thing in their life; rather, it was life itself (Deut 30:19–20).

Covenant Representative from the People (Deut 31–34)

Deuteronomy 31–34 highlights four aspects of Moses's life as it draws to a close. It describes how Moses selected Joshua as his successor, highlights a song Moses sang for Israel, recalls the blessing Moses spoke over God's people, and provides final details about Moses's death.

Moses Selects Joshua (Deut 31)

The Lord had prepared Joshua to succeed Moses. Joshua had led the war against the Amalekites (Exod 17) and also was one of the two faithful spies who spied out the land (Num 13–14). He had faithfully served Moses, and now he would lead Israel. Moses encouraged Joshua to be strong and courageous, even as Moses committed to the priests the sacred writings he had received from God under the inspiration of God's Spirit (Deut 31:7–13).

Moses Sings a Song (Deut 32)

Moses knew the people would forsake God after he died, so he recited a song for them that is recorded in Deuteronomy 32. Moses especially highlighted two truths. First, God was faithful; he always had been, and he always would be. Second, God's people often had proven unfaithful; they had been unfaithful from the beginning and even to that day struggled to trust God. As in Deuteronomy 9, Moses's purpose was not to belittle the Hebrews or condemn them; rather, it was to remind them of the importance of staying faithful to God. He was their strength, and he was their life.

Moses Speaks a Blessing (Deut 33)

Moses then recited a blessing over all Israel. He spoke to each tribe and pronounced a blessing on it. The people he led had often caused him much heartache, but Moses nonetheless loved them and anticipated their future walk with God.

Moses Sees Canaan (Deut 34)

Deuteronomy closes with the account of Moses's death. The Lord took him to the top of Mount Nebo, from where Moses could look across the Jordan Valley and see the entire range of the promised land. God would not allow Moses to enter the promised land, but God did by his grace allow his faithful servant to see the land he had promised to his people. Moses died on Mount Nebo, and the people mourned him for thirty days as Joshua assumed leadership.

Concluding Thoughts from Deuteronomy

As the book of Deuteronomy concludes, God's people are standing at the Jordan River waiting to cross, on the verge of inheriting the land God had promised to Abraham six centuries earlier. Moses has died, and Joshua has become the leader. Perhaps some wondered what the next chapter of their history would look like; the book of Joshua records those details for us.

Part Two

The Historical Books

These books trace the history of God's people as they entered the promised land, lost the promised land, and returned to the promised land.

Books Covered

Joshua
Judges, Ruth
1–2 Samuel
1–2 Kings
1–2 Chronicles
Ezra, Nehemiah, Esther

6

Joshua

As we begin the book of Joshua, one important fact to notice immediately is that the story God is writing continues directly from the end of Deuteronomy. In other words, the book of Joshua is a distinct book from Deuteronomy, but the story continues uninterrupted. Deuteronomy 34:1–6 describes the death of Moses; Joshua 1:1 begins with the words "Now after the death of Moses . . ." The book of Joshua bears an eyewitness flavor, and many believe, therefore, that Joshua or someone close to him recorded the account under the inspiration of the Holy Spirit.

The book of Joshua is a story of conquest and division. After the reconnaissance of the city of Jericho, Joshua takes the Hebrews across the Jordan River on dry land, thus launching the Entering Era (1405–1043 BC).[1] In three strategic military campaigns, the Hebrews achieved effective control of Canaan, and after doing so, they divided the land among Israel's twelve tribes.

The Plan Is Set (Josh 1–5)

Joshua Commissioned (Josh 1)

The Lord commissioned his new leader and encouraged him to be strong and courageous. Joshua should set his sights on the task that lay ahead.

---

1. Jones, *Puzzle of the Old Testament*, 71–88. This period covers the portion of history from Joshua up until the kingdom of Israel became united under Saul, its first king.

He should remember to follow the word of God carefully, and he should remember God was with him wherever he would go.

Joshua then summoned the heads of the tribes of Reuben, Gad, and Manasseh, tribes that had chosen to live east of the Jordan (Num 32). Joshua reminded them of their commitment to help their fellow Hebrews conquer Canaan. The leaders assured him of their support as God's purpose moved ahead.

Rahab Contacted (Josh 2)

Israel's first obstacle was Jericho, a mighty walled city just west of the Jordan River. Joshua dispatched two spies, who secretly entered the city and stayed at the home of Rahab, a prostitute.[2] Rahab hid the spies and then bargained for her life. She had saved their lives by hiding them, and now she asked them to save hers. More importantly, she confessed faith in the God of Israel (Josh 2:8–11). The people of Jericho had heard about the mighty acts God had performed in Egypt and in the wilderness, and their courage was gone. But whereas the other citizens of Jericho assumed the end was near, Rahab saw her chance. If the God of Israel was willing to accept her into his family, she wanted to join.

The spies assured Rahab they would spare her and departed. After escaping Jericho, the spies returned to the Israelite camp and informed Joshua that Jericho was theirs.

Jordan Crossed (Josh 3–4)

In Joshua 1:5, the Lord assured Joshua that just as he was with Moses, he would be with Joshua. The Lord demonstrated that power in various places throughout the book so that both the Hebrews and future readers could see that God's power now rested on Joshua. One way he demonstrated this was by miraculously parting the waters of the Jordan River so that the people could cross on dry ground. The Jordan River was overflowing its banks because of the spring runoff from Mount Hermon far to the north, but that proved to be no obstacle to God. Perhaps many Israelites saw in the crossing of the Jordan a parallel to their crossing the sea as they fled Egypt (Exod

---

2. Staying at the home of a prostitute ensured the spies' anonymity, since few at Jericho would have wanted to disclose they were at Rahab's house.

14). God had parted the waters for Moses, and now he parted the waters for Joshua. The same God was still at work, writing his amazing story! Joshua ordered the people to mark the spot of the crossing with a pile of twelve stones, one representing each tribe, so future generations would know of this amazing day.

Israel Consecrated (Josh 5)

Circumcision Reinstituted (vv. 1–9)

As the people entered the land, God commanded Joshua to circumcise all the men who had not undergone circumcision during their days of wandering in the wilderness (vv. 1–9). Joshua certainly must have wondered about the timing of this; nonetheless, the people obeyed. God had given Abraham circumcision as the seal of the covenant (Gen. 17), and now, as the people followed through on this act of obedience, God would bless them.

Passover Reestablished and the Manna Ceases (vv. 10–12)

The people celebrated Passover for the first time in the promised land. Exodus 12 summarizes the details of the original Passover; what an exciting moment it must have been for the people to celebrate Passover as a free people in the land of promise! Second, the manna ceased.[3] God had provided every step of his people's journey through the wilderness with manna, but now the manna ceased. Why? Because they were home! They no longer needed it, for they would eat the fruit of the promised land.

Captain of the Host of the Lord Revealed (vv. 13–15)

One night, as Joshua pondered the forthcoming battle with Jericho, he suddenly noticed a man standing opposite him. Joshua approached cautiously, asking, "Are you for us or for our enemies?" The answer he received was surprising. The one he faced had not come from the Israelite camp, nor

---

3. Exodus 16 first describes manna as God's provision for his people during their time in the wilderness. The people gathered it six days a week and had to trust God for their daily provision. For more detail, see ch. 2 of this book.

from the city of Jericho, but from heaven itself. He would be Israel's true leader into the battle against Jericho. The captain of the Lord's army instructed Joshua to remove his sandals, for the place he was standing was holy (Josh 5:15). His words recall God's words to Moses as Moses stood before the burning bush (Exod 3:5). Again, the text illustrates that the same God who worked in Moses was now at work in Joshua.

The Peace Is Secured (Josh 6–12)

The conquest of Canaan took place in three stages: the central campaign (Josh 6–9), the southern campaign (Josh 10), and the northern campaign (Josh 11–12). Israel's conquest of the land lasted approximately five to six years.[4]

The Central Campaign (Josh 6–9)

Victory over Jericho (Josh 6)

As the people marched against Jericho, God gave unusual battle instructions. They were to circle the city once each day for six days. On the seventh day, they were to circle the city seven times, followed by the blasts of the rams' horns and the shout of the people. As the people obeyed, God caused the walls of Jericho to fall in their place, and the people defeated the city and destroyed it. Rahab and her family were rescued, and she became a part of the amazing story God was writing. God in his grace took a prostitute from Jericho and not only made her part of his family but inserted her into the genealogy of the Lord Jesus Christ (Josh 6:23–25; Matt 1:5).

Victory over Ai and Bethel (Josh 7–8)

After such an astounding victory at Jericho, Israel's defeat at the hands of Ai, a relatively small town, was very disheartening. However, the Lord revealed to Joshua that Israel had sinned by keeping back some of the treasure of

---

4. Caleb's words to Joshua in Josh 14:7,10 provide a rough timeline for the conquest. Caleb said he was forty at the time the spies entered the land (Num 13) and then affirmed he was now eighty-five.

Jericho, which was supposed to be given to the Lord's storehouse. Achan, the guilty party, was revealed, and he and his family were put to death. God then gave the Israelites victory over Ai and nearby Bethel.

Treaty with Gibeon (Josh 9)

Gibeon was a large city on Canaan's central plateau. The Gibeonites controlled not only Gibeon but all other cities on the plateau. They recognized, however, the formidable force of Joshua and his army and acted deceitfully to secure a treaty with the Israelites. The Israelites failed God by failing to consult him prior to making a treaty with the Gibeonites. On the other hand, the treaty with Gibeon did put Canaan's central plateau under Joshua's control without a fight. He had effectively cut the land in half, isolating the southern region from the northern region. Although the Israelites had failed spiritually, God was still able to use the Gibeonite deception for his sovereign purpose in the story he was writing.

The Southern Campaign (Josh 10)

The kings of the southern region of Canaan were horrified when they learned Gibeon had sided with Israel. They knew the odds were already against them, and now a powerful ally had turned traitor. They marched against Gibeon, and the Gibeonites responded by asking Joshua to help them. Joshua's army attacked the coalition at dawn, and the Lord gave Joshua an astounding victory in which Joshua called for the sun to stand still in the sky, and the Lord made it happen![5]

Following this victory, Joshua and his army moved to the south, conquering the cities that had led the coalition along with other towns and villages. The southern region was now in Israel's hands.

The Northern Campaign (Josh 11)

A coalition of northern kings attempted to unite, using the same strategy the southern kings had unsuccessfully tried. Again Joshua attacked, and

---

5. The topography of the area makes it clear that when Joshua attacked, the sun would have been at his back and in the coalition's face. Thus, when Joshua called on the sun to stand still, the sun remained in his enemies' eyes all day.

again, God brought victory. Following the initial victory, Joshua's army then moved through the northern region, conquering the cities of the coalition and other towns and villages. The northern territory now lay in Israel's hands. Joshua 11:23 aptly concludes the account by telling us "so Joshua took the entire land, just as the Lord had directed Moses."

Summary of the Conquest (Josh 12)

Joshua 12 records the cities and regions of the thirty-one kings Israel conquered. When the Israelites had reached this point in the conquest, they had achieved effective control of the land. They were the dominant force, and no one could live there without interacting with them. At the same time, the Israelites did not control every square inch of the promised land. Pockets of people remained to be driven out, a necessity Joshua would address with the people.

The Partitioning Is Settled (Josh 13–22)

Joshua 13–22 records the division of the land by tribes. It also records a few other special allotments in the story God is writing.

Land for the Two and One-Half Tribes and Caleb (Josh 13–14)[6]

The tribes of Reuben, Gad, and half tribe of Manasseh settled east of the Jordan (Josh 13). Numbers 32 records how these tribes had requested to settle that territory; Joshua now formalized those allotments.

Caleb also received his portion of the land (Josh 14). Caleb, along with Joshua, had been one of the two faithful spies who gave the people of Israel a positive report (Num 13:30; 14:6–9). He had waited forty-five years to claim the promise he had seen back then, but now, he asked for Hebron, a difficult territory to conquer in the southern region. Joshua blessed Caleb, and the land became his. When God's people pursue God's plan, they achieve God's results.

---

6. The tribes of Manasseh and Ephraim came from Joseph's two sons (Gen 41:50–52). Since Joseph was one of the original twelve sons of Jacob, the biblical text often designates these two tribes as half tribes.

Land for the Nine and One-Half Tribes and Joshua (Josh 15–19)

The remaining nine and a half tribes received territory west of the Jordan. The tribe of Manasseh, due to its size, also received territory west of the Jordan, in addition to what it had received on the eastern side.

The people then allotted Joshua his portion (Josh 19:49–50). Joshua hailed from the tribe of Ephraim. He requested a particular piece of land within his tribal territory, and the people granted his request. Thus, as we look at Joshua 14–19, we see how the allotment of land to God's two faithful spies frames the allotment of territory in the promised land. What a great testimony of faith Joshua and Caleb continue to have in the incredible story God continues to write! Both Joshua and Caleb served God's purpose in their generation, as King David did later (Acts 13:36).

Land for Special Groups (Josh 20–22)

The law of Moses had prescribed cities of refuge to which people could flee if they accidentally brought about the death of another (Num 35). Joshua now completed this command by establishing six cities of refuge, three east of the Jordan and three west of the Jordan (Josh 20).

Joshua also allotted Levitical cities throughout the land (Josh 21). The law of Moses had instructed that the Levites would receive no land allotment; rather, the Lord was their portion. However, they needed a place to live, so Joshua appointed forty-eight cities for them among the twelve tribes. In a way, we may understand the Levites as serving as God's spiritual lamps or lights among the people.

Joshua dismissed the eastern tribes of Reuben, Gad, and the half tribe of Manasseh to settle their territory east of the Jordan River. Those tribes built an altar in the land of Canaan near the place they crossed the river. When the western tribes heard of it, they were concerned the eastern tribes were committing idolatry. However, upon investigation, they discovered the eastern tribes had established the altar only as a sign of unity between eastern and western tribes for generations to come.

The Proclamation Is Sounded (Josh 23-24)

The book of Joshua closes with two important speeches Joshua delivered to the people. He encouraged God's people to cling to the Lord and choose him in light of all God had done for them.

Joshua Challenges the Leaders to Cling to God (Josh 23)

As Joshua grew older, he summoned Israel together and encouraged the people to move ahead into all God had for them in the promised land. Joshua had allotted the tribal territories to the tribes and encouraged them to lay hold fully of the promise God had made to their ancestors. They needed to complete the conquest of the peoples who remained in their particular tribal territories.

Joshua reminded the people the Lord would be with them as long as they faithfully followed all the law of Moses commanded. They themselves had seen God's mighty power in giving them the land, and God would continue to be faithful to them if they were faithful to him. However, if they turned from the Lord, they would have no assurance God would continue to lead and guide them. Instead, the nations they were to drive out would become a snare to them.

Joshua Calls the People to Choose God (Josh 24)

Joshua summoned the people to Shechem, where they earlier had renewed the covenant (Josh 8:30-35) and where God had first told Abraham he would give him this land (Gen 12:6-7). As the people gathered in this historic place, Joshua recounted for them the amazing work God had done in making them a people. He recounted first how God had acted in history to redeem them (Josh 24:5-7). Through Moses and Aaron, God had led his people out of Egypt, led them through the sea, and closed it on the Egyptians. He had humbled a mighty nation and set his people free.

Second, Joshua recalled how God had sustained his people in hard times (Josh 24:8-10). He gave them grace as they journeyed through the wilderness, feeding them manna, providing water, and enduring their complaints. He also protected them from false prophets such as Balaam (Josh 24:9-10; see Num 22-24).

Third, God had dealt with his people by grace (Josh 24:13). He gave them cities they had not built and fed them with the fruit of vineyards and olive orchards they had not planted. He was a gracious God.

Therefore, in light of all that God had done, Joshua pressed the issue (Josh 24:14–15). They needed to forsake everything and anyone else they considered holy and place themselves fully in God's hands. Joshua wanted them to choose to serve God that day, while the evidence was still fresh in their minds as he recounted it for them. Joshua further added his own words of assurance, lest anyone doubt where he and his family stood: "As for me and my household, we will serve the Lord" (Josh 24:15). The people affirmed their allegiance to the Lord, and Joshua affirmed the covenant with them again that day.

Concluding Thoughts from Joshua

The closing verses of Joshua 24 record Joshua's death and burial. However, much more important is Joshua's legacy: "Israel served the Lord throughout the lifetime of Joshua and of the elders who outlived him" (Josh 24:31). At the beginning of the book of Joshua, we wonder whether Joshua will have what it takes to succeed Moses. At the end of the book, God's endorsement rings loud and clear. Joshua was up to the task, because he trusted in the God who called him and equipped him. God's promise to equip all his servants for all he calls them to do still stands today.

7

Judges, Ruth

Judges

IN OUR LAST CHAPTER, we noted how the book of Joshua immediately continues the story from Deuteronomy. The name of the biblical book changes, but the same story rolls on. So it is with the book of Judges; it follows immediately upon the book of Joshua, and begins with the words "After the death of Joshua . . ." (Judg 1:1).

The book of Joshua recorded the people's successes as they followed God's leadership. However, the book of Judges paints a sad spiritual picture. Indeed, the book of Joshua records the Hebrews conquering the Canaanites physically, but the book of Judges describes the Canaanites conquering the Hebrews spiritually. God's people did not drive out the inhabitants of the land, and for that, they paid a great spiritual price. Forgetting what God had done for them, the tribes of Israel turned from the Lord to worship regional idols. Occasionally during the book, a spiritual leader arose and ushered in a time of spiritual renewal, but for the most part, the book of Judges spans over three centuries of spiritual decline.

We do not know for sure who wrote the book of Judges. Some have suggested that perhaps Samuel, the last of the judges, recorded this portion of Israel's history.

A primary theme of the book of Judges is the recurring cycle of sin. Each cycle had four elements:

74

1. *Sin:* the people fall into sin and worship other gods.

2. *Suffering:* the Lord sends suffering on Israel, usually in the form of some oppressive nation.

3. *Supplication:* the people cry out to God and beg for him to intervene on their behalf, usually vowing they will serve him forever if he helps them.

4. *Salvation:* the Lord raises up a judge to deliver Israel and to set the people on a right spiritual path again.

We see this cycle over and over in the book of Judges.

Reasons for Israel's Spiritual Defeat (Judg 1–2)

As we look at Judges 1–2, we see Israel disobeyed God in two significant ways. First, the people disobeyed him by sparing the other nations militarily. Second, they disobeyed by serving the other nations spiritually. Their accommodation of these peoples led to their becoming like them.

Israel Disobeys by Sparing the Other Nations Militarily (Judg 1)

After a brief review of some victories in the book of Judges, the text reveals Israel's repeated failure to drive out the other nations. (Notice the repeated phrase "did not drive out" beginning in Judges 1:21.) God had promised to help them finish the task; unfortunately, too many considered the task either too difficult or not that important. Perhaps some reasoned they could live alongside the pagan population while continuing to practice their own worship of the one true God. Judges 2 would illustrate the folly of that sort of thinking.

Israel Disobeys by Serving the Other Nations Spiritually (Judg 2)

An angel of the Lord appeared to God's people and told them that because of their lack of obedience to God's command, he would no longer be with them to drive out the foreign peoples. Instead, these people would remain a source of temptation to God's people in the land. The chapter records how after Joshua's death, the people quickly fell into the cycle of sin, suffering, supplication, and salvation. The chart below summarizes the details of this recurring cycle in the book of Judges.

The Book of Judges	Step 1 Sin	Step 2 Suffering	Step 3 Supplication	Step 4 Salvation
Cycle 1	"The Israelites did evil in the eyes of the LORD" (3:7)	From Mesopotamia (3:8)	"They cried out to the LORD" (3:9)	"He raised up for them a deliverer" (3:9): Othniel
Cycle 2	"Again the Israelites did evil in the eyes of the LORD" (3:12)	From the Moabites, Ammonites, and Amalekites (3:13)	"The Israelites cried out to the LORD" (3:15)	"He gave them a deliverer" (3:15): Ehud
Cycle 3	"Again the Israelites did evil in the eyes of the LORD" (4:1)	From the Canaanites (4:2)	"They cried to the LORD for help" (4:3)	"The LORD, the God of Israel, has commanded" (4:6): Deborah and Barak
Cycle 4	"The Israelites did evil in the eyes of the LORD" (6:1)	From the Midianites (6:1)	"The Israelites cried out to the LORD" (6:7)	"The LORD is with you" (6:12): Gideon
Cycle 5	"Again the Israelites did evil in the eyes of the LORD" (10:6)	From the Philistines and Ammonites (10:7)	"The Israelites cried out to the LORD" (10:10)	"The Spirit of the LORD came upon Jephthah" (11:29): Jephthah
Cycle 6	"Again the Israelites did evil in the eyes of the LORD" (13:1)	From the Philistines (13:1)	Not mentioned	"He will take the lead in delivering Israel" (13:5): Samson

Revivals during Israel's Spiritual Decline (Judg 3–16)

Judges 3–16 highlights the ministries of twelve godly judges plus a few others. We will consider each in turn.

Othniel, Ehud, and Shamgar

Othniel was a relative of Caleb, one of the two faithful spies from Numbers 13–14. This meant he lived in Hebron, the inheritance Caleb received (Josh 14:6–14). Cushan-Rishathaim, a king from upper Syria, threatened Israel, but God used Othniel to subdue him.

In contrast to Othniel, who descended from the tribe of Judah, Ehud was a Benjaminite. God's calling to serve his people as a judge did not depend on one's tribal connection but on God's calling. The nation of Moab (the descendants of Lot, Abraham's nephew) threatened Israel, and God used Ehud to kill Eglon, king of Moab, and establish peace again in the region.[1]

Shamgar received only one verse of attention in the book of Judges (Judg 3:31), but the writer considered him important enough to mention. By God's grace, he achieved victory over the Philistines, one of Israel's neighbors and a constant enemy to the southwest.

Deborah with Barak (Judg 4–5)

When the Israelites again fell into sin, the Lord gave them over to Jabin, king of Hazor.[2] This time, God chose a woman named Deborah, who was judging Israel and serving as a prophetess (Judg 4:4–5). Deborah was from the centrally located tribal territory of Ephraim. Deborah contacted Barak, a military man from the tribe of Naphtali, which held the region above and around the Sea of Galilee (Judg 4:6–8).

The armies met in the Jezreel Valley, where the Lord gave Israel the victory. When Sisera, Jabin's general, tried to escape, he met his end at the hand of Jael, in whose tent he tried to hide as he fled Israel's army. Encouraged by this victory, the Israelites pressed on until they destroyed the king of Hazor. Deborah and Barak composed a song to commemorate the amazing victory God had given (Judg 5), and the land had rest for forty years.

---

1. I (Bryan) especially like Ehud because he was left-handed!

2. Joshua 11:1 also mentions a Jabin, king of Hazor, whom Joshua defeated. The name Jabin is a common name and here refers to another king who assumed power in Hazor when the Israelites lost control of it.

Gideon (Judg 6–8)

When the people again fell into sin, the Lord raised up Midian, a tribal people who did not claim any particular territory. This time, in response to the people's supplication, the Lord raised up Gideon, a member of the tribe of Manasseh.

Two items stand out in Gideon's call to service. First, he felt inadequate to receive such a commission from God. His hesitancy is similar to what many of us face when the Lord brings us challenges that seem too big for us. In the end, we, like Gideon, must recognize that when God calls us to a particular task or ministry, he equips us for that task or ministry.

Second, Gideon put a fleece before the Lord to ensure he was following the Lord in the right way (Judg 6:36–40). He asked the Lord to give him a clear sign—twice!—so he would know for sure he should fight against Midian. The text does not tell us that when we face difficult circumstances, we should put a fleece before the Lord. Rather, it simply states this is what Gideon did. However, once the Lord answered Gideon's requests, Gideon was ready to act.

Judges 7 records God's reduction of the size of Gideon's army from thirty-two thousand to ten thousand to three hundred. God wanted to bring victory for the Israelites, but he wanted Gideon and all the rest to see he alone was responsible for this great victory. As the men of Gideon's army drank water beside the spring of Harod near the edge of the Jezreel Valley, God chose his three hundred warriors depending on how they drank from the spring. Now supported by his three hundred "elite troops," Gideon attacked the Midianites, and the Lord brought victory.

The people wanted to make Gideon king, but he insisted the Lord was their king and refused kingship (Judg 8:22–23). Tragically, following Gideon's death, the people quickly lapsed into spiritual failure again.

Abimelech (Judg 9)

Gideon had refused the kingship of Israel, but one of Gideon's sons named Abimelech was more than willing to take it on. Unfortunately, Abimelech had an evil heart, and his leadership led to much contention. After ruling about three years (Judg 9:22), Abimelech died as he attempted to fight Thebez, an Israelite city.

Tola and Jair (Judg 10)

Judges 10:1–5 mentions the ministries of Tola and Jair, two judges from Issachar and Gilead, respectively.[3] We know little about what they accomplished except they served God's purpose in their generation. Following their ministries, Israel again lapsed into idolatry, leading to God sending the Ammonites from the east and the Philistines from the southwest.

Jephthah (Judg 11–12)

Jephthah came from the territory of Gilead, as did Jair. The text suggests God did not choose Jephthah as much as Jephthah's kinsmen did. Jephthah accepted the position as leader with the understanding that if he defeated the Ammonites, he would become ruler over Gilead. The tribes feared the Ammonites and quickly agreed.

Jephthah's victory over the Ammonites came at a great price. Jephthah vowed to the Lord that if the Lord brought victory, Jephthah would offer as a sacrifice whatever came out first to greet him when he got home. When his daughter came out first to greet him, Jephthah was crushed. However, he determined he would follow through on his rash vow and apparently sacrificed his daughter.[4]

Ibzan, Ilon, and Abdon (Judg 12)

God's purposes continued through Ibzan, Ilon, and Abdon, who hailed from Bethlehem, the territory of Zebulun in the north, and Pirathon in the land of Ephraim. Perhaps their ministries overlapped; indeed, it seems apparent some of the judges mentioned in the book reigned at the same time.

---

3. The land of Gilead does not refer to any specific tribe, but to a region east of the Jordan. Issachar's territory lay in Israel's northern central region.

4. Not all scholars believe Jephthah actually sacrificed his daughter. Some believe Jephthah made a careless vow and then foolishly followed it by sacrificing her. Others argue Jephthah did not actually sacrifice his daughter but dedicated her to the Lord as an assistant in the tabernacle. We can't resolve the issue with certainty, because even the text itself suggests Jephthah was not a deeply spiritual person.

Samson (Judg 13–16)

Along with Deborah and Gideon, Samson stands as one of the famous judges in the book of Judges. His rule lasted twenty years, and the major enemy during his day was the Philistines. Samson was part of the tribe of Dan, whose territory at that time lay in the Sorek Valley, west-southwest of Jerusalem.

Samson's Birth (Judg 13)

Judges 13 recalls the account of Samson's birth to parents who had been unable to have children. An angel of the Lord appeared to Samson's mother and told her she would bear a son. The angel gave specific instructions to dedicate the child to the Lord as a Nazirite (Num 6:1–21), that he might be wholly devoted to God all his life. One specific stipulation of Samson's Nazirite status was that he should never cut his hair; that fact would become tragically important later in his life.

Samson's Relationship with a Philistine Woman (Judg 14–15)

Judges 14 highlights Samson's relationship with a Philistine woman he met at Timnah, a city located in the Sorek Valley. Samson told his parents he wanted to marry her, and the author reveals the Lord was planning to use this occasion to bring his judgment on the Philistines.

Samson often displayed extraordinary levels of strength when the Spirit of God came upon him (Judg 15:9–20). He was able to kill a lion and a group of thirty Philistines, and later he killed a thousand Philistines with the jawbone of a donkey.

Samson's Downfall with Delilah (Judg 16)

Samson was able to do many mighty works, but in the end, his weakness for women led to his downfall. He fell in love with Delilah, a woman from the Sorek Valley (Judg 16). Delilah enticed Samson until he finally told her the secret to his strength: he was a Nazirite, and no razor had come upon his head. Samson carelessly shared his sacred secret with a Philistine woman who clearly intended to do him harm. The Philistines captured Samson, blinded him, and brought him in shackles to Gaza, a Philistine city.

The Philistines thought they had won; their god Dagon had given them victory over their enemy Samson! In the end, however, the Lord prevailed through Samson. The Philistines brought Samson into their Dagon's temple, thinking they would mock him; instead, Samson asked the Lord for strength and knocked down the pillars of the temple so that the temple collapsed, killing everyone inside. The Lord did use Samson one last time to bring judgment on the Philistines, but Samson also lost his life when the temple collapsed.

Results of Israel's Spiritual Departure (Judg 17–21)

Judges 17–21 forms a fitting, albeit tragic, end to the book. The chapters highlight Israel's spiritual departure from God's expectations religiously, morally, and civilly. Every aspect of society broke down as the people turned from God to worship the gods of Canaan or to worship the Lord in ways he had not prescribed.

Religiously: The Example of Micah and His Idolatry (Judg 17–18)

Judges 17 highlights the life of a man named Micah who was determined to worship God in his own way.[5] The story begins with Micah stealing 1,100 pieces of silver from his own mother; he later regretted it and confessed his sin to her. Grateful, she dedicated the silver to be used in making a molten image to worship the Lord. Of course, this violated the second commandment, which prohibited making any graven images. Micah also established one of his sons to be his own personal household priest.

One day a Levite visited Micah, and Micah determined he would make this Levite his own personal priest. This action also was a gross violation of the law of Moses, but "in those days Israel had no king; everyone did as they saw fit" (Judg 17:6). Without centralized political and spiritual leadership, the people failed to follow God's commands.

Judges 18 records the account of the tribe of Dan moving north to establish a new residence in the northern territory. They had lost their territory in the Sorek Valley and were seeking a new home (Josh 19:47–48). They ended up passing through Micah's territory and talking the priest into

---

5. This Micah is different from the prophet Micah, who ministered much later from 750 to 700 BC.

accompanying them to their new home in the north. The men of Dan also stole Micah's household idols and other religious objects that belonged to him. Again, all of this clearly violated the law of Moses.

Morally: The Example of the Levite and His Concubine (Judg 19–20)

Judges 19 describes a great moral outrage that occurred in the tribal territory of Benjamin. A Levite who was passing through with his concubine[6] was threatened in the Benjaminite town of Gibeah, and the people raped his concubine and abused her to death. As the word spread through Israel about the men of Gibeah's wicked actions, the other tribes demanded the Benjaminites turn over the worthless men who had done this. However, the tribe of Benjamin refused, and in response, all the other tribes went to war against Benjamin.

Initially, Benjamin succeeded in holding off the other tribes, but on the third try, Benjamin was overwhelmed and suffered a great defeat. Justice had apparently come, but this would not be the end of the story.

Civilly: Brides for the Benjaminites (Judg 21)

The victorious tribes faced a significant dilemma. On the one hand, they had defeated Benjamin and punished the guilty for their actions. On the other hand, their severe slaughter of Benjamin meant perhaps the tribe would face extinction. While the other eleven tribes had supported the decision to fight the Benjaminites, they now felt sorry for the low numbers of Benjaminites who remained. Consequently, they tried to think of a way that they could give the Benjaminite men their daughters in marriage in order that they might have more children. The problem was that all the other tribes had taken an oath that they would not give their daughters as wives to the Benjaminites!

The tribes first determined they would slaughter the citizens of Jabesh-Gilead, a city that had not participated in the battle and thus had not participated in the vow, and give the remaining virgins as brides to the Benjaminites. Outrageous? Yes! But it was the period of the judges, when everyone did as they saw fit.

---

6. A concubine was essentially a wife of lower status.

Second, the tribes concocted a plan whereby at the annual festival in Shiloh, as the daughters of Shiloh went dancing into the vineyards, each man of Benjamin would lie in wait in the vineyards, rush out, grab a woman, and race back to Benjamin with her. This way, it would appear the men of Benjamin were *taking* the women rather than the fathers of these women *giving* them to the Benjaminites. It was an obvious attempt to circumvent their vow, but this is what they did. The book of Judges closes with a very fitting verse: "In those days Israel had no king; everyone did as they saw fit" (Judg 21:25). Without good leadership, anarchy reigned as the nation went down the path of spiritual decline.

Concluding Thoughts from Judges

Again and again through the book of Judges, we see the cycle of sin, suffering, supplication, and salvation. Yet, we also see God's grace again and again coming to his people as they repented and he forgave them. A new judge brought peace for a time, but eventually, the people would fall back into sin and worship idols. The book of Judges highlights a battle for the minds of God's people; would they serve the God of Israel, or would they serve the gods of Canaan? Sadly, the generation that followed Joshua had forgotten his challenge (Josh 24:13–15).

As we said earlier, the book of Joshua records the Hebrews conquering the Canaanites physically, but the book of Judges describes the Canaanites conquering the Hebrews spiritually. As we come to the end of the book, many readers are no doubt shaking their heads. What in the world is going on? How can God's people behave this way? Perhaps most important of all, where is God in all this? For the answer to this question, we will turn to the book of Ruth, and find that God is just across the Jordan River in a land called Moab.

Ruth

It is quite providential that the book of Ruth follows the book of Judges in our English Bibles. By the time we get to the end of the book of Judges, we might wonder what in the world is going on. So much evil has occurred as the people experience spiritual decline when everyone does as they see fit (Judg 17:6; 21:25). The cycle of sin, suffering, supplication, and salvation continues to spin as a battle continues for the hearts and minds of God's people. Indeed, as we read Judges, we might wonder how God would ever use this period to prepare the world for his Son.

The short book of Ruth takes a huge step toward answering these questions. God's work is not finished, and none of this takes him by surprise. He is able to use anyone, even in the midst of turbulent times, who surrenders fully to him. The book of Ruth powerfully illustrates this principle.

The book's events occur during the time when judges governed Israel's twelve tribes (Ruth 1:1).[7] Ruth's love for God, her love for her mother-in-law Naomi, and ultimately her love for Boaz stand in stark contrast to the immorality that surrounded her due to the spiritual apostasy characterizing the Hebrews at this point in their history. Although Ruth is a gentile (a non-Jew), she becomes the great-grandmother of King David and, as a result, an ancestor of Jesus Christ. Her life powerfully illustrates God's heart for all peoples of the world.

Ruth's Resolve (Ruth 1)

The story begins in Bethlehem and initially centers on a couple named Elimelech and Naomi. Elimelech and Naomi had two sons named Mahlon and Chilion. In the course of time, a famine forced them to seek food elsewhere, so they journeyed across the Jordan River to the country of Moab. The family settled in Moab, and in the course of time, Elimelech died. Meanwhile, the two sons married Moabite women; Chilion married Orpah, and Mahlon married Ruth. Within the next ten years, both Mahlon and Chilion died, leaving Naomi bereaved and alone with only her two daughters-in-law. Naomi believed that perhaps the wisest course of action was for her to return to Bethlehem, while her two daughters-in-law returned to their own people and became reestablished into Moabite life and culture.

The two daughters responded quite differently. Orpah kissed her mother-in-law goodbye, choosing to return to her people and to her gods. However, Ruth insisted she would accompany Naomi back to Bethlehem. Ruth reassured her mother-in-law with her powerful statement: "Wherever you go I will go, and wherever you stay I will stay. Your people are my

---

7. Jones, *Puzzle of the Old Testament*, 71–88, includes Judges and Ruth as part of the Entering Era.

people, and your God is my God.[8] Where you die I will die and there I will be buried" (Ruth 1:16–17, Bryan's translation).

Ruth was affirming the life decision she had made when she married Naomi's son. Her future lay with Naomi and with Naomi's God who had become her God. The two of them returned to Bethlehem together.

Ruth's Reputation (Ruth 2)

Ruth 2 records how Ruth went to glean grain and happened upon the fields of a man named Boaz, a relative (Ruth 2:3). Bethlehem was a small town, where everyone knew everything about everyone, and Boaz had heard of Ruth and all she had done for Naomi. Boaz treated Ruth with favor, spoke kindly to her, and ordered his servants to treat her well. Ruth continued to glean in the fields of Boaz during the time of the barley and wheat harvests, which occurred during the late winter and spring seasons.

Ruth's Redeemer (Ruth 3)

The law of Moses provided that a near relative could function as "guardian-redeemer" (Ruth 2:20) for a relative who experienced debt or to assist a woman of his extended family who had become a widow. The law of Moses instructed that a widow could marry a brother of her deceased husband or another near relative to further her dead husband's name.

Following Naomi's suggestion, Ruth proceeded to the threshing floor where Boaz and his men were spending the night; the workers presumably were guarding the wheat harvest they had collected. Ruth quietly found the place where Boaz was asleep and lay down at his feet. Boaz was quite startled when he woke up to find a woman lying there! Ruth's words "spread the corner of your garment over me, for you are a guardian-redeemer" (Ruth 3:9) indicated a bold move for a woman in her culture. It is important to note, however, that Ruth was not merely offering herself sexually to Boaz. She was declaring her intent to become his wife since he was a near relative. In a response that reflected Boaz's godly character, he suggested the matter be settled the next day, because a nearer relative did exist. Nonetheless, he

---

8. Many translations render the phrase "your people *will be* my people, and your God *will be* my God," but the Hebrew clauses have no verbs, suggesting present tense.

knew that Ruth was a woman of noble character, for he said so himself (Ruth 3:11). The stage was set.

Ruth's Reward (Ruth 4)

Ruth 4 begins at the city gate, where citizens conducted the business of the community. Boaz spoke with the closer relative, who decided he could not redeem Mahlon's estate lest he jeopardize his own inheritance. At that point, Boaz announced his willingness to marry Ruth. He did so, and later, they had a son whom they named Obed.

However, Obed's birth did not mark the end of the story. Perhaps we expect the story will end with the words "and they lived happily ever after," and maybe they did. But the story God was writing was not finished. Ruth 4:17 tells us that Obed was "the father of Jesse, the father of David." Now we see why the story of Ruth is included in the Bible. Ruth's faithfulness to her mother-in-law led to her marrying Boaz and having his son, and ultimately she became a great-grandmother of King David. Further, she became an ancestor to the Lord Jesus Christ in the amazing story God was writing (Matt 1:5).

Concluding Thoughts from Ruth

We never know what God will do with a life lived totally for him. Ruth did not serve as a public official or a leader in her community. Her life was not marked by many of the things this world ascribes to greatness. Instead, she was a good, quality daughter-in-law who faithfully served her mother-in-law and followed her God. As she lived as a godly woman in her culture, God multiplied her life's impact. Ruth could not possibly have foreseen all that would come her way when she chose to follow Naomi to Bethlehem, but God did. We never know how God will use our lives of faithfulness either, but that is not the point. Our task is to serve him faithfully in whatever he calls us to do and leave the results to him. Ruth is a powerful example of what God can do with a life yielded to him.

8

1–2 Samuel

THE BOOKS OF 1–2 Samuel describe the transition from the rule of the judges to the rule of the kings. Samuel, the last judge, would anoint Saul, Israel's
first king. Saul was followed by David, the former shepherd. David's son
Solomon would become Israel's third king, as we will see in 1 Kings. With
the selection of Saul beginning in 1 Samuel 9, the Entering Era (1405–1043
BC) comes to an end, and the United Era (1043–931 BC) begins.[1]

We do not know who wrote the books of 1 and 2 Samuel; it is possible
Samuel wrote the first chapters of 1 Samuel. Indeed, 1 Samuel 10:25 and 1
Chronicles 29:29 refer to his writings, and perhaps it is the early chapters of
1 Samuel to which these texts refer. However, Samuel could not have written all of these books, since 1 Samuel 25:1 records his death.

1 Samuel

Samuel (1 Sam 1–8)

First Samuel 1–8 describes Samuel's birth and consecration, his confirmation as a prophet of God, and his cry to the Lord on behalf of Israel as
God's people faced challenges from the Philistines. First Samuel 8 describes
Samuel's cautionary words to the people as they considered becoming a
monarchy for the first time.

1. Jones, *Puzzle of the Old Testament*, 91–112.

Samuel's Consecration (1 Sam 1–2)

The book of 1 Samuel begins during the period of the judges. The tabernacle, God's dwelling place established in Exodus 25–40, stood at Shiloh, where Eli and his two sons Hophni and Phinehas served as priests. A man named Elkanah came up for the yearly festival at Shiloh with his wives Peninnah and Hannah. Peninnah had children, but Hannah did not and desperately wanted them. While at Shiloh, Hannah prayed to the Lord that he would give her a son. If he did, Hannah vowed she would dedicate that son to the Lord, and he would serve the Lord all his days. The Lord answered her prayer, and soon, Samuel was born. True to her word, after she weaned Samuel, Hannah returned him to Shiloh to serve the Lord.

Sadly, Samuel did not have good spiritual role models at Shiloh. Eli's two sons Hophni and Phinehas made up their own rules about sacrifice and practiced sexual immorality. Their father Eli did not discipline them enough while they were young, and now it was too late. A man of God came to Eli and told him God would judge his house for Eli's spiritual failures.

Samuel's Confirmation (1 Sam 3)

Samuel continued to minister to Eli at Shiloh. One night Samuel heard a voice, and assuming it was Eli, he ran to him and asked what Eli needed. After this happened three times, Eli discerned the Lord must be calling Samuel. The next time the Lord called, Samuel replied, "Speak, Lord, for your servant is listening" (1 Sam 3:10), an excellent response anytime we believe we hear God's voice. The Lord told Samuel he would raise up a true leader and bring the house of Eli to ruin. In the days that followed, all Israel saw God's hand on Samuel; he truly was a prophet of God.

Samuel's Cry (1 Sam 4–7)

First Samuel 4–7 depicts a time when Samuel indeed needed to cry to the Lord much on behalf of his people. Scholars have also called this section the ark narrative, because it describes a battle in which the ark of the covenant was captured and then restored to Israel.[2] The Philistines had arrived along the Judean coast around 1200 BC and threatened Israel's national

2. For a fuller discussion see Arnold and Beyer, *Encountering the Old Testament*, 173.

security. One day, after suffering defeat at the hands of the Philistines, the Israelites decided they would take the ark of the covenant into battle with them, because they believed doing so would ensure victory. Unfortunately, not only did Israel suffer a great defeat, but the Philistines captured the ark. The day of the ark's capture, Eli, Hophni, and Phinehas all died. The wife of Phinehas also died in childbirth that day. The judgment against Eli's house had begun.

The Philistines thought they had won a great victory over Israel's God and confidently placed the ark of the covenant in the temple of Dagon, their god, at Ashdod. However, God demonstrated his power over Dagon and over the Philistines as he struck them with a plague. The Philistines tried to move the ark to other Philistine cities, but each time, God's plague followed. First Samuel 6 records the return of the ark to Israelite territory, but not before the Philistines tried one last feeble attempt to convince themselves all God's judgment had happened by chance.

Twenty years later, Samuel led the Israelites in a time of rededication of the Lord. The Philistines, however, were determined to undo the damage of years prior and attacked Israel. The people cried to Samuel, but Samuel cried to the Lord, and the Lord brought victory. Samuel established a stone monument to commemorate God's victory. He named it Ebenezer, which means "stone of help" (1 Sam 7:12).

Samuel's Caution (1 Sam 8)

First Samuel 8 marks a turning point in Israel's history. Up until that time, God had ruled them through judges; however, moving forward, the people wanted a king. As Samuel grew older, the people saw Samuel's sons did not follow in his ways, and they did not trust them to provide good leadership as Samuel had. They asked Samuel to appoint a king over them.

Samuel hesitated to honor the people's request; he knew the problems having a king could bring. Nonetheless, the people were insistent. Samuel took the request before the Lord, and after declaring to the people all the challenges having a king would bring, he agreed to their request.

Significant in this chapter is verse 5; the people wanted a king so they could be "as all the other nations." When we stop to ponder the implications of that, it's sad. God's people wanted to be just like everybody else. They wanted to become more like the world than to have the world become more like them.

Saul (1 Sam 9–15)

With the beginning of King Saul's reign, we enter the United Era (1043–931 BC). A study of this period reveals three examples of kingship: Saul, David, and Solomon. As we study them, we will see each king had his strong points and weak points. In the end, however, the issue is how closely a king followed God and his commands. The king bore a heavy responsibility to set a good spiritual example.

Saul's Choosing (1 Sam 9–10)

First Samuel 9–10 records the account of Saul's selection as Israel's king. God so guided the circumstances that as Saul went looking for his father's lost donkeys, he crossed paths with Samuel, who anointed him as Israel's king (1 Sam 10:1). That anointing, however, was a private matter. The public anointing would come later at Mizpah.

Samuel called the people together and brought Saul before them. Saul stood taller than everyone else, and he looked like kingly material. In time, the people would learn whether or not having the stature of a king sufficed to be a great king. At this moment, however, all seemed good; Israel had its first king.

Saul's Crowning—Again (1 Sam 11–12)

In the early days of Saul's kingship, Nahash, king of the Ammonites to the east, threatened Jabesh-Gilead, a northeastern city of Israel. When Saul heard the news, the Spirit of the Lord came upon him, and he rallied Israel and defeated the Ammonites. In response, the people insisted on crowning Saul again; they would reconfirm the kingship at Gilgal down in the Jordan Valley.

In the context of Saul's reconfirmation as Israel's king, Samuel knew the time had come for him to step aside as Israel's leader. He recounted for the people Israel's history from the time they came out of Egypt until the present day, warning them that by choosing a king at this time, they had failed to accept God's plan for them.[3] In fact, when Samuel called to

---

3. Deuteronomy 17 presents criteria for Israel to consider when the time came to choose its first king. In light of this passage, it appears Israel choosing a king was not a sin; rather, choosing Saul was wrong, because it was not God's timing to give Israel a king.

the Lord to send rain on Israel's wheat harvest, the people knew they had sinned, for significant rain never fell that time of year.[4]

We may draw a good lesson on leadership from Samuel's words in 1 Samuel 12:23: "Far be it from me that I should sin against the LORD by failing to pray for you." What a great example for leaders today! Never forget to pray for the people you lead. When we do, we're not doing them a favor; rather, we're sinning if we don't.

Saul's Compromises (1 Sam 13–15)

First Samuel 10 mentioned how Saul had the stature of a king. In fact, during his reign, Saul won many battles against the Philistines and other neighboring nations (1 Sam 14:47–52). Nonetheless, 1 Samuel highlights two of Saul's spiritual compromises in particular that revealed the nature of his heart. These occur in 1 Samuel 13 and 15.

Saul Usurps the Priestly Role (1 Sam 13)

Samuel had told Saul he was coming and would meet with Saul and the people after seven days to offer a sacrifice to the Lord as they prepared to fight the Philistines. When the seven-day period was almost over, Saul apparently panicked and offered the burnt offering in Samuel's place. Samuel arrived and rebuked Saul, telling him his kingdom would not endure. Instead, the Lord would seek out a man according to his heart. It was already the beginning of the end for Saul.

Saul Disobeys God's Command Regarding the Amalekites (1 Sam 15)

The Lord instructed Saul through Samuel to be God's instrument of judgment against the Amalekites. Saul was to destroy everything—all the people and all their animals. Instead, Saul decided he had a better idea. He would spare Agag, king of the Amalekites, and also the best of the sheep, goats, and cattle to sacrifice to the Lord.

Samuel confronted Saul and asked him why he had disobeyed the voice of the Lord. Tragically, Saul provided only excuses—he really had obeyed

4. Typically, rain does not fall in Israel from mid-April at least until September or October. The wheat harvest would have concluded around late May.

the voice of the Lord, but just kept back some of the animals to sacrifice; in fact, the people had practically *made* him do it. Finally, Saul did confess his sin, but the text leaves us wondering whether he really confessed it only so Samuel and the others would honor him. As Samuel turned to depart, Saul reached for Samuel's robe and tore it. Samuel replied that it was fitting, for God had torn the kingdom from Saul.

First Samuel 15:22–23 sounds a sober warning, not only to kings like Saul but to all of us who would serve God faithfully:

> Does the LORD delight in burnt offerings and sacrifices as much as in obeying the LORD? To obey is better than sacrifice, and to heed is better than the fat of rams. For rebellion is like the sin of divination, and arrogance like the evil of idolatry. Because you have rejected the word of the LORD, He has rejected you as king.

In our culture today, we often think of "big sins" and "little sins." Someone has joked that the expression big sins normally designates what others do, whereas the words little sins refer to what they themselves do! The irony of Samuel's words to Saul are that most of us would put divination and witchcraft in the category of very bad sins. However, Samuel says that to disobey the voice of the Lord is as serious as divination or idolatry. For someone to know God's will and to deliberately turn away from it is as the sin of those who would try to contact an evil spirit. The Christian life is all about choosing to follow Jesus wherever he leads us.

David (1 Sam 16—2 Sam 24; also 1 Kgs 1–2)

From 1 Samuel 16 onward, the shift in the account moves from Saul to David. Ironically, Saul remained king throughout the end of the book of 1 Samuel; however, the story line makes it clear God was preparing Israel for David's reign.

David's Calling (1 Sam 16)

Even though Saul remained king, the Lord sent Samuel to Bethlehem to anoint one of Jesse's sons as the next king. Ironically, as Jesse's sons walked before Samuel, even Samuel fell into the trap of associating stature with competence. The Lord reminded Samuel that the Lord looked at a person's heart and not at the outward appearance. In the end, David was anointed as Israel's next king.

David's Victory over Goliath (1 Sam 17)

The famous story of David and Goliath illustrates David's heart even when David was a young man. As the Israelites drew up in battle against the Philistines in the Valley of Elah, the Philistines put forward their giant champion warrior, Goliath, to fight against an Israelite. Day after day, Goliath issued his challenge, but none dared to take him on.

One day, David arrived just as the Philistine was coming to issue his daily taunts. David was enraged, not on behalf of himself but on behalf of his God. How dare this Philistine taunt the armies of the living God? David told Saul he would fight the Philistine.

Why did David think he could win? David thought he could defeat Goliath based on God's past provision and protection. As David served his family as a shepherd, the Lord enabled him to defeat a lion and a bear. David knew that any God who could help him defeat a lion and a bear also could help him defeat a Philistine.

The battle did not last long and certainly did not turn out as expected. A well-placed stone from David's sling struck Goliath's skull, and when the giant fell to the ground, David did not give him time to recover. He ran to Goliath and beheaded him with his own sword. The Israelite army, energized by David's great victory, arose and chased the Philistines all the way down the Valley of Elah out to the coast. Further, David's victory over Goliath certainly got Saul's attention. However, it was the beginning of a relationship that would soon sour.

David's Struggles with Saul (1 Sam 18–27)

David's struggles with Saul began when Saul became jealous of David's success and fame. Although David spared Saul's life twice, he knew Israel's king was determined to get him. David even spent some time serving Achish, king of Gath and a leader of the Philistines.

Saul Becomes Jealous of David (1 Sam 18–23)

Saul placed David over Israel's army, and the Lord prospered David wherever he went. However, the praises of others turned Saul's heart against David, and he became jealous and fearful David would seize the kingdom from him. First Samuel 18–20 contains tragic episodes in which Saul continued to mistrust David and even try to kill him. Meanwhile, Jonathan, Saul's son, was one of David's closest friends and found himself caught in the middle of the struggle between his father and his friend.

David Spares Saul's Life Twice (1 Sam 24, 26)

The Bible tells of two occasions when David spared Saul's life when he could have killed him. The first one occurred when Saul was pursuing David in the wilderness of En Gedi. Saul entered a cave to relieve himself, unaware David and his men were in the cave. Instead of killing him, David sneaked up on Saul and cut off a piece of his garment to demonstrate he was close enough to kill him. When Saul had moved away from the cave and David perceived a safe distance between them, he shouted to Saul and showed him the evidence. Saul "repented" of his action toward David, but when the next opportunity presented itself, he pursued David again.

On the second occasion, Saul was pursuing David, and he and his army were asleep when David and his nephew Abishai sneaked into the camp. David and Abishai stood over Saul and Saul's general Abner and could have killed them both; instead, David and Abishai took Saul's spear and water jug and moved away. Again, when David woke them with a cry from a safe distance and showed Saul the evidence, Saul indicated some remorse, but by this point, David knew he could not trust Saul.

David Joins the Philistines (1 Sam 27)

David's mistrust of Saul led him to join the Philistines for a time. Achish, king of Gath, welcomed David, as they both had a common enemy—Saul![5] David joined the Philistines for a time, but when the time came for the Philistines to fight Israel, the Philistine leaders did not trust David to fight

---

5. "The enemy of my enemy is my friend" is the principle that applies here. David and the Philistines had a common threat in Saul and thus found an alliance to their mutual benefit.

alongside them and dismissed David and his men from the Philistine army (1 Sam 29).

Saul's Final Battle with the Philistines (1 Sam 28–31)

SAUL CONSULTS A MEDIUM (1 SAM 28)

The Israelites prepared to fight the Philistines in the Jezreel Valley in the northern central region. As they did so, Saul made another decision that again revealed his mixed heart. He decided to consult a medium in the village of Endor to see if she could conjure up Samuel from the dead to give him spiritual direction. The text records a dramatic encounter in which the Lord actually allowed Samuel to appear before Saul. Samuel denounced Saul's strategy and forecast that Saul would die the next day in battle. Sadly, even though Saul now knew if he went into battle he would die, he engaged the Philistines anyway the next day.

DAVID LEAVES THE PHILISTINES (1 SAM 29–30)

As the Philistines prepared for battle, many of their leaders decided they did not trust David. Achish, king of Gath, tried to persuade them, but in the end, he dismissed David and his men. In the providence of God, however, this proved a good thing. David did not end up siding with the Philistines against Saul, an action many Israelites likely would have viewed as treasonous. Instead, David was absent from the battle on the day Saul died.

David and his men returned to the city of Ziklag in the south and found the Amalekites had looted it and carried off its people. They pursued the Amalekites and were able to rescue their families and their possessions. Meanwhile, Saul was fighting the battle with the Philistines.

SAUL'S DEATH ON MOUNT GILBOA (1 SAM 31)

Meanwhile to the north, Saul fought the Philistines in the Jezreel Valley and fell wounded on Mount Gilboa. Rather than submit to Philistine capture and torment, he fell on his own sword and ended his life. The Philistines rejoiced while Israel mourned. It was a sad day for God's people, who had seen their first king come and go.

2 Samuel

David's Conquests (2 Sam 1–10)

Second Samuel 1–10 describes the victories God gave to David. As David assumed the kingship, he was able to win political, spiritual, and military victories.

Political Victories (2 Sam 1–5)

David becomes king over Judah (2 Sam 1–4). David heard the news of Saul's death and lamented Israel's fallen leader. Again, David revealed his heart; Saul had been his enemy, but Saul at one time had been his friend and his king. David's kinsmen from the tribe of Judah then anointed him as their leader and king. Meanwhile, up north, Saul's general Abner anointed Ishbosheth, Saul's oldest surviving son, as Israel's next king. A civil war ensued for a period of two years, after which Ishbosheth was killed.

David becomes king over all Israel (2 Sam 5). Following the death of Saul's son, representatives of all the tribes met with David and said they wanted David to rule them also. David accepted their request and then moved north, capturing Jerusalem and making it his capital. David established his palace there as well.

Spiritual Victories (2 Sam 6–7)

David relocates the ark (2 Sam 6). David had made Jerusalem his political capital; the moving of the ark of the covenant to Jerusalem would also make Jerusalem the nation's spiritual capital. After an initial setback, David succeeded in moving the ark to Jerusalem amidst great pomp and circumstance.

David receives a promise (2 Sam 7). Second Samuel 7 is another significant chapter in which David reveals his heart. It also contains an incredible promise God made to David—a promise that would last forever.

David marveled at the extent of God's blessing on his life. When he saw all God had given him, it bothered him that he lived in a nice palace while the ark of God sat in a tent. He determined he would build God a house, and Nathan the prophet told him to proceed. However, God did not want David to build him a house, for it was not God's timing. Nevertheless,

God appreciated the heart attitude that had led to such a decision. Instead, God would reward David by building him a house—a house of people. God promised his blessing would rest on David and his descendants forever.

God's incredible promise to David has important implications for the incredible story God was writing through his people. Ultimately, Jesus, who was from the line of David, would fulfill God's promise. In fact, the angel Gabriel alluded to this promise when he told Mary she would conceive and give birth to the Messiah (Luke 1:32–33).

Military Victories (2 Sam 8–10)

Following God's promise of blessing on David's life, David accomplished other military victories as well. Second Samuel 8–10 records victory over Edom, Ammon, Moab, Syria, and others. As long as David's heart followed the Lord, David experienced God's blessing. For Israel, it was not only the high point of the United Era, but it was the beginning of Israel as an empire.

David's Compromise (2 Sam 11–12)

Leadership brings with it many challenges; it also brings many temptations. We don't know all the circumstances that led to David's moral failure, but we do know that after that failure, nothing was ever the same. Up to this point in 2 Samuel, so much had gone right; after this, so much would go wrong. David experienced God's forgiveness, but the consequences haunted him the rest of his life.

David's Sin (2 Sam 11)

Joab, David's nephew and commander of his army, had Israel's troops away fighting the Ammonites, while David remained in Jerusalem. One night, he looked down from his roof and saw a woman bathing.[6] David inquired about her and found out she was Bathsheba, wife of Uriah, one of David's mighty men. At that point, of course, the situation should have ended, but

---

6. The Hebrew word literally means "washing herself" and does not imply Bathsheba was in a bathtub on her roof where anyone with a higher roof could see her. She may merely have rolled up her sleeves to put cool water on her arms.

David knew he had opportunity, because the woman's husband was away at war. David summoned her to the palace, and they had sexual relations.

When Bathsheba informed David she was pregnant, David knew he had a problem. He summoned Uriah home from the battle line and twice took steps to make it appear Uriah was the father. When these measures didn't work, he ordered Uriah placed in the front lines of the battle so he would die. Uriah died, David married Bathsheba, and their son was born. Perhaps David thought he had gotten away with his sins of adultery and murder, but he had not; God had seen the entire ugly incident (2 Sam 11:27).

God's Rebuke (2 Sam 12)

God sent Nathan the prophet to David. Nathan confronted David about his sin, and when David confessed his sin, Nathan informed him he would receive God's forgiveness. Nonetheless, consequences would ensue; the child born would die, and David would experience family struggles the rest of his reign.

David comforted his wife Bathsheba when their child died in fulfillment of God's word. In time, God gave them another son, Solomon, who would succeed David as king. God's grace intervened, but the situation was painful. It was also during this time that David wrote Psalm 51, expressing his deep sorrow over his sin.

The David and Bathsheba story illustrates two important principles. First, we might experience forgiveness, but we cannot choose the consequences. Anyone who decides "maybe I'll just go ahead and commit my sin and ask for forgiveness later" does so at the risk of terrible consequences. Sin will always take you farther than you want to go and cost you more than you want to pay. Don't go there!

Second, for those who already have gone down that road, the Bible calls us to cry out to God for forgiveness. God's grace can overcome the greatest sin. David knew that if God could forgive him, God could use him again (Ps 51:10–13). God's grace can redeem and restore us as well.

David's Consequences (2 Sam 13–24)

Nathan told David the sword would never depart from David's house because of his sin with Bathsheba (2 Sam 12:10). Much of the rest of 2 Samuel reads like a sad soap opera as the consequences of David's sin played themselves out among David's children. David's action would lead to the death of three more of his sons and terribly hurt one of his daughters.

Amnon and Tamar (2 Sam 13–14)

Second Samuel 13 records an incident in the life of Amnon, David's oldest son.[7] Amnon felt sexually attracted to his half-sister Tamar, and his lust led to his raping her. The text tells us David was very angry when he heard this news but apparently did nothing. We cannot help but wonder what lessons Amnon learned about women based on his observation of his father with Bathsheba. Ultimately, Amnon died at the hands of his brother Absalom, Tamar's brother, who took vengeance on him for violating his sister.

Absalom (2 Sam 15–19)

The relationship between David and his son Absalom became strained after the incident of Amnon and Tamar. In due time, Absalom staged a coup attempt for Israel's throne and chased his father out of Jerusalem. Ultimately, Absalom's delay in pressing the attack against his father saved the kingdom for David. Joab killed Absalom in battle, and a messenger brought the news to David that the kingdom was back in his hands. However, David had lost yet another son. Furthermore, tension among the tribes due to the civil war between David's forces and Absalom's forces would continue the rest of David's reign (2 Sam 19:41–43; ch. 20). The book of 2 Samuel ends with a few accounts of miscellaneous events in David's kingdom (2 Sam 20–24).

Concluding Thoughts from 1–2 Samuel

The books of 1–2 Samuel describe Israel's transition from a loosely organized league of tribes into a monarchy ruled by a king. First Samuel saw Saul, Israel's first king, come and go, a victim of his many poor choices. Second Samuel highlights David, Israel's second king, as a man after God's own heart. Nonetheless, one can only wonder how much greater David would have been had he not failed with Bathsheba.

---

7. The Bible records David's many children from at least six different women (2 Sam 3:2–5) prior to Solomon's birth from Bathsheba.

Second Samuel 7 is a key chapter that furthers the story God is writing through the Old Testament. Through the amazing covenant God made with David, God's purposes would continue and ultimately come to their greatest fulfillment in Jesus, the son of David and Son of God.

9

1–2 Kings

THE BOOKS OF 1–2 Kings are two different books in our English Bibles, but Jewish tradition refers to them simply as the book of Kings. The books together span three eras: the United Era (1043–931 BC), the Divided Era (931–586 BC), and the Scattered Era (605–538 BC).[1] First Kings 1–11 records the end of the United Era, 1 Kings 12—2 Kings 23 records the Divided Era, and 2 Kings 24–25 describes the Scattered Era.

First Kings begins with David's death and the ascension of Solomon to the throne of Israel (1 Kings 1–11). After Solomon passed away, a revolt divided the kingdom in two: the Northern Kingdom was called Israel, and the Southern Kingdom was called Judah, after its major tribe. The books of Kings alternately trace the reigns of the two kingdoms' rulers until Assyria conquered the Northern Kingdom in 721 BC. Second Kings' final chapters describe the last kings of the Southern Kingdom as Babylon captured Jerusalem in 586 BC and carried the people of Judah into exile, thus beginning the Scattered Era.

We do not know for sure who wrote the books of Kings and compiled all of the information found here. Clearly there are places where the writer refers to other sources used to write his Spirit-inspired account (e.g., 1 Kgs 11:41). Some early traditions suggest perhaps the prophet Jeremiah had a hand in writing the book of Kings, but we do not know for sure. We will

---

1. Jones, *Puzzle of the Old Testament*, 91–162.

treat 1 and 2 Kings as one book in this chapter due to the flow of the events in them.

United Era Concludes (1 Kgs 1–11)

David's Death and Charge to Solomon (1 Kgs 1–2)

In 2 Samuel 12, Nathan the prophet warned David the sword would not depart from his house. His words again proved true even as David lay dying. Adonijah, one of David's sons, attempted to seize the throne. David intervened and settled the issue by appointing Solomon as his successor. David then commissioned his son to follow the Lord faithfully so the Lord would carry out the blessings of the covenant he had given to David's line (2 Sam 7).

Solomon (1 Kgs 3–11)

Solomon's reign breaks into five parts: his wisdom (1 Kgs 3), his work (1 Kgs 4–8), his warning (1 Kgs 9), his wealth (1 Kgs 10), and his wives (1 Kgs 11).

Solomon's Wisdom (1 Kgs 3)

As Solomon began his reign, he went to Gibeon, a few miles north of Jerusalem, where he offered sacrifices at the tabernacle. (See also 2 Chr 1:3–6.) The Lord then appeared to Solomon in a dream and offered to give Solomon whatever he requested. In response, Solomon asked for wisdom (literally, "a listening heart"), and God assured him he would have it. That wisdom was first demonstrated by Solomon's judgment between two harlots who claimed the same baby. In a day without DNA analysis, fingerprinting, or knowledge of blood types, the king made the right decision. You may want to read the amazing story yourself in 1 Kings 3:16–28.

Solomon's Work (1 Kgs 4–8)

First Kings 4–8 focuses on two main areas: the team Solomon assembled to accomplish his work and the temple he completed to glorify his God.

SOLOMON'S TEAM

Solomon divided the land into twelve districts. Each district was responsible to provide for the king's needs one month out of the year. Scholars have noted that Solomon likely divided the land in this way to help people begin thinking in terms of being Israelites rather than belonging to a particular tribe. First Kings 4:29–34 again highlights Solomon's amazing wisdom.

THE TEMPLE

Solomon's father David had wanted to build God a temple, but God told him the timing was not right (2 Sam 7:4–7). Solomon reconfirmed his covenant with Hiram, king of Tyre, and contracted with Phoenician workers to provide materials and craftsmen to build the temple. First Kings 6–7 records the intricate detail as the temple was built essentially on the model of the tabernacle, only on a grander scale. At the dedication of the temple, Solomon led Israel in prayer, and the book of Chronicles records that fire fell from heaven and consumed the sacrifice, indicating God's approval (2 Chr 7:1).

Solomon's Warning (1 Kgs 9)

Following Solomon's dedicatory prayer, the Lord appeared to him and reassured him of his faithfulness to Solomon in the days ahead. However, he sternly warned Israel's king that failure to follow his commandments and statutes would result in Jerusalem's judgment.

Solomon's Wealth (1 Kgs 10)

First Kings 10 highlights the amazing wealth Solomon accumulated. His father David was the military man, conquering the surrounding nations and controlling the trade routes. Solomon now was able to exploit economically what his father had conquered militarily.[2] During the days of Solomon, his control of the trade routes led to great prosperity in the Israelite Empire. The text even records the queen of Sheba coming from her country and

---

2. We should remember David as the military man and Solomon as the economic man.

being overwhelmed at what she saw. The text records that so much gold was present that silver was worth very little during Solomon's day (1 Kgs 10:21).

Solomon's Wives (1 Kgs 11)

Solomon had begun well (1 Kgs 3), but he did not finish well. He abused the power he had and ended up with a thousand women at his disposal. Many of these wives were from foreign nations that worshiped other gods, and Solomon's accommodation of their worship east of Jerusalem on the Mount of Olives gradually led to his actual involvement in pagan worship. Solomon's kingdom began to crumble as subdued nations broke off and asserted their independence, and a prophet predicted one of Solomon's own leaders would eventually become king. At Solomon's death, the stage was set for trouble.

Divided Era (1 Kgs 12—2 Kgs 23)

First Kings 12 records the division of the kingdom during the reign of Rehoboam, Solomon's son. Rehoboam gathered all the tribes to Shechem in Israel's heartland and told them he planned to be even harder on them than his father had been. The northern tribes, perceiving Rehoboam didn't have the power to make them comply, revolted and formed their own nation. The Northern Kingdom took the name of Israel, while the Southern Kingdom took the name Judah after its major tribe, the tribe of David's line. The sections below highlight the differences between the Northern Kingdom and Southern Kingdom as we go through the Divided Era.

Comparing the Kingdoms of Israel and Judah

Israel

The Northern Kingdom of Israel featured three main characteristics. First, it was ruled by the strongest. Whoever was able to gain strength and seize power held power until he or one of his sons grew too weak to maintain it.

Second, Northern Kingdom dynasties were generally short-lived. Often the principle of "might makes right" prevailed as powerful generals overthrew weaker kings. There was no lasting loyalty on the citizens' part to any one bloodline.

Third, every one of the nineteen kings of the Northern Kingdom was evil. While some kings conquered territories and accomplished good things politically, militarily, or economically, in the end, every one of them received a negative spiritual evaluation from the writer of Kings.

Judah

Judah's three characteristics differed from that of the Northern Kingdom. First, in Judah, we have one continuous line—the line of David. God had made a promise to David that his descendant would not fail to sit on the throne (2 Sam 7), so in Judah, that was the case.

Second, a consequence of David's line ruling continuously meant that Judah had one continuous dynasty. Some kings were weaker than others, but their link to the line of David helped hold the Southern Kingdom together.

Third, the book of Kings records that out of the twenty kings of Judah, eight received a theologically positive appraisal from the writer of Kings, whereas the other twelve did not. Sadly, even David's line did not remain true to God.

Highlights from 1 Kings 12—2 Kings 23

Ahab and Jezebel (1 Kgs 16–22; 2 Kgs 9)

The Bible records Ahab as one of the worst kings Israel ever had spiritually (1 Kgs 16:33; 21:25–26). Not only was he an idol worshiper, but he added fuel to the pagan fire by marrying Jezebel, a devout Baal worshiper and Sidonian princess. Under the reign of Ahab and Jezebel, following God faithfully in the Northern Kingdom could mean persecution and even death. Nonetheless, God's purpose continued in the Northern Kingdom. Eventually Ahab lost his life in battle, and Jezebel later died when King Jehu assumed power.

The Ministries of Elijah and Elisha

The Lord sent Elijah to the Northern Kingdom of Israel at the beginning of
Ahab's reign (1 Kgs 17:1). God used Elijah to counteract Ahab's wickedness.
Elijah is perhaps best known for his contest with the prophets of Baal on
Mount Carmel (1 Kgs 18:19–40). Elijah proposed that fire fall from heaven
on the sacrifice of the one true God, and when it was Yahweh's turn, fire fell
from heaven. Sadly, Elijah was forced to flee when Jezebel became all the
more determined to kill him. Nonetheless, God protected his prophet and
encouraged him.

Elisha succeeded Elijah, and God used him to accomplish many
miracles among his people. Elisha, like his predecessor Elijah, attempted to
turn the people back to the God of Israel. Some scholars have drawn connections between the miracles of Elisha and the miracles of Jesus.

Assyria's Conquest of Israel (2 Kgs 17)

In 745 BC, Assyria became strong again when Tiglath-Pileser III began to
reign. Assyria initiated a westward expansion, and smaller kingdoms such
as Israel, Judah, and Syria needed to consider how they would respond.
In 721 BC, the Northern Kingdom of Israel fell to the Assyrians, and the
people were deported. It was the end of the Northern Kingdom, though
Judah would persist until 586 BC.

Second Kings 17:7–41 records the theological reason behind all of this.
God's people did not face judgment because Assyria was just too powerful; rather, "this disaster happened because the people of Israel had sinned
against the LORD their God" (2 Kgs 17:7). The people persistently rejected
God's grace and ignored God's prophets. In the end, they lost their kingdom.

King Hezekiah (2 Kgs 18–20)

When Hezekiah assumed power, Assyria was by far the most powerful
nation on earth. However, the Bible records an amazing victory that God
won on behalf of Hezekiah when the king chose to trust in his God against
Sennacherib, Assyria's king. The angel of the Lord decimated Sennacherib's
army, and the king went home in disgrace.[3]

3. Archaeologists have discovered an inscription in which Sennacherib talks about
the same battle. Interestingly, he concedes in the inscription that he could only "shut up

Josiah (2 Kgs 22–23)

Josiah was Judah's last good king. Although he became king at age eight, the Bible records that at age sixteen, he truly set his heart on following the Lord his God (2 Chr 8:3). He ordered the temple to be refurbished, and in the midst of that project, Hilkiah the priest discovered a scroll on which the law of Moses was written. Up until that point, Josiah had been a good king, following the Lord as best he knew. Now, however, he had the written word of God, rediscovered after who knows how long. Nonetheless, even a very positive influence like Josiah could not stem the tide of Judah's wickedness. When Josiah died in battle with the Egyptians in 609 BC, Judah's last four kings were not able to hold the kingdom together.

Scattered Era (2 Kings 24–25)

Second Kings 24–25 records three departures from Judah. The chart below illustrates the family tree of Judah's last five kings; unfortunately, none of the last four maintained the quality of Josiah.

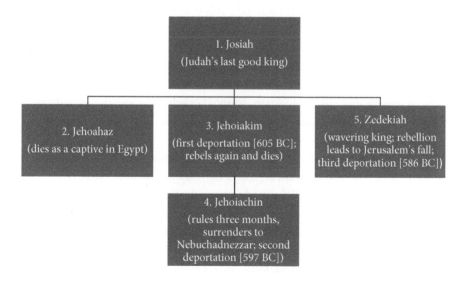

Hezekiah in Jerusalem like a bird in a cage"—a subtle admission that he was not able to conquer Jerusalem. See Arnold and Beyer, *Readings from Ancient Near East*, 146–47.

FIRST DEPARTURE UNDER JEHOIAKIM (2 KGS 24:1–7)

Judah struggled to live under foreign domination. When Jehoiakim rebelled against Babylon, Nebuchadnezzar, king of Babylon, advanced against Judah and took away some of the people to exile in 605 BC. The prophet Daniel was among those exiled at this time (Dan 1:1–2).

SECOND DEPARTURE UNDER JEHOIACHIN (2 KGS 24:8–16)

Jehoiachin, Jehoiakim's son and thus the grandson of Josiah, became king at age eighteen. Unfortunately for him, when he assumed power, the Babylonian armies were surrounding Jerusalem. Jehoiachin surrendered to King Nebuchadnezzar after three months (597 BC) and spent the next thirty-seven years of his life in a Babylonian prison (see next section).

THIRD DEPARTURE UNDER ZEDEKIAH (2 KGS 24:17—25:17)

When Zedekiah rebelled against Nebuchadnezzar, Nebuchadnezzar again marched against Jerusalem and Judah. This time, Jerusalem fell, the temple was destroyed, the city walls were broken down, and the people were deported. King Zedekiah saw his sons killed and then was blinded. The year was 586 BC, and it was the darkest hour in Old Testament history.

These events, like the destruction of the Northern Kingdom, happened because of the people's sin. Prophets such as Jeremiah warned the people of impending disaster if they did not turn back to God, but they refused to heed his counsel.

Ironically, after all this, the book of Kings ends with a note of God's grace. When a new Babylonian king, Evil-Merodach (605–562 BC), assumed the throne after Nebuchadnezzar's death, he released Jehoiachin from prison and allowed him to eat at the king's table the rest of his life (2 Kgs 25:27–30). Perhaps the Jews saw in this hope for the future. Interestingly, Babylonian administrative records have confirmed Jehoiachin's presence in the royal house, eating food from the king's table.

Concluding Thoughts from 1–2 Kings

At the beginning of this chapter, we described how the books of Kings cover all or parts of three eras. During the end of the United Era, Solomon saw much success, but he compromised and the kingdom suffered. During the Divided Era, eight kings of Judah attempted to hold things together spiritually, and when they trusted God and followed him, great things happened. Others, however, did not follow the Lord. Finally, the book of Kings records Israel's defeat by Assyria and Judah's defeat by Babylon. All this happened because the people turned from God.

At the same time, the amazing story God was writing continued. Through his people's successes and failures, he continued to prepare the world for the coming of Jesus. The line of Judah, which featured good kings and bad kings, continued by God's grace and ultimately would find its fullest expression in Jesus.

10

1–2 Chronicles

THE BOOKS OF 1–2 Chronicles are one book in the Hebrew Bible (Chronicles). One early tradition claims Ezra compiled the books, but we do not know for sure. In fact, scholars of these books often refer to the author as the Chronicler. What an interesting way to say "we don't know who wrote it"!

One interesting feature of these books is that they touch all eight Old Testament historical eras but focus primarily on the United Era (1043–931 BC) and the Divided Era (931–586 BC).[1] The first nine chapters highlight fifty-three generations that started with Adam and ended with Zerubbabel of the Gathered Era. The author then tells the stories of the three kings of the United Era before covering the reigns of the twenty kings who ruled Judah during the Divided Era.

At first glance, Chronicles appears very similar to Kings, but the books actually have distinct purposes. The author of Chronicles focused mainly on the kings of Judah, the Southern Kingdom, virtually ignoring the kings of the Northern Kingdom unless they happened to interact with a king of Judah. He also stressed Judah's spiritual condition, in contrast with the author of 1 and 2 Kings, who emphasized mostly the political condition of the divided kingdom. In short, we might say the Chronicler is trying to answer the question, "What great things was God doing through David's line?" If the narrative fits that purpose, it is part of Chronicles. The book of

---

1. See Jones, *Puzzle of the Old Testament*, 91–135.

2 Chronicles ends with a few verses related to the Scattered Era and only briefly hints at the coming of the Gathered Era.

1 Chronicles

Genealogies (1 Chr 1–9)

First Chronicles 1–9 highlights three main areas of genealogical interest. First Chronicles 1–3 takes us from Adam to the family line of David, from whose line Jesus, the Messiah, ultimately would come. First Chronicles 4–8 then highlights the twelve tribes of Israel, while 1 Chronicles 9 highlights in particular those who returned from Babylon.

Genealogy of the Coming Messiah (1 Chr 1–3)

As stated above, 1 Chronicles 1–3 takes us from Adam to the line of David. These early chapters focus on God's purpose to reach the world. The writer, in highlighting this family tree, records rather quickly many generations of God's faithfulness, which ultimately would culminate in the coming of Jesus, from the line of David. This genealogical record is continued to its fulfillment in Matthew 1 in the New Testament.

The chart below provides an overview in concise form.

Passage	Prophecy	Persons (Generation #)
1 Chr 1:1–4	Seed of Woman (Gen 3:15)	Adam (1) to Seth (11)
1 Chr 1:24–27		Seth (11) to Abraham (20)
1 Chr 1:34	Nation of Hebrews (Gen 12:2–3)	Abraham (20) to Israel/Jacob (22)
1 Chr 2:1		Israel/Jacob (22) to Judah (23)
1 Chr 2:3–5	Tribe of Judah (Gen 49:10)	Judah (23) to Hezron (25)
1 Chr 2:9–15		Hezron (25) to David (33)

Passage	Prophecy	Persons (Generation #)
1 Chr 3:1–5		David (33) to Solomon (34)
1 Chr 3:10–19	Family of David (2 Sam 7:12–13)	Solomon (34) to Zerubbabel (53)

Genealogy of the Twelve Tribes of Israel (1 Chr 4–8)

This section highlights various names and generations from the tribes of Israel. A couple points to note:

First, the tribe of Judah appears at the beginning of the genealogy, a fact that fits well with the Chronicler's purpose. Since his intent is to highlight the great things God was doing through David's line, why not start with Judah, the tribe of David?

Second, the tribes of Dan and Zebulun receive no mention. The text gives no reason for this omission, though Dan and Zebulun were part of the many northern tribes that were scattered during the days of the Assyrian conquest. This section also highlights God's continued purpose even for the remnants of those tribes he had scattered.[2]

Returnees from Exile (1 Chr 9)

God had judged his people and exiled them to Babylon. Nevertheless, as he had foretold through the prophet Jeremiah (Jer 25:11–12), he would bring them home after seventy years of exile. God's grace continued with this group of people.

United Era (1 Chr 10—2 Chr 9)

The United Era, as we have said, featured the ministry of the reigns of three kings: Saul, David, and Solomon. The writer of Chronicles touched on each one in order.

---

2. Various Scripture passages highlight the fact that some of the northern people came down and joined Judah around the time of the Assyrian invasion or right after the conquest; see for example 2 Chr 15:9; 30:1–22.

Saul (1 Chr 10)

The account of Saul begins with the battle of Mount Gilboa, where Saul lost his life in battle with the Philistines. Again, we must keep in mind the writer's purpose. The book of 1 Samuel highlighted the positive and negative aspects of Saul's reign, because that writer's purpose was to describe all of Israel's spiritual and political history. Here, the Chronicler's purpose is to get us to David's line. Consequently, he cuts to the heart of the matter. Saul's heart ultimately was not right with God, and therefore God took the kingdom from him and gave it to David.

David (1 Chr 11–29)

David's Conquests (1 Chr 11–22)

First Chronicles 11–22 highlights David's conquests in four areas: political, spiritual, military, and religious.

Political (1 Chr 11–12)

The text of Chronicles immediately moves to the coronation of David over all Israel, whereas 2 Samuel 1–4 describes it in stages. Again, we must keep in mind the writer's purpose to show the great things God was doing through David's line. The text records David's anointing, his capture of Jerusalem, the mighty men who served him, and his most trusted advisors.

Spiritual (1 Chr 13–17)

Again, we remind readers that the Chronicler's purpose was to highlight the great things God was doing through David's line. Not surprisingly, the writer devotes four chapters to describe David bringing the ark to Jerusalem. The writer included virtually everything that was in 2 Samuel 6 but also included the hymn the people sang on the occasion.

Second, the text highlights David's promise from God to establish a covenant with him forever (1 Chr 17). Second Samuel 7 also had recorded this as part of the history of David, but for the writer of Chronicles, this covenantal promise was critical. Ultimately, of course, it points not merely to David's son Solomon who would build the temple, but to Jesus, David's ultimate descendant and Messiah King.

MILITARY (1 CHR 18–20)

The writer of Chronicles recognized how God had blessed David in battle as well. As we highlighted in the previous chapter, David was the military man who expanded Israel's kingdom to the point of empire; Solomon his son was the economic genius who controlled the trade routes and exploited his empire for economic gain. These chapters highlight David's victory over nations that surrounded him: Philistia, Moab, Syria (Aram), Edom, and Ammon.

RELIGIOUS (1 CHR 21–22)

At first, we are somewhat surprised to read the account in 1 Chronicles 21 that highlights a failure of David. David ordered a census of all Israel, demonstrating his trust in his military might over his trust in God and God's protection and provision. However, the account also reflects David's heart. When Ornan,[3] a Jebusite who still lived just north of the city of David, offered to give David everything he needed for an offering to make peace with God, David responded that he would not offer the Lord his God burnt offerings that cost him nothing. Indeed, the Lord indicated his acceptance of David's offering by answering with fire from heaven that consumed the sacrifice (1 Chr 21:26). First Chronicles 22 records David's initial thoughts and preparations regarding the building of the temple. God had revealed to David that David's son Solomon would build the temple; nonetheless, David's heart for the Lord prompted him to help his son make preparations.

David's Conclusion (1 Chr 23–29)

Again, when we keep in mind the book's purpose—to highlight the great things God was doing through David's line—we understand how the book of 1 Chronicles ends. First Kings 1–2 provided only the basic information regarding the transition of power from David to Solomon. However, the Chronicler wanted to document these details much more completely, in

---

3. The alternate spelling Araunah appears in 2 Sam 24:18.

order that we might understand all the things David did to prepare the spiritual aspects of the kingdom for his son Solomon. First Chronicles 23–26 records David's special preparations with the Levites, Israel's professional ministers. He divided the Levites into various divisions and also gave instructions for the priests. Musicians from the Levites received their assignments, while others oversaw the gate, treasury, and other items. David also assigned other officials as ministering professionals who oversaw business and military matters (1 Chr 27). First Chronicles then closes with David's commissioning of Solomon to build the temple (1 Chr 28), along with his description of the contributions made to construct the temple. David offered a prayer of dedication, and the people established Solomon a second time as the Lord's choice (1 Chr 29).

2 Chronicles

Solomon (2 Chr 1–9)

The writer of Chronicles essentially followed the same pattern for Solomon's reign as did the writer of 1 Kings as he described Solomon's wisdom, work, warning, and wealth.

Solomon's Wisdom (2 Chr 1)

Solomon's request from God for wisdom at the beginning of his reign naturally was featured by the writer of Chronicles, who was eager to highlight the spiritual side of Israel's kings along with the great things God was doing through David's line. God's gracious offer was accepted by Israel's new king, and God granted his request for wisdom to rule Israel.

Solomon's Work (2 Chr 2:1—7:10)

Second Chronicles 2:1—7:10 describes the work Solomon commissioned for the temple in Jerusalem, along with Solomon's palace he would build as well. The Chronicler naturally highlighted in great detail all the work that went into completing the temple with its furnishings. The author included Solomon's dedicatory prayer and even added the note that fire fell from heaven to consume the burnt offering as God's glory filled the temple (2 Chr 7:1–2).

Solomon's Warning (2 Chr 7:11–22)

Following the temple dedication, the Lord appeared to Solomon and affirmed that the covenant he had made with Solomon's father David would now continue through him. Solomon's faithfulness would result in blessings for him and for Israel; disobedience and unfaithfulness would lead to disaster.

Solomon's Wealth (2 Chr 8–9)

Solomon's work also included other building projects. He completed his own palace but also rebuilt many cities throughout his kingdom. Second Chronicles 9 records the visit of the queen of Sheba (1 Kgs 10), who came and marveled at all she saw in Solomon's domain. The text also describes Solomon's great wealth, which God had given him as he continued the great work through David's line.

Somewhat surprisingly, 2 Chronicles 9 ends with an account of Solomon's death but never mentions the thousand women who led his heart astray to serve other gods. Again, we must remember the Chronicler's purpose. The writer was not highlighting a history of Israel; rather, he was highlighting the great things God was doing through David's line, and the spiritual failure of David or Solomon did not fall under that category. We do not see any record of David's adultery with Bathsheba, and we likewise do not see any record of Solomon's spiritual and moral failures. The author's intent is to exalt God, not to point out the failures of his kings.

Divided Era (2 Chr 10–35)

As we have mentioned throughout the chapter, the focus of the writer of Chronicles is the kingdom of Judah. Occasionally a king of Israel will cross paths with a king of Judah, and consequently he is mentioned as well. However, the purpose of Chronicles is to highlight the great things God was doing through David's line.

The chart below provides some detail regarding the Divided Era highlighted in 2 Chronicles. Following the chart, because the general outline of Chronicles overlaps with the books of Kings so much, we will highlight only special events that highlight the writer of Chronicles' spiritual focus.

Chapter of Scripture	Year (BC)	Kings of Judah (good kings marked with *)	Prophets of Judah whose ministries overlapped with Judah's kings
10–12	931	1—Rehoboam	Shemaiah
13	913	2—Abijah	
14–16	911	3—Asa*	Azariah, Hanani
17–20	872	4—Jehoshaphat*	
21	848	5—Jehoram	
22	841	6—Ahaziah	
22–23	841	7—Athaliah (queen)	
23–24	835	8—Joash*	
25	796	9—Amaziah*	
26	792	10—Azariah/Uzziah*	Isaiah
27	750	11—Jotham*	Isaiah, Micah
28	735	12—Ahaz	Isaiah, Micah
	722	Israel Falls	
29–32	715	13—Hezekiah*	Isaiah, Micah
33	697	14—Manasseh	Nahum (between 663 and 612 BC)
33	643	15—Amon	
34–35	641	16—Josiah*	Jeremiah, Zephaniah
36	609	17—Jehoahaz	Jeremiah

Chapter of Scripture	Year (BC)	Kings of Judah (good kings marked with *)	Prophets of Judah whose ministries overlapped with Judah's kings
36	609	18—Jehoiakim	Jeremiah, Habakkuk
36	598	19—Jehoiachin	Jeremiah
36	597	20—Zedekiah	Jeremiah
36	586	Judah Falls	Jeremiah, Obadiah; Joel (about 500 BC)

Jehoshaphat (2 Chr 17–20)

Jehoshaphat was a good king who followed the Lord. The writer of Chronicles highlights his eagerness to place the Levites in various cities so that the people of God would receive instruction from the word of God. Jehoshaphat also trusted the Lord when a large coalition of nations came against him from the southeast. As he trusted God, God brought victory.

Hezekiah (2 Chr 29–32)

The writer of Chronicles especially highlights the reign of Hezekiah. King Hezekiah possessed the faith to stand against the king of Assyria, and ultimately the Lord rewarded Hezekiah's faith by decimating the Assyrian army and sending Sennacherib home in disgrace. When Hezekiah became sick to the point of death, he prayed to the Lord, and the Lord graciously extended his life fifteen years. Hezekiah was not perfect, but he was a good king.

Josiah (2 Chr 34–35)

Josiah was Judah's last good king. The Bible mentions that when he turned sixteen he especially turned his heart toward God. Josiah's reforms included cleaning up the temple that had fallen into disrepair, and the cleaning process resulted in the discovery of the book of the law of Moses. This discovery further fanned the flames of Josiah's spiritual revival. Nonetheless, the wickedness set in motion by fifty-five years of his grandfather Manasseh's reign made it difficult for Josiah to undo all the spiritual damage. Josiah died in battle fighting the Egyptians, beginning Judah's downward spiral to exile in the Scattered Era.

Scattered Era (2 Chr 36:5–21)

The reigns of Judah's last four kings—Jehoahaz, Jehoiakim, Jehoiachin, and Zedekiah—transition us to the Scattered Era. Jehoiakim's revolt against Babylon led to the first deportation of Judean exiles (605 BC), although Jehoiakim was able to hang on to his throne for a while. But when Jehoiakim rebelled again, he had the good fortune to die before Nebuchadnezzar, king of Babylon, arrived back in Judah. Jehoiachin, Jehoiakim's eighteen-year-old son, would have to pay the price. After three months, Jehoiachin surrendered to the Babylonians (597 BC, the second deportation) and spent thirty-seven years in a Babylonian prison for his father's sin. About ten years later, after Zedekiah, Judah's last king, rebelled, Judah's kingdom came crashing down. The temple was destroyed, the walls were destroyed, and the people were deported (586 BC, the third deportation). It was a sad time in the story God was writing.[4]

Gathered Era (2 Chr 36:22–23)

In 539 BC, Cyrus, king of Persia, conquered Babylon. In the first year of his reign, Cyrus issued a decree that any Jews who wished could return and rebuild Jerusalem and its temple with Persian support. The book of Ezra records that almost fifty thousand people took Cyrus up on his offer and headed back to Judah (Ezra 2:64–65).

As the Chronicler closes his work, he makes it clear to his readers that Cyrus's decree did not happen simply because Cyrus was a nice guy. Rather, his decree happened "in order to fulfill the word of the LORD spoken by Jeremiah" (2 Chr 36:22). God was still writing his story, and as he did, he would continue to prepare the world for the coming of his Son.

How does Chronicles point to Jesus? First, it highlights Jesus's ancestry. Jesus hailed from the line of David, and the Chronicler continues to highlight the great works God was doing through David's line. The kings of Judah, of course, were imperfect people, with their faults often on display as

---

4. The book of Lamentations records the horror of Jerusalem's last days.

well. Nonetheless, the writer of Chronicles showed how from generation to generation, God continued to work and do a great thing among his people, and in particular through the line of David.

Second, after all the sadness of the final chapters, the book of Chronicles ends on a high note. The people of Judah are at last going home after exile! It is the beginning of the Gathered Era! Perhaps the writer of Chronicles wondered if this would be the time God would bring about his Messiah, the ultimate descendant of David. History would reveal that it was not yet time, but as God's purpose moved on, the coming of the Messiah grew ever closer.

11

Ezra, Nehemiah, and Esther

JEWISH TRADITION CONSIDERS THE books of Ezra and Nehemiah one book, and it makes sense to treat them together in one chapter because they go together. These men of God overlapped with respect to their ministries, and God powerfully used them in the incredible story he was writing. Meanwhile, back in Persia's royal court, God was still at work through a young Jewish woman named Esther, who found herself in an unlikely role— queen of Persia!—and embraced the situation to fulfill God's purpose.

Ezra

The book of Ezra details the first two returns of Jewish exiles to the promised land. Zerubbabel, a descendant of David, led the first return to Jerusalem in 538 BC, and ultimately God used him to lead the rebuilding of the temple. Ezra the priest and scribe led the second return in 458 BC and helped to renew the people's spiritual vitality. Tradition considers Ezra the author, and this is likely. The book of Ezra is part of the Gathered Era (538 BC–Christ).[1]

---

1. Jones, *Puzzle of the Old Testament*, 165–85.

Leader 1: Zerubbabel (Ezra 1–6)

Zerubbabel Returns to Jerusalem (Ezra 1–2)

Ezra 1:1 repeats the ending of 2 Chronicles 36. It highlights King Cyrus's decree that any Jew who wished could go home and rebuild Jerusalem and the temple with Persian support. Ezra 2:64–65 records how almost fifty thousand people headed back to Judah. Cyrus's decree was prophesied by Jeremiah (Jer 25:11), but Isaiah had mentioned Cyrus even earlier, around the year 700 BC (Isa 44:28, 45:1). God not only continued to prepare the world for the coming of his Son, but he sometimes announced his instruments ahead of time!

Zerubbabel Reconstructs the Temple (Ezra 3–6)

Dedication of the Temple's Foundation (Ezra 3)

The people returned and began to reestablish the temple's foundation. Once they had completed its foundation, they held a great celebration that featured both joy and sadness. On the one hand, people celebrated the great work God was doing. On the other hand, many remembered the temple's former glory and realized the sad price the nation had paid for its sin and unbelief.

Difficulty with Adversaries (Ezra 4–5)

Ezra 4:1–5 highlights the initial opposition the people faced when they began to rebuild Jerusalem and the temple. The rest of Ezra 4 (vv. 6–23) highlights how the trouble continued even into later generations.

The work stopped for approximately fifteen years until the year 520 BC. Right at this time, God raised up the prophets Haggai and Zachariah to encourage the people to complete the temple. When Judah's enemies again threatened to report them to the king, the work continued in faith. When the enemies did report them, a search of the royal Persian archives revealed the Jews did in fact have permission to build the temple. Armed with confirmation from the Persian king Darius, the Jews joyfully continued their work.

Dedication of the Temple (Ezra 6)

Once the Jews no longer faced opposition from the surrounding people, they were able to press on with all diligence. They completed the temple and dedicated it in the year 516 BC with great joy (Ezra 6:15). Following the temple's completion, the focus of the book of Ezra shifts from Zerubbabel's leadership to Ezra's leadership.

Leader 2: Ezra (Ezra 7–10)

The year was now 458 BC—eighty years after Cyrus's initial decree that the Jews could go home. Artaxerxes, Persia's fifth king, was now on the throne.[2]

Ezra Returns to Jerusalem (Ezra 7–8)

We first meet Ezra in Ezra 7:1. He was a priest and a scribe, an educated man with a zeal for spiritual things. Ezra 7:10 summarizes his life well: "Ezra had devoted himself to the study and observance of the Law of the LORD, and to teaching its decrees and laws in Israel." Ezra went up to Judah carrying the proclamation of King Artaxerxes with him, a proclamation that highlighted not only the king's permission but also his favor. The Persians probably thought they were gracious, and to some extent, they were. However, God's even more gracious hand was guiding the events of the story he was writing.

Participants of the Trip (Ezra 8)

Ezra 8 describes the journey of the 1,758 people who made the trip back to Judah. Ezra demonstrated his faith by refusing to have a guard detail accompany his group. In a day when a delegation might fear an attack from robbers, Ezra wanted to demonstrate his trust in God. The people arrived safely and gave glory to the Lord.

---

2. The accounts in the book of Esther took place during the reign of Xerxes, Persia's fourth king (486–65 BC).

Ezra Renews the People (Ezra 9–10)

Difficulty with Mixed Marriages (Ezra 9)

Soon after Ezra's arrival, the leadership informed him the people of Israel and even some of the priests and Levites had intermarried with the people of the land (Ezra 9:1). The book of Ruth had made it clear that foreigners were welcome among God's people if they chose to follow the God of Israel. However, the people of Judah had intermarried with the people of the land "with their detestable practices" (Ezra 9:1). Time and time again, when the Old Testament warned against marrying the people of the land, the issue was faith mixing, not race mixing.

Ezra was devastated and took the matter before the Lord. The people of God stood at a crucial crossroads: would they return to their failed sinful practices, or would they move ahead into all God had for them? Ezra knew he would have to deal with the people's marriages to foreign pagans.

Dedication of the People (Ezra 10)

Ezra's prayer was answered when the leadership informed him they would support him in his actions. Ezra then went to the people and admonished them for their sin in intermarrying with the people of the land and adopting their customs and worship patterns. The people repented and vowed to separate themselves from their pagan spouses. The text does not specifically say so, but it seems likely that foreign people were given the choice of remaining pagan or choosing to place their faith in God. Those who persisted in their Canaanite abominations were separated from Judah.

Believers today should not use this passage to condone divorce from an unbeliever. First Corinthians 7 makes it clear that once we are married to unbelievers, we should stay married insofar as it depends on us. The situation in Ezra 9–10 was a specific historical situation in which Ezra prayed to the Lord and the people resolved to separate themselves from the abominable pagan customs of the land. They did not wish to revert to their past sins but to move forward into what God had for them.

Concluding Thoughts from Ezra

How does the book of Ezra point to Jesus? First, it describes the people's return to the land so the story God was writing could continue. The people returned, rebuilt the temple, and began to reestablish the nation. Second, Ezra to some extent prefigures Jesus. Ezra was a priest deeply committed to God and his word (Ezra 7:10). He wanted to study it, live it, and teach it to others. As such, he modeled the work of his Lord, who would come about 450 years later. Jesus also had a passion for the word of God, and the book of Hebrews tells us that while Jesus hailed from the tribe of Judah, he nonetheless serves as our great high priest (Heb 7–10).

Nehemiah

The book of Nehemiah was probably written by Nehemiah himself, although some suggest Ezra may have collected Nehemiah's memoirs and written them down.[3] Nehemiah was a contemporary of Ezra, and likewise lived in the Gathered Era (538 BC–Christ).

In 444 BC, Nehemiah received permission from the Persian King Artaxerxes I to lead a third group of exiles from Babylon back to the promised land. We don't know how many Jews returned on this trip. Nonetheless, once there, Nehemiah set about to rebuild Jerusalem's wall—the wall King Nebuchadnezzar of Babylon had destroyed in 586 BC.

The book of Nehemiah highlights Nehemiah's leadership. Once Nehemiah's team completed the wall, Nehemiah led several spiritual reforms among the people. The book of Nehemiah describes Nehemiah's rebuilding of Jerusalem's wall, his renewing of God's covenant, and his reforming of Jerusalem.

Rebuilding of Jerusalem's Wall (Neh 1–7)

Commencement of the Wall (Neh 1–2)

The building of the wall was yet to begin, but in God's mind, it had already begun. He was preparing the way for this great work by guiding the events of history so that Nehemiah, a Jew, would end up serving as King

---

3. The repeating of the list of 50,000 returnees in Ezra 2 and Neh 7 make us think it's likely each man wrote his own work.

Artaxerxes's cupbearer. A cupbearer was an important official who spent much time at the king's side, and consequently, the king would get to know him very well.

When Nehemiah received word that Jerusalem was in distress, he prayed to the Lord and asked him to use him to bring about a solution. Three months later, the Lord gave Nehemiah an opportunity to speak to the king about his concern, and the king granted not only permission but full endorsement of the project. Nehemiah arrived in Jerusalem in the summer of 444 BC; he inspected the wall, devised a plan, and challenged the leadership to join him in rebuilding Jerusalem's walls. As with Zerubbabel's return in 538 BC, opposition to the Jews' work from the people of the land would soon begin.

Construction of the Wall (Neh 3–5)

Organizing the People (Neh 3)

Nehemiah 3 describes the organization of the workers and their faithful work around Jerusalem's perimeters.

Overcoming the Problems (Neh 4–5)

Nehemiah 4–5 describes the problems Nehemiah faced as people continued the work. The first set of problems was external; the people of the land frustrated the workers by constantly threatening and harassing them. In response, Nehemiah organized the workforce so that people would be ready to switch from workers to soldiers at any moment. The people worked in shifts around the clock so the work would progress faster.

Second, Nehemiah faced internal threats. In the midst of the wall building, Nehemiah discovered that the wealthy were exploiting the poor and taking advantage of them by charging interest, something the law of Moses prohibited. Furthermore, some of Judah's governors and officials were good leaders, while others were corrupt. Many times leaders will face either external opposition or internal opposition; Nehemiah faced both.

Completion of the Wall (Neh 6–7)

Sanballat, Tobiah, and Geshem continued their assault against the work of Nehemiah. However, their threats, attacks, and slander yielded no results, and the wall was completed in fifty-two days (Neh 6:15). Judah's enemies could do nothing except recognize that God's hand was upon the Jews. The date was August/September 444 BC.

Renewing of the Covenant (Neh 8–10)

Reading of Scripture (Neh 8:1–12)

Nehemiah, along with Ezra and other officials, gathered the people in Jerusalem. Ezra read from the book of the Law while those who stood around him conveyed the sense of it to the people who listened.[4]

The reading of the law of Moses brought great celebration but also much mourning. The people rejoiced to be back together in Judah, with the temple and the security a wall provided. However, for others, it was a reminder of how far they had fallen when they had taken their eyes off God's plan for their lives. Nehemiah reassured them that the joy of the Lord would give them strength to press on (Neh 8:10).

Restoration of Tabernacles (Neh 8:13–18)

Nehemiah 8:13–18 reveals a bit about how far the people had strayed. As they heard the word, they realized they were at the time of the Feast of Tabernacles, an important Jewish festival.[5] God's people really went all out to celebrate the Feast of Tabernacles; the text records that the people as a whole had not celebrated with such fervor since the days of Joshua.

---

4. The Hebrew word in Neh 8:8 is ambiguous. Some commentators believe those who assisted Ezra were merely elaborating on the basic sense of the meaning of the verses Ezra read. Others believe they were actually translating the law of Moses from Hebrew into Aramaic, the language of the common people of that time. Aramaic is a language similar to Hebrew (cf. Spanish and Portuguese).

5. The Feast of Tabernacles is also called the Feast of Booths; the Hebrew word is *sukkot*. It typically falls in September or October in the Jewish calendar and marks the fall harvest of fruits and vegetables. It also commemorates when the Israelites lived in tabernacles or booths as they journeyed through the wilderness (Lev 23:33–43).

Recommitment of the People (Neh 9–10)

The Levites led the people in a time of recommitment. Nehemiah 9–10 records a national confession of sin; God's people had been faithless despite God's faithfulness. The shame and disgrace that came from exile was their fault, not God's. Further, the Levites led all God's people in a vow of faithfulness. They spelled out specific stipulations, and all agreed to renew their hearts and follow the stipulations of God's covenant.

Reforming of Jerusalem (Neh 11–13)

Nehemiah 11–13 recounts three aspects of Nehemiah's reform in Jerusalem: counting the residents, celebrating the wall, and correcting the people's sins.

Counting the Residents (Neh 11)

Nehemiah 11 records an accurate counting of those who settled in Jerusalem and those who settled elsewhere. Allocation of the population was determined by the casting of lots, with God guiding the process so that his perfect will would be done. Now that Jerusalem's wall was in place and security was established, the people could again begin to establish the city.

Celebrating the Wall (Neh 12)

The celebration for the wall's dedication took place with great pomp and circumstance. Much singing and celebration ensued as the people marked the great victory God had won on their behalf.

Correcting the Sins (Neh 13)

Nehemiah 13 describes the steps this great reformer took to ensure the purity of God's people. Like Ezra, his contemporary, Nehemiah had to stand strong on his principles, principles rooted in God's word. Nehemiah had returned to Artaxerxes to give a report on Jerusalem's status. When he returned to Jerusalem, he found the house of God had been neglected and challenged the people to deal with it. He also had to stop Sabbath violations; the people were not resting on the Sabbath according to God's commandment (Exod 20:8–11). And Nehemiah, like Ezra, had to deal with the problem of God's people intermarrying with the pagan peoples of the land who did not convert to the Jewish faith. Nehemiah stood his ground, reminding the people their actions would lead to ruin just as they had before. In the end, they submitted to his leadership.

Concluding Thoughts from Nehemiah

Nehemiah, like Ezra, was a man of principle. He stood strong and faced much internal and external opposition. People who are leaders know that both kinds of opposition are challenging; yet, Nehemiah pressed on, and in the end, God used him to guide the people to take the appropriate next steps in the great story he was writing. Nehemiah thus did his part in God's plan to ensure the continuation of Judah as a pure nation, and as he did so, he helped prepare Judah and the world for the coming of Jesus.

Esther

The book of Esther follows the book of Nehemiah in our English Bibles. However, the events recorded in the book of Esther actually occur between the events in Ezra 6 and Ezra 7, that is, between the first return of the Jews to the promised land under Zerubbabel's leadership and the second return of the Jews to the promised land under Ezra's leadership. It is as if the Scripture is saying to us, "Okay, you've read the books of Ezra and Nehemiah and have seen what God was doing back in the promised land. But meanwhile, back in Persia, something else was happening that ensured Ezra's and Nehemiah's ministries would continue." In fact, the events of the book of Esther ensure the people of God continued! God used Esther to save her people from destruction as he continued to write his story.

Esther served as queen to the Persian king Xerxes (486–64 BC); the Bible calls him Ahasuerus. Esther's story begins in approximately 483 BC. Throughout history, God's people have faced opposition from people who sought to destroy them. The book of Esther highlights a time when God's people faced extermination. However, God's story would continue through a woman God used in an amazing way, beyond what she ever could have imagined.

We do not know who wrote the book of Esther; some have suggested Mordecai (whom we will meet in the book of Esther) or perhaps even Esther herself. The events take place in the Gathered Era (538 BC–Christ).[6]

Esther's Placement as the Queen (Esth 1–2)

The Demotion of Vashti (Esth 1)

The book begins with King Ahasuerus throwing a great party for the people of his kingdom. As the party continued, the king summoned his wife Queen Vashti to come appear before the people that all might see her beauty. Surprisingly, Vashti refused the request of her husband the king and would not come. Concerned over the possible ramifications of Vashti's decision as the news of her refusal spread, the king established that Vashti be deposed as queen and that the search begin immediately for a woman to replace her.

The Promotion of Esther (Esth 2)

The search began throughout Ahasuerus's kingdom for a woman charming, beautiful, and intelligent enough to serve as his queen. Esther, an orphaned Jewish girl being raised by her older relative Mordecai, was placed among the candidates. In the course of time, the king summoned her, and she found favor with the king and became his queen. Never in her wildest dreams would Esther have imagined such blessing! However, she soon would discover that with her position came great responsibility.

Haman's Plot against the Jews (Esth 3–8)

The Rage of Haman (Esth 3)

King Ahasuerus had an important official named Haman who craved admiration and adoration from the common people. However, Mordecai refused to bow to Haman and this angered Haman greatly. Haman models for us a classic example of racism; in his anger over Mordecai's actions, he made the assumption that all the Jewish people were just like Mordecai. Haman went to the king and told him there were rebellious people in the land. Further,

---

6 Jones, *Puzzle of the Old Testament*, 165–85.

Haman told the king he had a plan for the peoples of the land to destroy the Jews and plunder their property that no further harm would come to the king. The king signed the edict, and it was distributed through the land.

The Response of Mordecai (Esth 4)

The Jewish people now faced extermination on the date the decree had determined. Anyone who wished could take up his sword and kill Jews and plunder their property without penalty. Mordecai sent word to Esther and encouraged her to go speak to the king; however, Persian protocol dictated that no one came into the king's presence uninvited. Anyone who did faced possible death unless the king extended his scepter to that person. A key verse in this passage is Esther 4:14, which recounts Mordecai's words to Esther: "Who knows but that you have come to your royal position for such a time as this?" What some may have seen as a beauty contest, Mordecai saw as the hand of God. Esther determined she would go to the king at the risk of her life.

The Requests of Esther (Esth 5–8)

Queen Esther went before the king, who saw her and extended his scepter to her. She asked that the king and Haman attend a banquet she was preparing. Haman initially felt honored, but when he later saw Mordecai the Jew still refusing to bow to him, the anger he felt overshadowed the honor he had received. Meanwhile, the king discovered Mordecai had actually saved his life on an earlier occasion and instructed Haman to parade Mordecai around the town square with great honor. We can only imagine how little Haman enjoyed doing that!

At a second feast Esther prepared for the king and Haman, she revealed her Jewish identity and revealed Haman's plot against the Jews. The king in a rage ordered Haman executed and then exalted Mordecai, who received charge of Haman's estate. The potential damage, however, was far from over. According to Persian custom, an edict signed by the king could not be changed.[7] Thus, Esther urged that the king sign a counter decree that

---

7. This custom also became an issue in the book of Daniel. King Darius issued a foolish decree he could not cancel when Daniel violated it (Dan 6:7–9, 12, 15).

Jews who were attacked could take up the sword and avenge themselves on their enemies.

Mordecai's Proclamation about the Feast (Esth 9–10)

Mordecai Defeats Israel's Foes (Esth 9:1–19)

The king's counter decree yielded its desired effect. The Jews were able to defend themselves and took vengeance on their enemies. What Haman had meant for evil, God turned around and worked for good.

Mordecai Declares the Feast of Purim (Esth 9:20—10:3)

The Hebrew word *purim* literally means "lots." Haman had cast lots to determine the best day to annihilate the Jews; the Jews now named the feast "lots" to commemorate how God had turned Haman's evil intent into the salvation of the Jews. Even in modern times, Jewish people continue to celebrate Purim, which usually falls around mid-February in our calendar.

Concluding Thoughts from Esther

As we said at the beginning of the chapter, the books of Ezra and Nehemiah show how God used these men to further his purpose back in the promised land. However, in between the events of Ezra 6 and 7, events back in Persia took place that would seriously impact the ministry of Nehemiah and Ezra. God raised Esther to prominence in the Persian court so that he could use her to save his people.

One of the amazing ironies in the book of Esther is that God's name never appears in the book. For this reason, some Jews believed the book of Esther did not belong in the Bible. However, when we read the book, we cannot escape the obvious presence of God. He is in every event, in every meeting, to his glory. And through his leading of Esther and his guidance of the events in the book, God's purpose continues, his people continue to exist, and the story continues to move toward the coming of Jesus Christ.

Part Three

The Poetical Books

These books contain some of Israel's
ancient wisdom in poetic form.
They discuss deep philosophical questions
such as why the righteous suffer;
offer songs to God on many topics;
present concise, practical truths for life;
reflect on what gives life ultimate meaning; and
ponder the joy of romantic love within marriage.

Books Covered

Job
Psalms
Proverbs
Ecclesiastes
Song of Solomon (a.k.a. Song of Songs)

1 2

Job

THE BOOK OF JOB was probably written early in the Something Era (2090–1445 BC).[1] Indeed, some commentators believe it even precedes the book of Genesis.[2]

Why do bad things happen to good people? We all know accounts of people who suffer incredibly even though their lives suggest they do not deserve such suffering. That question has been around since the beginning of time, and the book of Job brings it into dramatic focus.

The book begins by documenting the sufferings God allowed Satan to inflict upon Job. After four rounds of advice from his friends, Job learned powerful lessons about God and about himself. Afterwards, God restored Job's family and fortune.

A Sad Prologue (Job 1–3)

The book's first three chapters prepare us for the rest of the book. They deal with Job's character, Job's calamity, Job's comforters, and Job's curse.

---

1. Jones, *Puzzle of the Old Testament*, 35–48.

2. The Hebrew of the book of Job is quite old and difficult to navigate. The reference to the Temanites, descendants of Jacob's brother Esau (Gen 36:9–11), and the reference to the book taking place in the land of Uz (Job 1:1; compare Lam 4:22) suggest the account may have taken place in the land of Edom.

Job's Character (Job 1:1–5)

The text says about Job that he was "blameless and upright; he feared God and shunned evil" (Job 1:1). Job worshiped his God faithfully and also interceded for his children, lest they might have forgotten to repent for sins they had committed.

Job's Calamity (Job 1:6—2:10)

A day came when all the angels of God, including Satan, the adversary and accuser, presented themselves before God.[3] When God pointed out Job's faithfulness to Satan, Satan suggested Job had good reason to love God. After all, God had essentially spoiled him rotten! God had given Job family, wealth, and a good name and had sheltered him from misfortune. Satan insisted that if those blessings were removed from Job's life, Job would curse God to his face.

First Attack of Satan (Job 1:6–22)

The Lord instructed Satan that he could touch anything Job had but warned him not to touch Job physically. In response, Satan brought waves of calamity against Job's property and family. Job lost his ten children, his many servants, and all his livestock. In response, Job worshiped anyway and did not sin against the Lord. He recognized God's prerogative to bring blessing or to take it away. It was a tough lesson, but Job passed the test.

Second Attack of Satan (Job 2:1–10)

When Satan again appeared before the Lord, the Lord pointed out Job's faithfulness. In response, Satan insisted Job would curse God to his face if Satan was allowed to afflict his body. Again, the Lord gave permission; note that whatever comes our way, Satan can act only as God allows him to do so.

Satan struck Job with boils from the top of his head to the soles of his feet. The boils were severe, and the pain was great. Job's wife suggested he

---

3. Some commentators have wondered how Satan could actually come into God's presence, but when one considers that God is omnipresent (i.e., he exists everywhere), Satan is always in God's presence.

curse God and die, but Job refused and insisted that would not be right. Still, he must have wondered what was going on and why he was suffering so.

Job's Comforters (Job 2:11–13)

Job's three friends Eliphaz, Bildad, and Zophar came to visit him because they heard of his pain. At first, they did not recognize him due to the boils that covered his body. They sat respectfully in silence for seven days when they saw how great his pain was. Ironically, when they began to speak, they added to their friend's misery rather than helping him.

Job's Curse (Job 3)

Job began by cursing the day of his birth (Job 3:1). He described the pain and suffering he was experiencing and did not understand why. This basic question in Job's heart is a question we all face at some point in life: "Why do bad things happen to seemingly good people?" Job's friends would try to give an answer, but God would give the ultimate answer.

A Series of Dialogues (Job 4:1—42:6)

Job Listens to His Comforters (Job 4–37)

Job 4–37 comprises a dialogue between Job and his friends. In Job 4–14, the first round of dialogues, Eliphaz speaks, followed by Job's response. Then Bildad speaks, followed by Job's response. Finally, Zophar speaks, followed by Job's response. With each speech, although the words vary somewhat, the accusation was essentially the same. Each of the friends believed that somehow, Job must have sinned and therefore deserved his suffering. In response, Job confessed he did not know of a sin he had committed to deserve his body being covered with boils. He questioned his friends, and he even questioned God to a point. However, Job's faith shines through in his words in Job 13:15: "Though He slay me, yet will I hope in him." Job ultimately trusted that God knew what he was doing, but he did want to know God's purpose behind it.

In the second round of dialogues (Job 15–21), the pattern was the same. Each of Job's friends spoke, followed by Job's response. Again, Job spoke words that help us understand his theology: "I know that my redeemer lives, and that in the end he will stand on the earth. After after my skin has been destroyed, yet in my flesh I will see God" (Job 19:25–26). Through the pain, somehow Job knew God was working through the process. In the end, Job's day of redemption would come. Some commentators have seen in the word "redeemer" a reference to Jesus, but this is probably premature. Most likely Job was referring to God as his ultimate Redeemer. Job believed God somehow would sort things out in the end, though he certainly did not see how.

The third round of dialogues (Job 22–31) included only Eliphaz, Bildad, and Job. Again, as in the first two rounds, the friends offered no real answer. They chastised Job for what they saw as boldness or arrogance, but in the end, they had no new counsel to add. They insisted Job must have done something to deserve his fate. In response, Job asserted his innocence, and pleaded with God to show him what was going on.

In the fourth round, we meet a new figure: Elihu (Job 32–37). Commentators have noted that Elihu's words are fairly on target. Elihu chastised Job's friends because they had no answer for Job, but he also charged Job with self-righteousness. Job was not God, Elihu argued, and therefore, Job really did not have the right to insist that God explain to him what was happening in his situation. God was God, and Job needed to remember that. It wasn't wrong for Job to ask God what God wanted to teach him through difficult circumstances, but in Elihu's judgment, Job had pressed his own innocence too far. Elihu's words paved the way for God's intervention in the closing chapters of the book of Job.

Job Learns from His God (Job 38:1—42:6)

First Lesson (Job 38:1—40:5)

Suddenly God intervened and began to speak to Job. His words "I will question you, and you shall answer me" (Job 38:3) must have created in Job a sense that this was not going to end well! God's first question—"Where were you when I laid the earth's foundations?"—revealed God's majesty over and against Job's smallness. Again and again through chapters 38 and 39, God put unanswerable questions before Job. Job did not control the forces of nature, Job did not control the stars, and Job was very small in the face of an all-powerful God. Job responded in 40:4: "I am unworthy—how can I reply to you?" But God was only half finished.

God knew he was getting through to Job; however, he would now drive home his point. He asked Job a question: "Would you discredit my justice? Would you condemn me to justify yourself?" (Job 40:8). He then continued with more questions and observations that highlighted his own majesty and power over and against Job's relative insignificance.

At the end of God's second series of questions, Job responded in humility. He wanted God to instruct him so that he could learn from him rather than challenging God's ways. Job repented deeply before God; he now understood that God did not owe him an answer for everything that happened to him.

A Sensational Epilogue (Job 42:7-17)

The book of Job closes with two events: God's rebuke of Job's friends and God's restoration of Job's fortunes.

Rebuke of Job's Friends (Job 42:7-9)

The Lord told Eliphaz, Bildad, and Zophar (note that Elihu was not mentioned!) that they had not spoken the truth concerning him. Therefore, he instructed them to ask Job to pray for them and for him to bring an offering on their behalf. The friends obeyed, and God received their offering.

Restoration of Job's Fortunes (Job 42:10-17)

Following the testing of his servant, the Lord restored Job's fortunes. Job was comforted by his friends and lived out his days with a new perspective on the God he served.

Concluding Thoughts from Job

The book of Job presents powerful lessons about God's sovereignty. Like Job, perhaps we wonder why bad things sometimes happen to good people. Perhaps we are walking with God, and we wonder why bad things happen to us sometimes. In the end, the book of Job reminds us that God does not answer to us. We may count on him to work all things together in our lives for our good and for his glory (Rom 8:28), but that does not mean we will like or enjoy everything he brings or allows to come our way.

Challenges will come to people who don't know God and to people who do know God. When God's children face difficult circumstances, knowing that Satan can bring to us only what God allows may be comforting. Job often asked God why he suffered, but in the end, Job knew God was guiding his life, and the same is true of us as we live in the great story God is writing.

13

Psalms

THE BOOK OF PSALMS is different from any other book of the Bible. It is the longest book of the Bible for one thing, but that's not what makes it unique. What makes it unique is how the book of Psalms comprises a collection of Israel's hymns and songs. Many have described this as Israel's ancient hymnal. Like our collections of hymns, those in the book originated over many centuries. Many of them came from the United Era (1043–931 BC),[1] though many psalms originated after that and some even before.

The psalms speak to many hearts today, because they speak to such a variety of human circumstances. If we wake up in the morning and just cannot help but praise God, we can find a psalm to help us do that. If we are feeling the weight of our sin and want to confess it to God, we can find a psalm to help us confess our sin. If we are feeling discouraged and need God's comfort, we can find psalms that will help us experience that comfort. If we are frustrated, angry, or the victims of injustice and we cry out to God for vindication, we can find a psalm that will help us do that. Again, just like many of our modern hymnals that have a wide range of hymns from various centuries, even so the book of Psalms represents that in Scripture.

---

1. Jones, *Puzzle of the Old Testament*, 91–112.

Who Wrote the Psalms?

The author of most of the psalms was King David, who is credited with almost half of them; however, other writers also contributed to the work. Moses is credited with writing Psalm 90; the sons of Korah, first mentioned in Numbers 16, are credited with approximately a dozen psalms, as is Asaph, one of David's worship leaders (1 Chr 16:4–5). A significant number of psalms are anonymous. We don't know who wrote them, but they continue to speak to us.

How Does Hebrew Poetry Work?

When we stop to consider that the book of Psalms represents ancient Hebrew poetry, we might ask the question how ancient Hebrew poetry differs from our modern poetry. One significant way is that the feature of rhyme rarely makes a difference in Hebrew; instead, the Hebrew poets were more concerned about the meter or rhythm of their poetic lines. We will discuss key elements below.

Parallelism

The Hebrew authors often employed an important feature called parallelism. Parallelism is when two or more consecutive lines or verses complement each other in some way. The two lines might essentially repeat the same idea, or in some cases they issue a sharp contrast. Two examples appear below:

> Example 1: His delight is in the law of the LORD, and on His law he meditates day and night (Ps 1:2).

> Example 2: The LORD knows the way of the righteous, but the way of the wicked will perish (Ps 1:6).

In the first example from Psalm 1:2, the two lines are synonymous. The righteous man delights in God's word, and the parallel thought reflects that he meditates on it day and night. That's how he shows his delight in God's word. On the other hand, verse 6 points out how the Lord knows the way of both the righteous and the wicked; because the righteous and the wicked take two very different approaches to life, they arrive at two very different destinations. Psalm 1:6 contrasts the two, but the two verses are still parallel. Scholars call the first example synonymous parallelism and the second example antithetic parallelism.

Acrostics

Another feature of the book of Psalms that is not obvious to English readers is the phenomenon of acrostics, or alphabetic poems. The Hebrew alphabet has twenty-two letters, so when we see a twenty-two-verse psalm we may suspect (and usually correctly) that the psalm is an acrostic. Verse 1 begins with *aleph*, the first letter of the Hebrew alphabet. Verse 2 begins with *beth*, the second letter of the Hebrew alphabet. Verse 3 begins with *gimel*, the third letter of the Hebrew alphabet, and so on throughout the psalm. The psalmists' tender care with which they crafted their psalm to God, incorporating this alphabetic dimension, speaks to their labor of love. This special gift to God was worth the effort![2]

What Do the Psalm Headings Mean?

Many of the psalms have headings on them (e.g., Pss 4–9, 16, 74). Scholars believe these probably represent some kind of musical notations or the kind of psalm the psalm is, but we really do not know. Sometimes, a psalm heading will include a historical note that tells us when the psalm was written or the occasion of the psalm's writing. For example, Psalm 3 was written by King David at a time he was fleeing from Absalom (2 Sam 15–18). Knowing that helps to interpret the psalm. Psalm 51 was written by David after he was confronted by Nathan, the prophet, over David's adulterous relationship with Bathsheba (2 Sam 12). Again, understanding the historical situation helps us to interpret the psalm. Some scholars have suggested that maybe the headings to the psalms were added later, but the headings are in all of the earliest manuscripts, so it is probably safe to assume they are inspired as well.

---

2. The parallel would be if we were to write a twenty-six-line poem to the Lord with the first line beginning with *a*, the second line beginning with *b*, the third line beginning with *c*, etc.

What Kinds of Different Psalms Do We Have?

Scholars have identified seven different basic psalm types into which any psalm typically fits. They are discussed briefly below.

Hymns

Hymns are psalms of praise and thanksgiving. This category is one of the most significant categories of the psalms. Hymns may be individual songs to God or they may reflect corporate worship. Some examples include Psalms 8, 100, 136, and 150, although there are many more.

Wisdom Psalms

Wisdom psalms generally provide reflections on life. The psalmist pondered life and wrote down his thoughts as he understood them. Examples of wisdom psalms include Psalms 1, 14, and 73.

Lament Psalms

Lament psalms are psalms in which the writer pours out his heart to God in sorrow and lament. Typically these psalms have three features. First, the writer expresses his lament. Second, he expresses his trust in God as he focuses on God's truth. Third, there is often at the end of the psalm some kind of praise as the psalmist works through his lament to praise God. Examples of lament psalms include Psalm 3 and Psalm 22.

Penitential Psalms

At first glance, people might confuse lament psalms with penitential psalms, because both categories express sorrow to the Lord. However, penitential psalms focus on sorrow for one's sin. A lament may be sorrow over a tough situation or something that has happened, but a penitential psalm focuses on conviction of sin and pleads to God for forgiveness. A famous example of a penitential psalm is Psalm 51, where David begged the Lord for forgiveness after his sin with Bathsheba.

Imprecatory Psalms

Imprecatory psalms are those psalms that sometimes make us uncomfortable when we read them. Imprecatory psalms call for God's judgment upon people who have wronged the psalmist or the psalmist's people. Sometimes the psalmist expresses strong thoughts, as he does, for example, in Psalm 35:4–6:

> May those who seek my life be disgraced and put to shame;
> may those who plot my ruin be turned back in dismay.
> May they be like chaff before the wind,
> with the angel of the LORD driving them away;
> may their path be dark and slippery,
> with the angel of the LORD pursuing them.

Another really tough example is Psalm 137:8–9:

> Daughter Babylon, doomed to destruction,
> happy is the one who repays you
> according to what you have done to us.
> Happy is the one who seizes your infants
> and dashes them against the rocks.

Christians usually have a hard time reconciling such thoughts with the gospel of Christ, where Jesus encouraged us to pray for our enemies (Matt 5:44). Indeed, we might say that as the psalmists lashed out in hate and anger, they did not always display godly characteristics. At the same time, we may commend them, because they committed their cause to God and asked God to take action. Ultimately, vengeance was the Lord's prerogative, not theirs (Rom 12:18–19).

Royal Psalms

Royal psalms speak of Israel's king. A great example is Psalm 2, which most commentators interpret as a psalm sung at the coronation of a new king. Other examples would be Psalms 93, 97, and 99, which proclaim the Lord's reign as King of the nations.

Messianic Psalms

Messianic psalms are psalms that find their ultimate fulfillment in Jesus Christ. Messianic psalms are different from prophecy in that in messianic psalms, the psalmists use words to describe their own life situations, but God guided their words in such a way that centuries later, the New Testament writers could find fulfillment in Jesus. Because Jesus is the King of kings, we find that sometimes royal psalms overlap with messianic psalms. Examples of messianic psalms appear below.

Psalm 2: Jesus as God's Son

As stated above, Psalm 2 celebrated the coronation of the king. However, the New Testament writers especially focused on verse 7: "You are my son; today I have become your father." They saw in this psalm an expression of Jesus as God's Son. Jesus was already God's Son, but God powerfully demonstrated Jesus's sonship when he raised him from the dead (Acts 13:32–33).

Psalm 16: Jesus as Risen

In Psalm 16, David described his own situation. He thanked the Lord for his life, yet he knew God had more for him beyond the grave. God would not abandon him to Sheol but would receive him to glory (16:8–11). On the day of Pentecost, Peter explained to the crowd that ultimately these verses spoke of Jesus, who could not stay in the grave but rose on the third day (Acts 2:25–32).

Psalm 22: Jesus the Crucified

David was experiencing a painful situation when he wrote Psalm 22. As he poured out his lament to God, he felt God had forsaken him (22:1). He said he felt it was as if he were totally surrounded by evildoers (22:12–13). He felt as if he were pierced through and could see his bones (22:16–17). He felt so discouraged that it was as if people were mocking him and gambling for the last of his clothes (22:18).

The psalm is remarkable in that it is not a prophecy per se, for King David knew nothing about crucifixion. However, a thousand years later, as Jesus hung on the cross, David's figurative words became words Jesus literally fulfilled through his suffering.

Psalm 22: David's Lament Fulfilled in Jesus

Psalm 22	Fulfilled in Jesus
v. 1: "My God, my God, why have you forsaken me?"	Matt 27:46: Jesus quotes the verse as he is dying.
vv. 7–8: "All who see me mock me; they hurl insults, shaking their heads. 'He trusts in the LORD,' they say, 'let the LORD rescue him. Let him deliver him, since he delights in him.'"	Matt 27:41–43: Chief priest, scribes, elders use this language to mock Jesus on the cross.
vv. 14–18: "I am poured out like water, and all my bones are out of joint. My heart has turned to wax; it has melted within me. My mouth is dried up like a potsherd, and my tongue sticks to the roof of my mouth . . . . A pack of villains encircles me; they pierce my hands and my feet. All my bones are on display; people stare and gloat over me. They divide my garments among themselves, and they cast lots for my clothing."	Jesus's body is twisted on the cross. His strength gradually dries up, and he experiences dehydration. His hands and feet are pierced with nails. People stare at him. Matt 27:35: Soldiers cast lots for Jesus's clothes

Psalms 45 and 110: Jesus as the King

Psalm 45 and Psalm 110 both refer to Jesus's kingship. Again, we can thank the New Testament writers for seeing this parallel. In Psalm 45:6–7, the psalmist described the king's throne that lasted forever and ever. The writer of Hebrews, however, specifically applied these words to Christ (Heb 1:8–9). Psalm 110 also provides words the New Testament writers later saw as applying not only to David but also to Jesus. Jesus was David's Lord, even though he was David's descendant (Ps 110:1; Matt 22:41–45). He was also designated God's high priest forever according to the order of Melchizedek (Ps 110:4; Heb 6:20; 7:1–3). As the early church sang their hymns of praise to God and his Son, the Lord Jesus Christ, they couldn't help but see in the psalms many references to their Lord and Savior.

Concluding Thoughts from the Psalms

As we close this chapter on the book of Psalms, we'd like to offer another suggestion to you. Try reading the psalms devotionally and praying the words back to God. For example, when you read Psalm 1, read the first verse and then ask the Lord not to allow you to walk down paths with wicked people and entertain their counsel, let alone mock the things of God. Read verse 2, and ask him to give you a delight for the word of God that results in meditating on it day and night. Read verse 3, and claim God's promise that you can become like a strong tree planted by channels of water that yields its spiritual fruit in its time. Continue through the psalm until you have prayed its entire contents back to God. As you do that, you'll be identifying with ancient worshippers of God, who expressed their thoughts to him in this way thousands of years ago.[3]

3. For further reading, see Arnold and Beyer, *Encountering the Old Testament*, 279–89; Bullock, *Encountering the Book of Psalms*.

14

Proverbs

THE BOOK OF PROVERBS, like the book of Psalms, is quite unique to the Scriptures. Although we can certainly read straight through its thirty-one chapters, doing so often provides us little context for the Proverbs. Nonetheless, the book of Proverbs contains a collection of powerful insights to live life practically and in a wise manner.[1] King Solomon is credited with writing almost the entire book of Proverbs. Proverbs 1:1—22:16, as well as chapters 25–29, all come from his hand. Chapter 30 is the work of an otherwise unknown individual named Agur, and Proverbs 31 comes from a man named Lemuel. Proverbs 22:17—24:34 is entitled "Sayings of the Wise," from an unknown group of sages. The book's significant link to Solomon means that most of it comes from the United Era (1043–931 BC).[2]

What Are Proverbs?

Proverbs represent catchy ways to describe powerful truths. The book contains 915 verses, and its proverbs represent time-tested truths that Solomon and others encouraged people to apply to their lives. As people apply these truths, they embrace the life God expects his people to live.

Are proverbs absolute truths we can claim, or are they timeless maxims that are almost always true but not necessarily true in every situation?

1. For an excellent layman's study on Proverbs, see Powell, *Wise Up*.
2. Jones, *Puzzle of the Old Testament*, 91–112.

Scholars have debated this issue. Certainly Christian parents have leaned on Proverbs 22:6 ("Start children off on the way they should go, and even when they are old they will not turn from it") as they try to raise their children for Christ, only to find a child strays from the Lord. Does that mean God's promise failed? Therefore, some have said the proverbs are simply time-tested truths, though they might not prove true in every circumstance.

Another more likely explanation is that the proverbs are all absolutely true, but they have to all be taken together. In other words, when parents do their job diligently and the children respond to their parents' godly instruction, then life as it was meant to be ensues, and the proverbs are true.

Regardless of which interpretation we take, it would be folly to suggest that proverbs are mere options for life. Rather, these represent excellent counsel for anyone seeking to live a God-honoring life.

Themes of Proverbs

Rather than going through the book of Proverbs chapter by chapter, we will attempt to summarize the main themes found in Proverbs below. Other themes appear, but these are the main ones.

Our Relationship with God

The book of Proverbs encourages us to trust in the Lord with all our hearts (3:5–6). He will direct our steps as we do so. Further, the book of Proverbs also tells us that the fear of the Lord is the beginning of knowledge and wisdom (1:7; 9:10). It is our relationship with the Lord from which our wisdom comes (2:6). Indeed, our relationship with the Lord is not the most important relationship in our life; rather, it is life itself. (See also John 17:3.)

Marriage and Family

While it is true some leaders of ancient times had multiple wives, the book of Proverbs assumes monogamy as the norm. The husband and wife work together, and he who finds a wife finds a good thing (18:22). In fact, a prudent wife is a gift from the Lord (19:14). The book of Proverbs closes with a poem about a virtuous woman, the kind of woman a man should pursue (31:10–31).

Fidelity is important to any marriage. The book of Proverbs warns against the immoral woman, who may lead a man's heart astray if he is not guarding his heart and guarding his marriage (7:4–5). As Solomon looked out his window one day, he saw a young man who passed down the road of the immoral woman, a place he never should have gone. In the end, he paid a terrible price (7:6–27). The book of Proverbs, with its stress on the importance of marriage and the reality of temptation, encourages us to guard our marriages as the treasures they are.

Regarding the area of family, the mother and father work together to educate the children. Proverbs 1:8 encourages children to listen to their parents' teaching. The parents are a team as they raise their children to follow the Lord. Children need to honor their parents, respect their authority, and follow their counsel, lest they bring shame and grief to themselves and their parents (10:1).

Wisdom

The book of Proverbs is clear that wisdom comes from God (2:6). At the same time, wisdom is something for which we should seek diligently (2:1–5). In Proverbs 8, wisdom becomes personified and speaks to any who would listen. God's wisdom is available to all who will draw near and lay hold of it.

Proverbs 1:7 and 9:10 remind us that the fear of Lord is the beginning of knowledge and wisdom. The Christian life requires more than knowledge; it requires wisdom that enables us to apply knowledge correctly.

The Fool and the Sluggard

Proverbs talks about fools and sluggards. In both cases, folly and laziness are chosen outlooks. The book is not making fun of people who have a lower aptitude; rather, it ridicules those who choose to go through life avoiding their responsibility or loving sleep too much. In the end, they are sure to realize the folly of their actions.

The book of Proverbs sadly records how some fools actually seem to like their folly (15:21). The sluggard, meanwhile, makes up excuses for not getting things done (22:13) and is always thinking about getting just a few more minutes of rest (6:9–10). As a result of such folly and sluggardness, the work they should be doing comes to ruin (24:30–34).

As we read the verses about the fool and the sluggard, we might find ourselves laughing if the situation really were not so tragic. At the end of life, such people have nothing to show for their lives.

Concluding Thoughts from Proverbs

The book of Proverbs is cited a few places in the New Testament. Although the book's main purpose is not to point to Jesus but to highlight the proper path for life, we do find a few places where the New Testament writers make a connection. Paul cited Proverbs 25:21–22 as he urged the Roman believers to love their enemies (Rom 12:20). The writer of Hebrews mentioned Proverbs 3:11–12 as he reminded his readers that the Lord disciplines those he loves (Heb 12:5–6). Peter used Proverbs 11:31 to emphasize the great price of securing our salvation (1 Pet 4:18), and both Peter and James instructed their readers to be humble, because God opposes the proud but gives grace to the humble (Prov 3:34; Jas 4:6; 1 Pet 5:5).

Sometimes when we choose to live according to biblical principles, people suggest we are living a "sheltered" life and missing out on all life has to offer. However, God's way is not the sheltered way; it's the right way. God created life, and God created our lives. He wants us to live them on purpose and for a purpose, and books such as Proverbs help us know the paths he wants us to choose and the paths he wants us to avoid.

15

Ecclesiastes

JEWISH AND CHRISTIAN TRADITION ascribe the authorship of Ecclesiastes to King Solomon, and many allusions in the book appear to support this likelihood. The writer had reigned as Israel's king, had accumulated much wealth, and had many wives. Assuming Solomon is the author, the book was written toward the end of the United Era (1043–931 BC).[1]

Solomon used the name Qohelet (often translated "the teacher") to describe himself. He showed the apparent meaninglessness of life from both his own experiences and his observations of others. After leading people down one dead-end road after another, seeking for life's true meaning, he concludes people can find meaning only when they live life in reverence to God and obedience to him.

The Teacher's Cry (Eccl 1:1–11)

Solomon began with the assertion that everything is meaningless (Eccl 1:2–3). The Hebrew word translated "meaningless" can also mean "futility" and elsewhere is sometimes translated "mist," indicating the temporary aspect of life.[2] The preacher asserted that life lived under the sun has no ultimate meaning.

1. Jones, *Puzzle of the Old Testament*, 91–112.

2. Interestingly, Abel, the second son of Adam and Eve, had this word as his name. Indeed, his time in the biblical text was very short—like a mist—although he was

The Teacher's Concern (Eccl 1:12—12:8)

Solomon began this section by saying, "I, the Teacher, was king over Jerusalem. I applied my mind to study and to explore by wisdom all that is done under the heavens. . . . All of them are meaningless, a chasing after the wind" (Eccl 1:12–14). Solomon would testify for the rest of this section from his own personal experience and from his private observations. As king of Israel, he had opportunity both to experience and to observe many things and to ask important questions about life's ultimate meaning.

The Teacher's Personal Experience (Eccl 1:12—2:26)

Solomon began by recounting his own personal experience in four areas of life: wisdom, pleasure, folly, and labor.

Wisdom (1:12–18)

The word translated "wisdom" occurs four times in these seven verses. Solomon affirmed that he set his mind to know wisdom as he attempted to know life's meaning. However, he concluded with a refrain that would become common in his book: "all is vanity and striving after the wind" (Eccl 1:17). Solomon affirmed that much wisdom brought much grief, as people became more aware of the pain and suffering in the world.

Pleasure (Eccl 2:1–11)

Solomon used the terms translated "pleasure" several times in these eleven verses. As king, he did not need to refrain from pursuing any pleasure, for he had the resources and the time to pursue them. In the end, however, he concluded that "everything was meaningless, a chasing after the wind" (Eccl 2:11).

Folly (Eccl 2:12–17)

The words translated "fool" or "folly" occur six times in these six verses. If meaning to life could not be found in wisdom, perhaps it could be found

---

commended for his faithfulness to God (Heb 11:4).

in senseless folly! However, that road as well proved a dead end: "all of it is meaningless, a chasing after the wind" (Eccl 2:17).

Labor (Eccl 2:18-26)

The words translated "toil" or "labor" abound in these nine verses. If meaning to life did not come through pursuing pleasure, perhaps it came through hard work. In the end, however, Solomon concluded that "this too is meaningless, a chasing after the wind" (Eccl 2:26).

The Teacher's Private Observation (Eccl 3:1—12:8)

Solomon now moved in this section from his personal experience to his private observations. The words translated "I have seen" or "I looked again" occur sixteen times in this section.[3] In general, Solomon pursued the same lines of investigation he had in the first section. He looked at wisdom but concluded it did not bring ultimate meaning to life. He looked at leisure or pleasure and made a similar conclusion. Folly as well led only to trouble, and hard work ultimately may not pay off.

The key to Solomon's conclusions in all of these areas was his understanding of death. Death came to all people indiscriminately; rich people might live only a short life, and their descendants would squander the money their ancestors had worked so hard to earn. On the other hand, Solomon knew of scoundrels who lived a long life. Where was the justice in all of that? Even King Solomon in all his wisdom struggled to understand it. As Solomon observed rich and poor, strong and weak, good and evil, he observed that death came to all people regardless of their status. How unfair life could be! It seemed perhaps all was meaningless.

The Teacher's Conclusion (Eccl 12:9-14)

Ecclesiastes 12:8 concluded again with the familiar words "'Meaningless! Meaningless!' says the Teacher. 'Everything is meaningless!'" Consequently, we might wonder what Solomon might have to say in the last six verses to tie his thoughts together.

---

3. Eccl 3:10, 16, 22; 4:1, 4, 7, 15; 6:1; 7:15; 8:9, 10, 17; 9:11, 13; 10:5, 7.

The Preacher's Legacy (Eccl 12:9–12)

Ecclesiastes 12:9–12 describes Solomon's legacy. He was a wise man who taught his people much. At the same time, he seemed to warn against too much study or inquiry into life. How would it all end?

The Teacher's Challenge (Eccl 12:13–14)

In the closing verses, Solomon finally tied everything together. People needed to fear God and keep his commandments, no matter who they were, no matter what their status (Eccl 12:13). They were to fear God, because ultimately God would bring every deed under his judgment (Eccl 12:14).

Why does Solomon conclude with these two short verses? Because they are the only path left that makes sense. The book of Ecclesiastes is not like the book of Romans. In the book of Romans, Paul lays out a logical argument and builds his case point by point. In Ecclesiastes, Solomon takes us to the dead ends of all of our humanistic thinking, until at the end only one path remains—the path of fearing God and following him.

Concluding Thoughts from Ecclesiastes

The book of Ecclesiastes points to many paths people in this world pursue. In the end, for Solomon, every path of life lived under the sun ends up meaningless. On the other hand, life that is lived above the sun (that is, with a heavenly perspective) gives life meaning. In terms of Ecclesiastes pointing to Jesus, we might conclude that life lived with the Son (Jesus) is the only way to gain ultimate meaning.

16

Song of Solomon

THE FIRST VERSE OF the book ascribes the authorship to King Solomon. As such the book falls in the United Era (1043–931 BC).[1] The Hebrew title of the book is "Song of Songs," which is the Hebrew way of saying "the best song."[2] Over the generations, many Jewish and Christian scholars have attempted to spiritualize the language of Song of Solomon. Jewish scholars have suggested the poem provides a picture of God's love for Israel, his bride. Some Christian interpreters have viewed the song as a metaphor of the love between Christ and his church. However, it seems most likely that a straightforward interpretation of the language is intended. The book exalts the joy of sexual love in marriage.

The Song of Solomon details Solomon's love for his Shulamite bride.[3] The story unfolds in the form of a stage presentation with the speaking roles alternating between Solomon, his bride, and a chorus of the daughters of Jerusalem.

---

1. Jones, *Puzzle of the Old Testament*, 91–112.

2. Compare the expressions King of kings and Lord of lords, which refer to the greatest king and the greatest lord.

3. The word Shulamite may refer to a woman from an unknown site named Shulem. Others have interpreted it as a form of the Hebrew name Solomon (*Shlomo*). In this latter understanding, the word would simply mean Mrs. Solomon or Solomon's lady.

The Courtship of King Solomon and the Shulamite Woman (Song 1:1—3:5)

The Desire of the Woman (Song 1:1-4)

The woman's desire for her husband begins the song. She desired his kisses and his embrace and wanted him to draw her after him.

The Descriptions of the Woman and the King (Song 1:5—2:17)

In this section, the king and the Shulamite woman exchanged loving descriptions of each other. Solomon described the woman as beautiful in every way. As he looked at her, he loved her (1:5-15). In response, Solomon's lady had the same attitude toward him. He was handsome, and she loved him and all his features. They delighted in each other as a married couple should (1:16—2:17).

The Dream of the Woman (Song 3:1-5)

Solomon's lady despairingly declared, "All night long on my bed I looked for the one my heart loves; I looked for him but did not find him" (Song 3:1). When she found him, she would not let him go.

The Wedding of King Solomon and the Shulamite Woman (Song 3:6—5:1)

Solomon Travels to His Bride (Song 3:6-11)

Solomon's wedding provided an interesting variation from weddings we are accustomed to seeing today. Everyone was looking for the groom rather than looking for the bride! Note the words in Song of Solomon 3:6-7: "Who is this coming up from the wilderness . . . . Look, it is Solomon's carriage." The king drew much attention as he arrived at his wedding.

Solomon Talks about His Bride (Song 4:1—5:1)

Five times in this section, Solomon used the words "my bride" to designate his beloved. In this section, Solomon described his bride in great detail. He loved every aspect of her! Many of the images sound quite foreign to us, but they make sense in a shepherding culture of the Middle East. Solomon described his bride as "altogether beautiful" (Song 4:7).

The Marriage of King Solomon and the Shulamite Woman (Song 5:2—8:14)

King Solomon and his wife celebrated their marriage in the remaining chapters of the book. Their celebration included both their admiration for each other and their affection for each other.

Their Admiration (Song 5:2—7:8)

In Song of Solomon 5:2—6:3, Solomon's wife described her husband in great detail. She described him as "radiant and ruddy, outstanding among ten thousand" (Song 5:10). Again, the images she used may seem foreign to us, but make more sense in a Middle Eastern culture. For example, Solomon's assertion "Your hair is like a flock of goats descending from Gilead" (Song 6:5) calls to mind black goats walking on a hill. The appearance of moving goats in tight formation reminded him of the way his beloved's hair flowed in the breeze.

In Song of Songs 6:4—7:8, Solomon again described his wife using many of the same images he had used earlier. He used the word translated "beautiful" four times. Husband and wife stood captivated in the love of the other and truly admired each other.

Their Affection (Song 7:9—8:14)

The book closes with the section that describes Solomon and his wife's affection for each other. She desired to be with him and longed for him (Song 7:11–13). Song of Solomon 8:6–7 likewise describes the intimate bond that existed between them. They had the right to be jealous for each other's love. The sacred love between husband and wife should not be broken.

Concluding Thoughts from Song of Solomon

As stated earlier, some interpreters have seen in Song of Solomon a meta-phorical understanding of Christ's love for the church. We have argued that this is probably not so; at the same time, we do well to remember that our marriages do comprise a picture of Christ and the church (Eph 5:21–33). The way we live with our spouse demonstrates to the world the love Jesus has for his bride.[4]

---

4. Some point out the difficulty in holding up Song of Solomon as an example of sexual joy within marriage when Solomon had one thousand wives and concubines (1 Kgs 11:1–3). The point is well taken. The words themselves, however, and the affirmation of the two lovers nonetheless provide a good picture of romantic love within marriage.

Part Four

The Prophetic Books

These books highlight the messages of the prophets, men whom God called to proclaim his word. The prophets spoke of God's judgment against sin, as well as the ultimate salvation of God's people.

Books Covered

Isaiah
Jeremiah, Lamentations
Ezekiel
Daniel
Hosea, Joel, Amos
Obadiah, Jonah, Micah
Nahum, Habakkuk, Zephaniah
Haggai, Zechariah, Malachi

17

Isaiah

ISAIAH PROPHESIED DURING THE reigns of four kings of Judah: Uzziah, Jotham, Ahaz, and Hezekiah. Isaiah prophesied during the Divided Era (931–586 BC),[1] and his ministry occurred from approximately 740 to 690 BC As stated, his ministry overlapped with the reign of Hezekiah, Judah's famous king. Likewise, the Assyrian conquest of the Northern Kingdom of Israel in 721 BC also occurred during the reign of Hezekiah and the ministry of Isaiah.

The Messianic Hope (Isa 1–12)

Isaiah 1–12 forms the first unit of the book and provides a great introduction to the book. In these first twelve chapters, Isaiah speaks much about the sin problem in Judah, but he also heralds a great day when the Messiah (Jesus), God's Anointed One, will come. Isaiah foresaw a day when the nations would stream to Jerusalem and the word of God would go forth from Jerusalem to reach the nations (2:1–4). He described the Branch of the Lord, a servant of God who would lead the people tenderly as God had led them in the wilderness (4:2–6). He described the birth of Immanuel in a prophecy to King Ahaz that ultimately would be fulfilled in Jesus (Matt 1:22–23).[2] Isaiah

1. Jones, *Puzzle of the Old Testament*, 113–35.

2. Many Isaiah scholars see a "fill-full-ment" (or secondary fulfillment) in Matt 1. They suggest Isaiah's words had an initial fulfillment during Ahaz's days, but Jesus's birth

also described the birth of a Son who would reign on David's throne and establish justice and righteousness in the earth as he took the government on His shoulders (9:6–7). Finally, Isaiah again used the branch image to describe one who would come from the stump of Jesse and bring peace on earth and restoration of harmony and nature. All the nations would look to the root of Jesse, and he would reign with justice and righteousness (11:1–10). Isaiah's words, of course, find their fulfillment in Jesus.

Oracles against the Nations (Isa 13–23)

Isaiah 13–23 contains Isaiah's oracles against other nations. These eleven chapters demonstrate Isaiah's conviction that God is Lord of all nations, not merely of Israel and Judah. In the ancient world, many societies believed that their gods controlled their own lands, but their power or sovereignty didn't extend into the territory of others. The biblical prophets are unique in asserting God's sovereignty over the entire earth.

As Isaiah described various nations, he indicated God's judgment would come upon them. Whether they were large or small, they would face God's righteous wrath. Even mighty nations such as Assyria and Babylon would not escape; God had made them what they were, and in his perfect timing, he would bring them down.

The Little Apocalypse (Isa 24–27)

Isaiah 24–27 is often called the little apocalypse, because it sounds so much like the book of Revelation. Especially in Isaiah 24, the images of the sun growing dark and the earth shaking, splitting, and falling call to mind the apostle John's cataclysmic description of the end of human history.

Isaiah 24 described God's final judgment of the earth. One's social, economic, or political status did not matter; God's judgment was thorough and impartial, and he would judge sin wherever he found it. At the same time, his people would know his salvation. He would prepare a beautiful banquet for them and swallow up death forever (25:6–8). The people would celebrate with song, and God would raise the dead and usher them into his everlasting kingdom (26:19–20). Lastly, Isaiah described how God would

---

filled it even more full of meaning and took it to a greater level of fulfillment.

destroy Leviathan (a poetic name for Satan),[3] restore his people once again, gather them one by one, and bring them home (27:1, 12–13).

False Trust (Isa 28–33)

Isaiah described the people's shallow spirituality. They had an essentially nursery-rhyme level of understanding (28:9–13), and their religion consisted of traditions they had learned from memory, not from careful study of God's word (29:11–14). Judah's spiritual shallowness led it to trust in other nations such as Egypt for protection rather than looking to the Lord (Isa 30–31). At the same time, Isaiah described a righteous kingdom that would come one day, using words that probably described Jesus's reign (Isa 32). Isaiah closed the section with a final word of woe against Assyria. Assyria thought it was great, but it was merely an instrument in the hands of a sovereign God (Isa 33).

Judgment and Salvation (Isa 34–35)

Isaiah 34–35 ties together the prior section (Isa 28–33). Chapter 34 describes the judgment God will bring on the whole world (and Edom in particular), while chapter 35 highlights the day of redemption God will bring. The land will enjoy prosperity and renewal, and God will bring spiritual renewal to his people as well.

Historical Interlude (Isa 36–39)

Many Bible interpreters believe Isaiah intentionally reversed the order of events in Isaiah 36–39. From analysis of the historical data, we may conclude the events of chapters 38 and 39 preceded the events of Isaiah 36 and 37. This is not a mistake. In the first half of the book, the major power was Assyria, so Isaiah put the story of King Sennacherib's invasion and defeat at the hands of God first to tie off the Assyrian section of the book. Second, Isaiah then included the events of 38–39 to anticipate Judah's exile to Babylon.[4] God had granted Hezekiah a fifteen-year extension of life, but

---

3. Leviathan is here described as both a serpent and a dragon, which parallels John's description of Satan in the book of Revelation (Rev 12:9; 20:2).

4. For more details, see Beyer, *Encountering Isaiah*, 142–45.

Hezekiah responded pridefully when a Babylonian delegation visited his realm. Thus, Isaiah 36–39 not only is a historical interlude, but it forms a bridge between Isaiah 1–35 and Isaiah 40–66.

The Great Future for God's People (Isa 40–66)

Isaiah 40–66 mixes prophecies about the people's return from their future Babylonian captivity with prophecies about the coming Messiah and the end times. In 539 BC, Cyrus, Persia's king, defeated Babylon, and during the first year of his reign, he allowed almost fity thousand Jews to return to their homeland (2 Chr 36:22–23; Ezra 1:1). As Isaiah looked ahead to this grand day of redemption, he must have rejoiced knowing that one day, his people would come home from exile.[5]

One of the most important features of Isaiah 40–66 is the servant passages or servant songs. These are found in Isaiah 42:1–4; 49:1–6; 50:4–11; and 52:13—53:12. Some also include Isaiah 61:1–3 in this collection even though the word servant does not occur in the passage.

Isaiah 42:1–4

Isaiah described how God's servant would have God's Spirit upon him. He would serve faithfully but quietly. Nonetheless, he would accomplish great results without drawing undue attention to himself. The Gospel writer Matthew said Jesus fulfilled Isaiah's words when he went about performing great works but urged people to be quiet about them (Matt 12:18–21).

Isaiah 49:1–6

Isaiah initially identified this servant passage as referring to God's servant Israel (49:3); yet, the servant had a mission to Israel! The apostle Paul clarified the difficulty in Acts 13:47, when he explained that the faithful remnant who followed Jesus represented the true servant of God. Within the

---

5. Some scholars in the past two centuries have suggested perhaps Isaiah the prophet did not write the entire book of Isaiah. They argue he wrote only the first half of the book, and someone else or perhaps a number of people wrote Isa 40–66. In general, it is fair to say that if we allow God to be God, and believe that he knows the future and can reveal it to his servants the prophets, the problem with Isaiah writing the entire book disappears. For more discussion see Beyer, *Encountering Isaiah*, 154–59.

group that carried Jacob's bloodline was a group that also displayed faith in Jacob's God.

Isaiah 50:4–11

Isaiah's next portrayal of the servant described the servant as suffering greatly for his faithfulness. Nonetheless, the servant, knowing that God had called him to this ministry, was determined to carry it out faithfully, and he did so. Some of the language in this passage reminds us of the suffering of Jesus at his arrest, although the New Testament doesn't specifically cite this passage.

Isaiah 52:13—53:12

This prophecy of Isaiah comprises the most famous of the servant songs. Indeed, The New Testament writers saw many parallels between the description of the servant and the life and ministry of Jesus Christ. The servant grew up simply and had no special attractiveness that people should be drawn to him (53:2). Furthermore, he suffered in the place of people, who really were the ones who deserved God's punishment (53:4–6). He silently went to his death, even though he had committed no wrong (53:7–9). In fact, to some extent, his death was God's doing (53:10). Nonetheless, the servant would ultimately be vindicated, and he would see the results of his labors (53:11–12).

Isaiah's words powerfully foreshadow Jesus's life and work.[6] The New Testament writers again and again cited this passage as they described Jesus's humble ministry, his suffering in the place of sinners, his innocent death according to his Father's plan, and his triumph and exaltation.

Isaiah 61:1–3

Isaiah 61:1–3 described one whom God had anointed to preach good news to the poor and to make things right again in society. As Jesus began his public ministry and returned to his home town of Nazareth, he read this passage when called on to read in the synagogue. He referenced himself as

---

6. For a complete discussion and chart on how Jesus fulfilled Isa 52:13—53:12, see Beyer, *Encountering Isaiah*, 209–12.

the fulfillment of these prophetic words, though many of the people from his hometown did not receive his words well (Luke 4:16–30).

The Consummation of Human History (Isa 65–66)

Isaiah closed his book by looking far ahead to the future, when God would establish his kingdom forever and create a new heaven and a new earth (Isa 65:17–25). Isaiah even used words to describe a great campaign God would launch to reach the world with the news of his glory (66:19–20). Isaiah's words sound strikingly like the Great Commission Jesus gave his disciples in Matthew 28:18–20.

Concluding Thoughts from Isaiah

The prophet Isaiah had a profound impact on the story God is writing. He especially impacted the New Testament writers; statistically speaking, one out of every seventeen verses in the New Testament is either a direct quote from or an allusion to Isaiah's words. Isaiah spoke powerfully to God's people as he challenged them to follow the law of Moses, but he also looked ahead to the great day God was planning when he would bring his ultimate Servant, the Lord Jesus Christ, to secure the salvation of all who would place their faith in him.

18

Jeremiah and Lamentations

Jeremiah

THE EVENTS OF JEREMIAH's prophetic ministry occur at the end of the Divided Era (931–586 BC) and the beginning of the Scattered Era (605–538 BC).[1] Jeremiah began his ministry during the reign of King Josiah (640–609 BC), the sixteenth king of the Southern Kingdom of Judah and Judah's last great king. His ministry continued until after Jerusalem's final fall at the hands of the Babylonians in 586 BC. Jeremiah prophesied that God would send the Babylonians because of Judah's sin. At the same time, he also provided hope by proclaiming God's promise to restore the people to their land after seventy years of captivity (Jer 29:10–14).

Introduction: Jeremiah's Call (Jer 1)

Most Bible commentators believe Jeremiah was between sixteen and twenty-five years old when God called him to ministry. Such an age would be considered quite young for someone to assume such a task; however, that fact did not bother God. The Lord informed Jeremiah about the plans he had had for him even before Jeremiah was born (1:4–5). Jeremiah protested he was too young, but God assured him of his presence and challenged him to speak to the people all God commanded him (1:6–10, 17–21).

1. Jones, *Puzzle of the Old Testament*, 115–35, 139–62.

Judah's Sin: A National Focus (Jer 2–33)

Rejection of God (Jer 2–24)

At numerous points in Jeremiah 2–24, Jeremiah challenged the people about their rejection of God and God's statutes. In doing so, Jeremiah challenged the prevailing false theology that since God had given the people the temple, the priesthood, and the kingdom of David, they had nothing to fear and could live as they pleased. However, Jeremiah told the people none of those things mattered in view of the people's abandonment of God (7:3–7). It was all just ritual and amounted to nothing! In response, the people formed a conspiracy against Jeremiah and attempted to get rid of him (11:18–23).

Rebuke from God (Jer 25–29)

Jeremiah continued to warn the people that they would face terrible consequences if they did not turn back to God. Some of the people thought God was merely scolding them, but Jeremiah warned them the exile would last seventy years (25:11–12). He would make Jerusalem like Shiloh, Israel's former spiritual center in the days of Joshua and Samuel (26:4–6).[2]

Meanwhile, as waves of Judeans began to face deportation to Babylon, false prophets in Babylon and in Jerusalem assured people everything would be okay. They suggested God had given them a spiritual slap on the wrist, but within two years he would bring them home (28:1–4). In response, Jeremiah wrote a letter to the captives in Babylon, again assuring them they would spend seventy years in Babylon (29:10). Nonetheless, God had wonderful plans to give them a future and a hope (29:11).

Restoration by God (Jer 30–33)

Following the strong words of judgment, Jeremiah turned to prophesy a wonderful day of restoration God would bring at the end of that time. One particular highlight was Jeremiah 31:31–34, where Jeremiah announced a new covenant God would inaugurate with his people. This covenant would eclipse any covenant he had held with Israel prior to that time, and

---

2. For more information on Shiloh's role early in Israel's history, see Josh 18:1–10 and 1 Sam 1:3—3:21.

it would feature forgiveness of sin and people's personal knowledge of the Lord. Over six centuries later, as Jesus shared the last supper (i.e., a Passover meal) with his disciples, he announced that the good days of Jeremiah's new covenant had come (Luke 22:20). The writer of Hebrews also echoed Jeremiah's words, likewise applying them to the church (Heb 8:8–12).

Jerusalem's Siege: A Local Focus (Jer 34–44)

Jeremiah 34–44 contains some of the saddest material in the book of Jeremiah. It describes the people's persistent rebellion despite Jeremiah's persistent warnings. In the end, they would pay the high price of exile. Even then, however, they chose to place the blame elsewhere.

Before the Final Siege (Jer 34–36)

Jeremiah 34–36 described the reigns of two rebellious kings of Judah: Zedekiah and Jehoiakim. Zedekiah initially tried to lead his people in an act of repentance by freeing the Hebrew slaves that had been unduly enslaved (34:8–11); however, the people immediately showed their hypocrisy and forced them back into slavery. Jeremiah pronounced the people's own "release"—to slavery and destruction at the hands of the Babylonians! Their unwillingness to free their slaves, even at this most desperate time, revealed their hardness of heart.

During Jehoiakim's reign, Jeremiah saw a glimmer of hope. God commanded the prophet to write down his words and share them with Judah's leadership, and many citizens initially received the prophet's words well (36:1–18). However, when Jehoiakim heard Jeremiah's words, he cut up the scroll piece by piece and burned the pieces in the fire, showing his utter contempt for God's word through his prophet (Jer 36:21–26). Jehoiakim's rebellion would lead to Nebuchadnezzar's second attack against Jerusalem, an attack during which Jehoiakim apparently died, leaving his eighteen-year-old son Jehoiachin in charge (2 Kgs 24:1–6).

During the Final Siege (Jer 37–39)

Jeremiah 37–38 records final dialogues between Jeremiah and Zedekiah, Judah's last king. Zedekiah clearly seems to have understood that Jeremiah spoke the truth; yet, the king lacked the courage to follow through on Jeremiah's counsel. Jeremiah passionately encouraged the king to surrender, promising that if he did, Jerusalem would be spared (38:17–20). Sadly, the king refused, and in the end, he and Jerusalem paid a terrible price.

Jeremiah 39 records Jerusalem's destruction. The city fell, Zedekiah was captured, Zedekiah's sons were killed, Zedekiah was blinded and led into captivity, and the temple was destroyed. It was the darkest hour in Old Testament history and provided the occasion for the writing of the book of Lamentations.

After the Final Siege (Jer 40–44)

In the aftermath of Jerusalem's destruction, King Nebuchadnezzar of Babylon appointed a man named Gedaliah as governor over Judah; however, some Judeans did not respect his leadership, and after a period of only seven months, Gedaliah was assassinated (41:1–3). Many people now feared for their lives; Nebuchadnezzar had hardly left the land and they had murdered his appointed governor!

The Judeans sought Jeremiah's counsel as to what to do next, and Jeremiah encouraged them to stay in Judah (42:7–12). Even though the people had already vowed to do whatever Jeremiah said (42:1–6), they did not expect him to answer this way and refused to heed his counsel (43:1–4). Instead, they took the prophet with them as prisoner to Egypt, lest he tell the Babylonians where they were going (43:6). Even in Egypt, the people continued to blame Jeremiah and God for their predicament rather than focusing the blame where it belonged—on themselves and on their own wickedness (44:15–19).

Jeremiah's Sermons: An International Focus (Jer 45–51)

Like many other prophets,[3] Jeremiah also included prophecies concerning other nations. God was their God as well, and he would deal with them as he saw fit. Egypt would experience God's judgment (Jer 46:13–24), as would the Philistines (47:1–4) and the Moabites (48:1–7). Likewise, other kingdoms such as Ammon, Edom, Syria, Kedar, Hazor, and Elam would know God's power (49:1–39).

---

3. Isa 13–23, Ezek 25–32, Amos 1–2, Zeph 1–2.

During Jeremiah's ministry, the primary threat was the nation of Babylon. Jeremiah saved words of judgment against this kingdom for last (Jer 50–51). As Jeremiah spoke these words, Babylon was the most powerful kingdom on earth, but when God was through with Babylon, he would humble the nation. Jeremiah's words were fulfilled when the Persians conquered the city of Babylon in 539 BC and ended the Babylonian Empire (Dan 5:30–31).

Conclusion (Jer 52)

Jeremiah 52 again describes Jerusalem's fall, and contains much of the same material as 2 Kings 25 and Jeremiah 39. One noteworthy item is the book's somewhat optimistic ending (52:31–34). King Jehoiachin, who had been deported and imprisoned at age eighteen, was released at age fifty-five after thirty-seven years of exile and ate regularly at the king of Babylon's table. The new king, Evil-Merodoch, granted Jehoiachin a full pardon and honored him this way.[4]

Concluding Thoughts from Jeremiah

Jeremiah prophesied for approximately forty years, and as far as we can see, very little spiritual fruit came from his ministry. However, we would be remiss if we assumed the only impact of his ministry lay in his generation. Through the ages, many have read the prophet's words, learned from them, and changed their lives accordingly.

Much of Jeremiah's message was negative, but he did hold out hope that one day, the Lord would raise up a righteous Branch of David, who would once again bring justice and righteousness to God's people (23:5–6; 33:15–17). This Branch of David—the Lord Jesus Christ—initiated the new covenant at the Last Supper (Jer 31:31–34; Luke 22:20), and one day, he will return to reign as King of kings and Lord of lords.

---

4. Interestingly, Babylonian economic records confirm Jehoiachin's presence at the king's table.

Lamentations

Both Jewish and Christian tradition ascribe the authorship of the book of Lamentations to Jeremiah, and most evangelical commentators have found little reason to disagree with that. The book describes the period around 586 BC and immediately after, during the events of Jerusalem's fall that brought the Divided Era (931–586 BC) to an end and launched the Scattered Era (586–38 BC).[5]

The book is laid out in five chapters, each of which is a funeral dirge. The twenty-two verses in chapters 1, 2, and 4 follow an alphabetic acrostic pattern, with each verse using the next letter of the Hebrew alphabet.[6] Chapter 3 follows this pattern, except that there are three verses for each Hebrew letter.[7] Chapter 5 contains twenty-two verses but is not an acrostic. The layout of Lamentations provides interesting discussions for scholars, but we still do not know what Jeremiah's purpose was in arranging his material this way.

The book of Jeremiah warned Judah about Jerusalem's impending fall, and the book of Lamentations described its horror. Jeremiah had warned the people again and again, but they had not listened. Now, they faced the awful reality of a ravaged city and destroyed temple. Somehow, "I told you so" just didn't seem to fit as the prophet bemoaned Jerusalem's sad state.

Jerusalem's Ruin (Lam 1)

Lamentations 1:1–11 describes a lament for Jerusalem; verses 12–22 describe a lament by Jerusalem, in which Jerusalem personified speaks. The word affliction occurs three times in the first eleven verses (vv. 3, 7, 9). The language is of a people struggling to deal with the awful reality of destruction and ruin.

---

5. See Jones, *Puzzle of the Old Testament*, 139–62.

6. The parallel in English would be writing a twenty-six-line psalm in which the first line begins with the letter *a*, the second line begins with the letter *b*, the third line begins with the letter *c*, and so on throughout the alphabet.

7. For Lam 3, which has sixty-six verses, the pattern is tripled. Verses 1–3 each begin with *aleph*, the first letter of the Hebrew alphabet. Verses 4–6 each begin with *beth*, the second letter of the Hebrew alphabet, etc.

God's Retribution (Lam 2)

The book of Lamentations repeatedly emphasizes the people's sorrow and horror. At the same time, it never places the blame on the Lord. Rather, the text describes how God brought the judgment "in the day of his anger" (2:1, 21–22) that came about because of Judah's sin.

Jeremiah's Recollection (Lam 3)

God's people faced crushing sadness. At the same time, Jeremiah, in the depth of his sorrow, reflected on truth and recognized there was still hope as long as the people turned to God: "Yet this I call to mind and therefore I have hope: because of the LORD's great love we are not consumed, for his compassions never fail. They are new every morning; great is your faithfulness" (3:21–23). These powerful words of truth broke through Jeremiah's sadness and enabled him to go on at a time when many would have thought there was no point in going on.

Over two millennia later, Thomas Chisholm (1866–1960) would write the words to the popular church hymn "Great Is Thy Faithfulness" based on this text. Since its composition, the hymn has encouraged many who struggle with difficult circumstances. The hymn reminds us that if people in Jeremiah's day could claim this truth as they went through the darkest hour in Old Testament history, then certainly God's people today can be encouraged, whatever challenges they are facing.

God's Reasons (Lam 4)

Jeremiah decried the people's destruction: "The punishment of my people is greater than that of Sodom" (4:6). They suffered greatly because of their sin. Furthermore, the prophet affirmed Judah's leadership had failed miserably (4:13–15). Judah's leaders had failed their people and led them into ruin.

Jerusalem's Request (Lam 5)

The closing chapter continues to describe the agonies of war. Jeremiah's words "remember, LORD, what has happened to us" (5:1) called on the Lord to look upon his suffering people as they faced the shame and indignity of the horrors of war. As Jeremiah closed his book, he pleaded with God:

"Restore us to yourself, LORD, that we may return; renew our days as of old"
(5:21). He dared not imagine that the Lord might have abandoned them
forever (5:22).

Concluding Thoughts from Lamentations

The book of Lamentations describes in detail the tragedy God's people faced
as they tried to pick themselves up after the agony of destruction. Jeremiah
put the blame squarely on God's people, for the Lord had only done what
he had promised to do—judge his people for their sin. At the same time, the
glorious hope of Lamentations 3:21–23 reminds us that God's faithfulness
is great and that he stands ready to forgive us if we will only turn back to
him with all our hearts and ask his forgiveness.

19

Ezekiel

JUDAH'S DEPORTATION TO BABYLON took place in three stages. The first deportation under King Jehoiakim took place in 605 BC and included Daniel and his friends (Dan 1:1–2). The second deportation took place in 597 BC, under King Jehoiachin, Jehoiakim's son (2 Kgs 24:10–17). The third deportation took place in 586 BC, when Nebuchadnezzar destroyed Jerusalem and the temple (2 Kgs 25:1–21). The prophet Ezekiel was part of the second deportation in 597 BC.

Ezekiel 1:1 mentions "the thirtieth year," and most interpreters believe this refers to the thirtieth year of Ezekiel's life. This would mean he was twenty-five years old when he went into exile in 597 BC. Also, according the law of Moses, priests would begin their temple service at age thirty. Of course, with Ezekiel living in Babylon, there was no chance of that. Instead, God took the opportunity to call his would-be priest to a prophetic ministry. Ezekiel's ministry took place during the Scattered Era (605–538 BC).[1]

Introduction (Ezek 1–3)

Ezekiel 1:1–3 describes the prophet's context. The year was 592 BC, and as Ezekiel turned thirty, his prophetic ministry began. Ezekiel 1:4—2:10 describes the prophet's calling. God showed Ezekiel an incredible vision of heaven, including the majestic Lord of the universe. As Ezekiel gazed at the

---

1 Jones, *Puzzle of the Old Testament*, 139–62.

glory of God, he fell on his face (1:28). The voice that spoke to him told him he would face challenges from Israel, a rebellious house, but that he should stand strong (2:1–10).

Ezekiel 3 describes the prophet's commission. He was to serve the role of a watchman, who preached to the exiles that God was about to bring destruction on them if they did not repent. Whether they listened or not, however, God would hold Ezekiel accountable for faithfully presenting the message (3:11, 17–21).

Prophecies of Retribution (Ezek 4–32)

Against the Nation of Judah (Ezek 4–24)

The book of Ezekiel has forty-eight chapters, and the first twenty-four, after dealing with Ezekiel's calling, focus on prophecies against the nation of Judah. The tone of the book is somber.

Jerusalem's Scattering (Ezek 4–7)

The Lord gave Ezekiel various prophetic images and visions to communicate the fact that he would scatter his people to the winds. In fact, several times in this section the expression "scatter to the wind" occurs (5:2, 10, 12; 6:8). Some of God's people were already in exile, whereas others remained in Jerusalem. Nonetheless, God's judgment would continue. Seven times in chapters 6 and 7, God used the expression, "And you will know that I am the LORD."[2] Judgment would bring a personal knowledge of the Lord, but tragically, that knowledge would come too late for God's people.

Jerusalem's Slaughter (Ezek 8–19)

God again presented to Ezekiel a series of visions and prophetic words to describe the incredible slaughter that was coming upon God's people. In Ezekiel 9:6, God's command "slaughter the old men, the young men and women, the mothers and children" sounds extremely harsh, and even Ezekiel thought so. In response, God explained to him that Israel's sin was

---

2. Ezek 6:7; 10:10, 13, 14; 7:4, 9, 27.

exceedingly great. The time had come for them to face the sad consequences of their evil actions.

Jerusalem's Sin (Ezek 20–23)

The year was now 590 BC. These chapters highlighted the people of God's abominable sins. God called to Ezekiel (20:4) to "confront them with the detestable practices of their ancestors" and of Jerusalem "to confront her with all her detestable practices" (22:2). He compared Israel and Judah to two wicked sisters in Ezekiel 23, and God again told his prophet to "confront them with their detestable practices" (23:36).

Jerusalem's Siege (Ezek 24)

The year was 588 BC when a delegation came to the prophet Ezekiel. They brought a sad announcement: "The king of Babylon has laid siege to Jerusalem this very day" (24:2). It was the beginning of the end for Judah's beloved capital city.

Against the Neighbors of Judah (Ezek 25–32)

Ezekiel, as the prophets Isaiah, Jeremiah, Amos, and Zephaniah had done, included a section in his book that described God's judgment against neighboring countries. God was Lord of all nations, whether those nations recognized it or not, and this theme is a common one in these prophetic books.

Ammon, Moab, Edom, and Philistia (Ezek 25)

Ezekiel focused first on the countries that neighbored Judah. The Ammonites and Moabites were descended from Lot, Abraham's nephew (Gen 19:36–38). The Edomites were descended from Esau, Jacob's brother (Gen 25:30; 36:1). The Philistines had landed along the Israelite coast around 1200 BC and immediately had become a problem for God's people, especially during the reign of King Saul, Israel's first king (1 Sam 13:3–5; 14:1–23; 17:1–52; 31:1–10). Ezekiel announced God's judgment on all these nations.

Tyre and Sidon (Ezek 26–28)

The year was 586 BC, the same year as Jerusalem's fall. Ezekiel announced the judgment of Tyre and Sidon, two Phoenician cities that lay along the coast of the Mediterranean Sea. These cities had become rich and, consequently, had become proud. God would humble them.

Egypt (Ezek 29–32)

The prophecies of Ezekiel 29–32 come from various dates ranging from 587–70 BC; nonetheless, they focus on Egypt, one of the major powers of the ancient world. Centuries earlier, the Egyptians had enslaved the Hebrews for over four centuries (Exod 1:8–14; 12:40). During the days of the Divided Era, Egypt occasionally made attacks on Israel and Judah. However, this great empire was no match for the Lord; he would humble them in his perfect timing.

Promises of Restoration (Ezek 33–48)

Ezekiel 33 comprises a turning point in the book of Ezekiel. Ezekiel 4–32, while containing some positive prophetic words, is largely negative, focusing on the coming judgment both of God's people and of the nations. However, beginning in chapter 33, God began to describe through Ezekiel the amazing future God was creating that included his people and other people that they might not have even imagined. In numerous places in these chapters, God described his restoration of Israel. The year was 585 BC (33:21), just shortly after Jerusalem's fall. God was already planning the renewal.

To Regather the People (Ezek 33–39)

God promised to rescue his people from distant countries and bring them to their own land. He would seek out the lost and bring back those he had scattered (34:12–16). He would restore life in the land to what it was formerly; in fact, conditions would even be better than in earlier times (36:9–11). They would again be his people, and he would be their God (36:19–28). He would bring them back into their land and give them security on every side (37:11–14, 21). Finally, when he did so, they would know he was the Lord their God (39:23–29). Just as they had come to know his wrath and judgment, now they would come to know his mercy and grace as the day of salvation dawned.

To Rebuild the Temple (Ezek 40–46)

The year was now 572 BC (40:1). God came to Ezekiel and told him to write down everything he said regarding the coming temple God would build in the age to come. The details are exceedingly specific, and many Christians find them difficult to read and absorb. We must remember that Ezekiel, as a priest, would have taken great interest and delight in describing for his audience the dimensions and characteristics of the new temple. This was a role Ezekiel had hoped to do during his lifetime, and although he would not, he would be able to help others anticipate its coming one day.

Ezekiel described in great detail (and probably with great joy) the measurements of the new Jerusalem and its temple (Ezek 40–43). Again, we must remember that such details were important to a priest, however confusing we might find them.

Ezekiel also described the future role of priests (Ezek 44) and princes (Ezek 45–46). In past times, a tension often existed between the palace and the priesthood, between king and priest; however, in these days, perfect harmony would exist between the offices. Such wording foreshadows the ministry of Jesus, who reigns as King of kings and as our great High Priest, thus bringing the offices together into one. Both the priests and the princes would have a hand in renewing Jerusalem and the temple.

To Reapportion the Land (Ezek 47–48)

In the closing chapters, Ezekiel described the incredible renovation God would do in the land he called his own. Living water would flow from the temple, flowing all the way to the Dead Sea and making it fresh (47:1–12).[3] The boundaries Ezekiel outlined of the land of God's people (47:13–23) described a vast expanse, the greatest the nation of Israel had known. God told the people to divide it up by lot, and to ensure foreigners had a proper place among his people (47:22–23).

---

3. The extent of the miracle may be understood when one ponders that the Dead Sea is almost 35 percent saline today.

Ezekiel then described the division of the land by tribe (48:1–9). The special portion allotted to the priests was described in 48:10–20 and tribal portions in 48:23–29, with the prince receiving a special portion near the sanctuary as well (48:21–22).

Ezekiel closed his prophecy with words concerning the new Jerusalem and restored Israel (Ezek 48:30–35). He described the twelve gates of the city that would be named after the twelve sons of Jacob. His doing so reminds us of the incredible promise God made to Abraham in Genesis 12:1–3. Those verses stand as a defining moment in God's redemptive purpose, because the rest of Scripture talks about unpacking those verses. In the new Jerusalem Ezekiel described, Abraham's great-grandsons have their names on the city gates. What a legacy!

Scholars have debated the meaning of Ezekiel 40–48. Some have interpreted those verses literally, understanding them to refer to a millennial kingdom with a restored temple. Others understand them to describe heaven in a spiritual sense. Still others have thought perhaps they describe the ideal heaven as Ezekiel would have seen it. In the end, we do not know for sure, but Ezekiel 48:35 is helpful. The prophet closed his work by saying, "The name of the city from that time shall be 'The LORD is there.'" That's what makes heaven heaven; it's not about gold, it's not about goods, it's not about the size of a mansion. Heaven is heaven because God is there. God's people will be with him forever, and nothing else will matter.

Concluding Thoughts from Ezekiel

Ezekiel focused mainly on Israel's judgment and restoration, but he did prophesy a bit about Jesus's life and ministry. He spoke of the peace and harmony that would come with a coming Davidic ruler, which was certainly a prophecy of Jesus (37:24–25). Scholars of the book of Revelation, the last book of the Bible, have also noted that the apostle John uses much imagery from Ezekiel.[4] Perhaps John and Ezekiel saw the same visions. If so, and this is likely, then it appears Ezekiel was privileged to see the glory of Christ as he would finally reveal himself. Ezekiel fell on his face as he saw his vision of God, just as all will one day fall on their faces before the King of kings and Lord of lords.

---

4. The following passages provide a good representative sample: Ezek 1:5–10 and Rev 4:6–7; Ezek 1:13 and Rev 4:5; Ezek 39:17–20 and Rev 19:17–18; Ezek 48:30–35 and Rev 21:12–13.

20

Daniel

THE EVENTS OF THE book of Daniel took place during the Scattered Era (605–538 BC) and just a little bit into the Gathered Era (538 BC–Christ).[1] The Assyrians had conquered the Northern Kingdom of Israel in 721 BC and scattered its people (2 Kgs 17). The Chaldeans, often called the Babylonians,[2] came to power in 626 BC, and soon overthrew the Assyrian Empire in 612 BC. King Nebuchadnezzar II of Babylon came to power in 605 BC, and under his leadership, the Babylonian army invaded Judah. Three deportations of exiles occurred in 605 BC, 597 BC, and 586 BC. Daniel, deported to Babylon by Nebuchadnezzar after Judah's first defeat in 605 BC, wrote this book from Babylon, and his ministry lasted seventy years.

The book of Daniel divides neatly into two sections. Daniel 1–6 deals more with God's work among individual people, while Daniel 7–12 records prophecies about God's people in general.

The People (Dan 1–6)

Daniel 1–6 comprises six accounts that highlight God's work in the lives of individuals. God's people encounter various enemies of the faith, who

---

1. Jones, *Puzzle of the Old Testament,* 139–62 and 165–85. The events of Dan 10–12 were predicted in 536 BC.

2. "Chaldean" describes the particular ethnic group that lived in the region of Babylon. "Babylonian" describes the region that comprised the center of the empire.

persecute them and even attempt to put them to death. Nonetheless, as God's people stand for him in faith, he brings deliverance. Those who oppose him receive his judgment.

Daniel's Deportation and Dedication (Dan. 1)

Daniel 1 records how Daniel and many other citizens of Judah were exiled in 605 BC during the reign of King Jehoiakim, king of Judah. Perhaps somewhat surprisingly, Nebuchadnezzar ordered that many of the youths of the Judean court be trained to serve in the Babylonian court, and Daniel and his friends Hananiah, Mishael, and Azariah[3] found themselves in such a position.

Daniel and his friends determined they did not want to defile themselves with the food and drink the king required of them, but preferred keeping the Jewish dietary laws from the law of Moses. As these four men proved faithful in relatively small spiritual things, God laid a foundation in their lives for greater works he would do later. Daniel 1 reminds us to be faithful in little things, because small acts of faithfulness can lay a foundation for bigger spiritual things God wants to do in and through us.

Nebuchadnezzar's First Dream (Dan 2)

Daniel 2 records how Nebuchadnezzar had a dream that greatly troubled him. When he insisted his nobles and wise men prove their powers by not only interpreting the dream but by telling him what it was, they replied that only the gods could do such things (Dan 2:4–11). Nebuchadnezzar became angry with them, because after all, he was paying them for their connections with the gods! He ordered the death of all Babylon's wise men, and this order would have included Daniel and his friends.

However, the Lord revealed both the dream and its interpretation to Daniel, who announced it to the king, thereby saving his life and the life of his friends. Daniel explained that Nebuchadnezzar's amazing dream of a statue corresponded to four earthly kingdoms that would be superseded by the kingdom of God one day.

3. Daniel 1:7 records how Daniel and his friends received Babylonian names. Daniel's was Belteshazzar, Hananiah's was Shadrach, Mishael's was Meshach, and Azariah's was Abednego. Interestingly, the three friends are known by their Babylonian names in Dan 3, whereas Daniel generally continues to be called Daniel.

The significance of Nebuchadnezzar bowing before Daniel is perhaps lost on the modern reader. Imagine some of the most powerful Muslim rulers of the world bowing down before the God of Billy Graham!

Nebuchadnezzar's Demand (Dan 3:1—4:3)

As Daniel interpreted Nebuchadnezzar's amazing dream of the statue in chapter 2, he told the king that the king was the head of gold (Dan 2:38). Perhaps Nebuchadnezzar went home that night and decided he would build a statue of gold in his own honor so everyone could worship it. At any rate, the king ordered a statue of gold erected on the plane of Dura outside Babylon and ordered his leaders to bow before it when they heard the sound of various musical instruments.

Daniel's friends Shadrach, Meshach, and Abednego refused to worship the image; they would not bow before the king's idol, even if it meant death.[4] When Nebuchadnezzar ordered God's three faithful servants thrown into a burning fiery furnace, the Lord's angel intervened and spared the men's lives, and Nebuchadnezzar again glorified God and humbled himself before him.

Nebuchadnezzar's Second Dream (Dan. 4:4-47)

In Daniel 4, we actually read the testimony of a pagan king who has seen the power of God. Nebuchadnezzar recounted how he had another dream, and none of his wise men or court magicians could interpret it! However, Daniel again interpreted the king's dream, warning him that God had placed him on his throne and could remove him if he did not humble himself. A year later, Daniel's warning proved true when the king walked upon the roof of his palace in pride. God humbled Nebuchadnezzar by taking away his sanity and making him like a wild animal. After a period of time, God restored Nebuchadnezzar's sanity and kingdom to him, and the king yet again gave glory to the God of Daniel.

---

4. Commentators have wondered why Daniel is not included in Dan 3's account. We ultimately do not know; perhaps he was on an assignment that took him outside the region of Babylon.

Belshazzar's Defeat (Dan 5)

In the year 539 BC, Belshazzar was serving as Babylon's last king.[5] One night, as Belshazzar threw a party for a thousand of his nobles and ladies, he blasphemed God by taking the sacred vessels that had seen service in the Lord's temple in Jerusalem and using them to worship idols. As Belshazzar's nobles and ladies watched in horror, the fingers of a man's hand wrote words on the wall over Belshazzar's head.[6]

Naturally, Belshazzar wanted to know the meaning of the words, but when none of his wise men could interpret the words, he grew more frightened than ever. At his queen's request, Belshazzar summoned Daniel, and indeed, Daniel was able to read the handwriting on the wall. First, however, Daniel brought a scathing indictment against Belshazzar for his failure to learn anything from the lesson of his grandfather-in-law Nebuchadnezzar. God had humbled Nebuchadnezzar and taught him the meaning of humility, but Belshazzar had learned nothing from Nebuchadnezzar's tragic example. Daniel explained that the inscription meant Belshazzar's kingdom was coming to an end, that he was found lacking before God, and that the Medes and Persians would receive his kingdom. That very night Daniel's words proved true; Belshazzar was killed, and Darius the Mede took over the kingdom.[7]

Daniel's Deliverance (Dan 6)

By this time, Daniel was an old man, perhaps around eighty years old.[8] Nonetheless, King Darius noted Daniel's talent and decided to promote him as leading commissioner over the entire empire. This did not sit well with the other nobles, who no doubt wanted a local, not a foreigner, ruling them.

---

5. Belshazzar was technically the crown prince, the son of Nabonidus. However, Nabonidus had appointed Belshazzar as co-regent when Nabonidus went into a self-imposed exile. (He was an unpopular king in Babylon.) Belshazzar's ruling as co-regent explains why Belshazzar said whoever could interpret the handwriting on the wall would rule as one of three (not as one of two) in the kingdom (Dan 5:7).

6. The Aramaic original literally says that Belshazzar saw the palm of the hand that was writing. This suggests the king was directly underneath the writing.

7. Many scholars connect Darius the Mede with Cyrus the Persian, the first king of the Persian Empire.

8. Assuming Daniel was in his teens in 605 BC, in 539 BC he would have been close to eighty.

However, they could find no fault in any of Daniel's work. As they considered how they might bring Daniel down, they saw what they considered a potential flaw in his character: Daniel was zealous about worshiping his God.

Daniel's enemies proposed to King Darius that the king establish a law that anyone praying to any man or god except for the king for the next thirty days be thrown into a den of lions. Darius, perhaps in a moment of egotism, agreed to the plan, only to realize later to his chagrin that the law trapped his best commissioner.

God's purpose for Daniel was not finished. When Daniel was thrown into the lions' den, God shut the lions' mouths and delivered Daniel from harm. The king then threw Daniel's enemies into the lions' den, and the lions destroyed them. At the end of Daniel 6, King Darius, as Nebuchadnezzar before him, praised the God of Daniel.

Prophecies (Dan 7–12)

The four prophecies of Daniel 7–12 in many ways parallel the stories of Daniel 1–6. Whereas the stories of Daniel 1–6 speak about God's great work in individual lives, the prophecies in Daniel 7–12 focus on God's great work in his people as a whole. At the same time, the kinds of challenges Daniel and his friends faced are the same kind of challenges God's people would face on the national level. When they face persecution from hostile forces, what will they do? They will stand with God and his promises! These prophecies reveal great, mighty, and even frightening events that would happen in the days after Daniel, but they also speak powerful assurances that God remains in control and that nothing can defeat his purposes.

Prophecy about Four Beasts (Dan 7)

In 553 BC, Daniel had a vision of four beasts that appeared from the sea. The first one was like a lion, the second like a bear, the third like a leopard, and the fourth too terrifying to describe. However, God's messenger explained to Daniel the meaning of the vision. Four kingdoms would arise, but the kingdom of God would surpass them all.

Scholars have wrestled with the identity of the four kingdoms. Some say the kingdoms are Babylon, Persia, Greece, and Rome; others say the four kingdoms represent Nebuchadnezzar, Media, Persia, and Greece. All agree, of course, that the kingdom of God overcomes all earthly kingdoms.

Prophecy about Two Animals (Dan 8)

In 551 BC, Daniel saw a vision of a ram and a he-goat. The ram represented the Medo-Persian Empire and the he-goat represented the empire of Greece under Alexander the Great. Just as the goat defeated the ram, so Greece would defeat Persia. Daniel also spoke of terrifying events that would accompany the kingdom of Greece following the death of Alexander the Great. Under one successor in particular—Antiochus Epiphanes IV—persecution of the Jews would result in desecration of the temple for a period of about three and a half years. However, God would thwart Antiochus's purpose and bring him down.

Prophecy about Seventy Weeks (Dan 9)

In 539 BC, the year Babylon fell to Persia, Daniel was praying as he studied the book of Jeremiah and read the prophecies of seventy years of exile for Jerusalem.[9] He recognized the exile could potentially end soon if he and others prayed for God to fulfill his word. Daniel prayed and asked God to intervene on behalf of his people and his beloved city Jerusalem.

In response, God sent the angel Gabriel with a prophecy about seventy periods of seven (or perhaps seventy weeks) that would yet come in the future. During this period, God's people would face incredible opposition, but God would bring judgment on those who persecuted his people.[10]

Prophecy about One Man, Two Kings, and the Time of the End (Dan 10–12)

In 536 BC, around the time of the Jewish festival of Passover, Daniel saw an amazing vision of an individual man standing on the banks of the Tigris (10:4–21). When we read the description of this individual and compare it

9. This would mean Daniel was reading what we call either Jer 25 or Jer 29.

10. Some evangelical scholars see this prophecy fulfilled in the great tribulation period prior to the second coming of Jesus. Others see it fulfilled during the days of Antiochus Epiphanes IV around 165 BC.

with Revelation 1, it seems clear Daniel saw a vision of the risen Jesus.[11] An angelic messenger then began to reveal to Daniel what was going to come in the days ahead.

The focus of Daniel 11–12 is on the king of the south and the king of the north. The king of the north probably represents a group of people known as the Seleucids, from whom Antiochus Epiphanes IV came. The king of the south refers to Egypt. Daniel 11–12 stands unique in that it is a very specific prophecy, with amazing details provided about the intrigue between these kingdoms as they battled for power in the ancient world.[12]

Daniel provided great detail about the period we know as the intertestamental period, the period between Malachi and Matthew in our Bibles.[13] At some point, he shifted to speak of the time at the very end of history.[14] Daniel 12:1–3 records an account of the final battle between God's forces and the forces of evil. God prevailed, of course, and Daniel described a day when people would rise to a resurrection of either blessedness or judgment.

The rest of the chapter highlights Daniel's conversation with the angelic messenger, who told Daniel he did not need any further explanation about the details of the vision he had seen. Rather, Daniel would enter into the Lord's rest at his death and one day rise to celebrate the resurrection and the triumph of God with others. Perhaps the angel's words provide a gentle reminder to Christians today who wish to try to sort out every detail of the end times. In the end, we know God wins, and perhaps that should be enough.

Concluding Thoughts from Daniel

Daniel served faithfully and finished well. His service to God as far as we see it began in the courtroom of Babylon, though it probably began much earlier as he first learned and meditated on the Scriptures. When the book

11. Cf. Dan 10:5–6 with Rev 1:13–16.

12. Daniel's prophecy in Dan 11–12 seems to have served as a prototype for individuals in the period between the testaments who came along and copied the style. They were not writing under the inspiration of the Holy Spirit as Daniel was, but they tried to mimic his approach.

13. Some have erroneously called this period the silent four hundred years, but God was actively at work preparing the world for the coming of Jesus. God was bringing the world under one world power (Rome) and one international language (Greek).

14. Scholars see this shift either at 11:36, 11:40, or 12:1.

closes, Daniel is in his eighties, and he is still serving God faithfully. What an example for us today!

Daniel's prophecies also contain powerful insights about the kingdom of God. Many times today, we may wonder where God has gone when we see the enemy seemingly making advances into our Christian culture. We must remember it was much worse for Daniel and his friends. Nonetheless, God's purposes will come to pass.

How does the book of Daniel point to Jesus? We've already mentioned Daniel 10 and Daniel's vision of Jesus. Daniel 7:9–14 also highlights the vision Daniel had of Jesus coming before his Father, the Ancient of Days, and receiving the kingdom.[15] When we face hardships in life, we need to go back to a central truth of Scripture: Jesus is coming again, every eye will see him, the victory is won, and the outcome is not in doubt.

15. When one compares Dan 7:9–14 with Rev 4–5, it is clear Daniel and John saw the same vision.

21

Hosea, Joel, and Amos

CHRISTIANS OFTEN CALL THE last twelve books of the Old Testament (Hosea–Malachi) the Minor Prophets. This is somewhat unfortunate, since the prophets' messages are quite powerful. It also seems a bit odd in that many of them are longer than New Testament letters such as Colossians or Philippians, and we never refer to any of those as Minor Letters! In Jewish tradition, these books are called the Book of the Twelve. In our discussion of these prophets, we will divide them up into groups of three in the order they appear in our Bibles.

Hosea

The prophet Hosea ministered during the Divided Era (931–586 BC).[1] God called Hosea to marry Gomer, a woman who would cheat on him and break his heart. God used the physical adultery in Hosea's life to confront the spiritual adultery occurring in the Northern Kingdom during the reign of Jeroboam II (793–53 BC). As Gomer had strayed from Hosea, so Israel had strayed from God. Likewise, as Gomer's adultery broke Hosea's heart, Israel's spiritual adultery broke God's heart.

---

1. Jones, *Puzzle of the Old Testament*, 113–35.

Introduction (Hos 1:1)

The first verse of the book provides the basic context for Hosea's message. It is the word of the Lord, which God communicated to Hosea. The kings mentioned in verse 1 help us to date Hosea's ministry to shortly before Samaria's fall in 721 BC.[2]

The Picture of Israel's Unfaithfulness (Hos 1–3)

In Hosea 1–3, Hosea's sad marriage to Gomer forms the backdrop of God's message to Israel. As God's people saw Hosea's heartache, perhaps at least some saw the heart of God for his people.

Hosea's First Marriage to Gomer (Hos 1–2)

Gomer's Physical Adultery (Hos 1:2–9)

The Lord commanded Hosea to marry Gomer, who was called "a promiscuous woman" (1:2). Gomer bore three children, and the language of the text leaves it ambiguous as to whether or not the second and third children were Hosea's. Each of the children received a symbolic name that denoted a coming judgment of God upon his people. The name Jezreel described the valley of Assyria's decisive victory over the Northern Kingdom. Lo-ruhamah ("not pitied") highlighted the end of God's compassion for Israel. Finally, Lo-ammi ("not my people") indicated God's separation from his people as he judged their sin.

Israel's Spiritual Adultery (Hos 1:10—2:23)

Hosea 1:10—2:23 describes both God's anguish for his people and his love for his people. In powerful, graphic language, God recounted Israel's wickedness and announced he would bring judgment on her for her spiritual adultery (2:1–6). Israel had not recognized the God who had given her everything she had but instead had credited those gifts to Baal (2:8).

Nonetheless, Israel's gracious God also announced through Hosea Israel's coming restoration (Hos 2:14–23). In tender language, he described

---

2. Arnold and Beyer, *Encountering the Old Testament*, 431.

how he would win Israel back to him and marry her: "I am going to allure her: I will lead her into the wilderness and speak tenderly to her . . . . I will betroth you in faithfulness" (2:14, 20). Israel would be his people once again, and he would be their God.

Hosea's Second Marriage to Gomer (Hos 3)

God commanded Hosea to take Gomer back. She apparently had strayed from him and found herself in a situation where she was to be sold into slavery. The text does not specifically mention Gomer by name, but the woman has to be Gomer to fit the analogy. God was calling Israel back to himself, just as Hosea was calling Gomer back to himself.

Hosea still loved Gomer despite her unfaithfulness. He bought her for himself at a generous price and brought her home to be with him again. The spiritual application was that God likewise would one day take Israel back to himself again.

The Proclamation of Israel's Unfaithfulness (Hos 4–7)

Hosea announced, "The LORD has a charge to bring against you who live in the land: there is no faithfulness, no love, no acknowledgement of God in the land" (Hos 4:1). The word translated "charge" implies that God was in effect bringing the Israelites into court for their wickedness. He was bringing charges against them, and in this section, we will mention two.

The Charge of Spiritual Harlotry (Hos 4–5)

Hosea warned that spiritual harlotry had led Israel astray. There was no knowledge of God in the land, which led to the people disrespecting God's word. Once they had abandoned God and his word, faithfulness and morality would be gone. This charge of Hosea's occurs over and over in this section (Hos 4:10, 11, 12, 13, 14, 15, 18; 5:3, 4).

The Charge of Spiritual Hypocrisy (Hos 6–7)

Hosea called the people to return to the Lord (Hos 6:1). The Lord stood ready to accept them if they would only turn to him, and Hosea's language indicated the restoration might come rather quickly if the people repented. Sadly, Israel did not return to the Lord, and did not cry out to him from their hearts (Hos 7:10, 14). They spurned God's gracious offer and remained in their sin.

The Punishment of Israel's Unfaithfulness (Hos 8–10)

Hosea announced that the time of Israel's punishment had come. Hosea's words "now he (God) will remember their wickedness and punish their sins" (Hos 8:13) are repeated in Hosea 9:9. Israel's punishment had arrived. God had given time to repent, but they chose not to, and now they would face his judgment.

God would use the nation of Assyria as an instrument of judgment against Israel. In 721 BC, the Assyrian army conquered Samaria, the capital of the Northern Kingdom, and scattered the people. Second Kings 17:7–41 described this event as the judgment of God against a people who stubbornly refused to listen, despite his continued warnings. Assyria would swoop down on them like an eagle (8:1), and fire would come upon their cities (8:14). They would wander among the nations (9:17), and their king would be removed (10:14–15). The Assyrians ruled through fear and intimidation; their own records, which archaeologists have discovered, described them as a brutal people.[3]

The Pardon of Israel's Unfaithfulness (Hos 11–14)

The closing chapters of Hosea take us in a new direction. Although these closing four chapters occasionally point to God's frustration at his people or his judgment, in general we see a turn toward the positive. Hosea described God's compassion, care, and call to his people. He also described God's rescue of Israel from Egypt. He had brought them out of Egypt and established them in the promised land, but they abandoned him and worshiped the Canaanite god Baal instead. God's sense of justice demanded that he bring judgment, though he longed to be gracious to them (11:8).

Hosea described God's care of Israel since the land of Egypt. He had brought them out and given them his commands, and they were not to know any God except him. However, despite his care for them as they left

---

3. Arnold and Beyer, *Readings from Ancient Near East,* 137–47.

Egypt and in the wilderness, they became satisfied once they reached the promised land, and their hearts became proud (Hos 13:4–6). They forgot the God who had given them everything they had, and they would soon learn the hard way that their actions had consequences.

God's Call to Israel (Hos 14)

Hosea called Israel to return to the Lord. They had stumbled in their iniquity, but if they took genuine, heartfelt words of repentance with them, God would receive them back again (Hos 14:1–4). God promised to restore blessing to his people, and he would establish a close relationship with them again. Hosea closed his message to Israel by reminding God's people that they should have nothing to do with idols but should trust totally and completely in the Lord their God. His ways and his ways alone were right and good (14:8–9).

Concluding Thoughts from Hosea

Hosea's book portrays his sad marriage to Gomer with all its pain and anguish. Through his pain, Hosea began to learn more about the heart of God as God's heart ached for his own people. Perhaps some Israelites came to repentance; the book of Chronicles suggests perhaps this was the case (2 Chr 15:9; 30:1–11). Unfortunately, the vast majority of Israelites did not.

The book of Hosea demonstrates in a powerful way that God cares deeply for people—even people who have strayed far from him. The Bible teaches us that all of us have sinned and fall short of the glory of God (Rom 3:23). It's tempting to look at other people and compare ourselves with them; instead, we should compare ourselves with God's holy, righteous standard. When we do, we realize that on our best days, we fall far short of God's expectation. We all stand in desperate need of a Savior and are part of a group known as "ungodly," for whom Christ died (Rom. 4:5).

Joel

Bible scholars have dated Joel's ministry as early as 900 BC and as late as 400 BC. The most likely date of his ministry is during the Gathered Era

(538 BC–Christ).[4] During Joel's lifetime, Assyria's locust plague came upon the Southern Kingdom of Judah, and Joel used that event to warn God's people of an even greater potential judgment—the very judgment of God. Joel's name means "Yahweh is God." He ended, however, on a note of hope by pointing to both the first and second comings of the Messiah.

Ruin from the Lord (Joel 1:1—2:11)

Description of the Locusts (Joel 1:1–7)

Joel described the locusts as coming in waves. One wave of locusts was followed by another, resulting in utter devastation to the crops. Joel indicated the extreme rarity of such an event; no one alive could remember when things had been so bad, and people who experienced it would be telling their grandchildren about this great day.

Destruction by the Locusts (Joel 1:8—2:11)

Joel highlighted the utter devastation. The land of Judah was largely given to shepherding and farming, and without food, the animals had nothing to eat, so both groups suffered. Joel called the leadership to proclaim a solemn assembly to cry out to God (1:14). He saw in Judah's sufferings a shadow of the coming day of the Lord (1:15).

Return to the Lord (Joel 2:12–17)

God called the people through Joel to return to him with all their hearts (2:12). If they genuinely repented, they could count on God's grace and compassion to prevail. Joel called every element of society to join in calling on God for mercy and relief (2:15–17).

Response of the Lord (Joel 2:18—3:21)

The Lord's response would happen in two stages. Joel first focused on the immediate blessing God could bring to the society (2:18–27). In the closing

---

4. Jones, *Puzzle of the Old Testament*, 165–85; Arnold and Beyer, *Encountering the Old Testament*, 434.

verses of the book, Joel looked ahead to describe the ultimate blessing God would bring his people (2:28—3:21).

God's Immediate Blessing (Joel 2:18–27)

God promised he would respond to his people's cries. He would make up to them the years the locusts had eaten (2:25). Many people today have claimed the spirit of these words as they look to rebuild their own lives. God is indeed able to redeem, to restore. When the day of blessing came, people would see God's presence and know he was God (2:27).

God's Ultimate Blessing (Joel 2:28—3:21)

Joel first described a great spiritual outpouring that would come upon God's people (2:28–32). All humanity at every level would experience the blessing of God's Spirit. God also described great wonders in the heavens and on earth that would occur in this great day of God. In Acts 2, on the day of Pentecost, the apostle Peter stood up and addressed the crowd in Jerusalem. The Holy Spirit had fallen on the early church, and people declared in many different languages the glories of God. Peter explained that this occurrence was the fulfillment of Joel's prophecy of the outpouring of God's Spirit.

Some interpreters believe the signs and wonders described referred to Jesus's second coming. It is also possible these signs referred to such things as the earthquake and darkness that came upon Jerusalem at the time of Jesus's death (Matt 27:45).

Joel 3 describes God's ultimate blessing that will appear at Jesus's second coming. Judah's neighbors would face God's judgment. God would gather them together and judge them for their actions. On the other hand, the nation of Judah would be inhabited forever.

Even today, different groups claim ownership of various plots of land in the Middle East. This struggle for specific land and territory is often something quite foreign to us. However, in its cultural context, we see more clearly how God has given specific land as a blessing to his people. Consequently, Joel's closing words would have been powerful and reassuring.

Concluding Thoughts from Joel

As Joel described the awful effects of the plagues of locusts on Judah, he recognized a greater judgment that lay ahead for the world. He urged his people to consider that fact and exhorted them to plead to God for mercy and grace, whether for deliverance from the locusts or deliverance from final judgment. In the end, however, he pointed his listeners to the coming Messiah, the Lord Jesus Christ, who would pour out his Spirit to accomplish his purposes and one day return to judge the world.

Amos

The prophet Amos ministered during the Divided Era (931–586 BC).[5] Most likely he ministered somewhere around 770–750 BC.[6] Amos lived in the town of Tekoa, located about seven miles south of Jerusalem. He was a southern citizen whom God sent to the Northern Kingdom to preach a message of judgment. Focusing on the issue of social justice, Amos warned the Northern Kingdom of God's coming judgment that would result in Assyria carrying Israel into exile. After a series of messages focusing largely on Israel's impending doom, Amos ended his book with a declaration of hope and promised God's future restoration of his people.

Introduction (Amos 1:1)

Amos prophesied during the reigns of Uzziah/Azariah, Judah's tenth king (792–40 BC), and Jeroboam II, Israel's thirteenth king (793–53 BC). Jeroboam's reign featured political and military stability in the Northern Kingdom, but the people had fallen into spiritual corruption.

The Roar of God's Judgment (Amos 1–2)

Amos described the Lord as roaring from Zion (1:2); he then proclaimed doom and destruction against Israel's neighbors. Each one of them would receive God's punishment for their sins. At first, Amos's listeners, the people of the Northern Kingdom, probably thought, "Hey, this guy's okay!

5. Jones, *Puzzle of the Old Testament*, 115–35.
6. Arnold and Beyer, *Encountering the Old Testament*, 436.

He's condemning all our neighbors!" However, after proclaiming God's judgment against seven neighboring nations, Amos then focused on the nation of Israel (Amos 2:6–16). Israel was guilty of social injustice, and God would deal with them for their wickedness. They had forgotten the Lord, and consequently, the nation was going down fast.

The Reasons for God's Judgment (Amos 3–9)

In this section, Amos preached three distinct messages to God's people. He then proclaimed details of five visions God gave him. Through them all, he focused on the reasons God was bringing judgment against a sinful people.

Amos Preaches Three Messages (Amos 3–6)

Amos 3 described Israel's future ordeal. God would punish them for their sins. He had a special relationship with them that exceeded his relationship with all of the families of the earth; that fact made his people especially responsible to him (3:2).

In Amos 4, the prophet focused on Israel's past offenses. He described how he had brought famine, drought, and plagues against God's people, but they did not return to him (4:6, 8–11).

Amos 5–6 highlighted Israel's present opportunity: they should seek God, that they might live (5:4, 6, 14). Turning to idols and false religious centers would get them nothing but trouble; turning back to God would bring them life.

Amos Proclaims Five Visions (Amos 7:1—9:10)

God showed Amos a vision of locusts (7:1–3) and a vision of fire (7:4–6). Each of these visions foretold devastating conditions that loomed before the Northern Kingdom. When Amos pleaded with God to be merciful, God determined he would not bring these judgments against Israel. However, God showed Amos another vision of a plumb line (7:7–9). Just as the plumb line revealed the straightness or crookedness of a wall, so the word of God revealed Israel's spiritual crookedness. He would tear the nation down and start over.

God then showed Amos a basket of summer fruit (8:1–3). A basket of fruit signified that the harvest time had come; fittingly, Amos used this as a parallel to highlight that the time of God's judgment had come.

In the prophet's concluding vision (9:1–10), he described the Northern Kingdom's altar that had been built as an alternative to the temple of Jerusalem. Amos announced its destruction. Further, God would judge people no matter where they ran. Ironically, the only way to escape God's judgment was to admit that there was no escape and run to God, begging for his mercy and pardon.

The Restoration after God's Judgment (Amos 9:11–15)

After much prophecy of doom and gloom, Amos concluded his message on a high note. The day would come when God would restore the line of King David again, and other nations would turn to God with hope. In Acts 15, as the early church began to include gentiles (non-Jews), many Jews wondered why this was happening. The apostle James, the Lord's half-brother, stood up and explained to everyone that they were seeing the fulfillment of these verses from Amos. God's restoration would include his own people but also would reach people who formerly were not his people.

Concluding Thoughts from Amos

Amos railed powerfully against the social injustice of his day. He saw its impact on society and called people to humble themselves before God. At the same time, he pointed ahead to a great day of restoration. One day, God's mercy and grace would extend to all nations, not merely to Israel. Such words may have astounded the prophet's hearers, just as this phenomenon astounded the early church. Nonetheless, God's great care for people extended beyond the boundaries of Israel and Judah, and Amos announced that one day, all people everywhere would see the power of God. The ultimate display of God's love for all people everywhere would come through his Son Jesus Christ.

22

Obadiah, Jonah, and Micah

Obadiah

OBADIAH WAS WRITTEN AT the end of the Divided Era (931–586 BC) and the beginning of the Scattered Era (605–538 BC).[1] It is the shortest book in the Old Testament. The book of Genesis recorded how Isaac the patriarch had two sons, Esau and Jacob. Esau became the father of the people known as the Edomites, while Jacob became the father of the Israelites. Over the centuries, these two people groups fought each other regularly.

Jerusalem fell to the armies of King Nebuchadnezzar of Babylon in 586 BC. At that time, the Edomites intervened on behalf of Babylon, helping to cut down Judeans as they fled in the direction of Edom. The prophet Obadiah viewed Edom's participation in the battle as a betrayal of a brother. He prophesied that one day, Edom would experience final defeat and Judah would experience ultimate victory.

Condemnation of the Edomites (Obad 1–16)

The book of Obadiah is straight and to the point: one day, the Edomites will experience God's judgment, even as Judah experiences God's salvation. Obadiah essentially deals with the what and why questions in his book.

1. Jones, *Puzzle of the Old Testament*, 137–62.

What? (Obad 1–9)

Obadiah announced Edom's impending judgment. In fact, the Lord's message had already gone forth (v. 1). The Edomites lived high in the clefts of the rock and thought no one could ever bring them down to the ground (v. 3). However, the Lord said he would do that very thing (v. 4). Edom's destruction would prove thorough and complete.

Why? (Obad 10–16)

Obadiah declared the primary reason for Edom's judgment: "violence to your brother Jacob" (v. 10). The Hebrew word translated "violence" is *hamas*, a word that denotes unjust violence of any kind.[2] Edom had stood by and done nothing when foreigners had conquered Jerusalem (v. 11).

Obadiah warned the Edomites not to gloat over Judah's loss and urged them to quit adding to Judah's misery. Obadiah further described the day of the Lord that was coming upon all the nations, and Edom would not be omitted (vv. 15–16). The nations would experience God's judgment for their wickedness, and Edom, who had betrayed his Jewish brother, would also.

Consolation for the Israelites (Obad 17–21)

As he had done in the first section, Obadiah dealt with the what and why of Edom's judgment and Judah's deliverance.

What? (Obad 17–20)

Obadiah affirmed the house of Jacob would be delivered (v. 17). God would use them to bring judgment on the Edomites (vv. 18–20). Those who had lived in Judah would occupy the vanquished territory that had once been Edom. This expansion into Edom would accommodate many Jewish refugees as they returned from all over the world to the promised land. However, Edom would come to an end.

---

2. The Arabic word *hamas*, which is used of the modern terrorist group, is a related word.

Why? (Obad 21)

Obadiah closed his book with a powerful comment: "The kingdom will be the LORD's." Ultimately, God's salvation would bless his people greatly. However, more than anything else, God's victory on behalf of his people would bring glory to him.

Readers may wonder how exactly Obadiah points to the coming of Jesus. Admittedly, this book does not do so like many other Old Testament books. At the same time, the story God was writing provided for Edom's defeat, so the history of God's people could continue. The Lord would bring restoration, and as he did, he would pave the way for the coming of his Son.

Jonah

The book of Jonah falls in the Divided Era (931–586 BC).[3] Most Bible scholars date Jonah's life to the early eighth century BC (800–770 BC). The book presents Jonah's ministry in narrative form. As we read it, we find that Jonah had a message to preach, but he also had a lesson to learn.

At the time of Jonah's ministry, the nation of Assyria was becoming strong and soon would become the dominant power of the ancient Near East. The Assyrians were bloodthirsty and vicious, and hatred for the Assyrians no doubt motivated Jonah to resist God's call to preach forgiveness to the nation that would one day destroy the Northern Kingdom of Israel. Jonah's hatred so blinded him to God's purpose that when the Assyrians responded to God's love and forgiveness, Jonah wanted to die rather than celebrate.

Jonah's Disobedience to God (Jonah 1)

Jonah's Call (Jonah 1:1–2)

We learn in the book's opening verse that God came to Jonah with a calling. That calling was unmistakable: "Go to the great city of Nineveh and preach against it, because its wickedness has come up before me." God wanted to warn Nineveh, Assyria's great but wicked city, of its impending doom, and he would use Jonah to do so.

---

3. Jones, *Puzzle of the Old Testament*, 113–35.

Jonah's Course (Jonah 1:3)

Jonah, however, had other plans. He did not want to follow God's plan, so instead he rose to flee to Tarshish, on a course due west rather than north and northeast. Jonah wanted to get as far away as possible from his calling, perhaps to get as far away from God as possible.

Jonah's Consequences (Jonah 1:4–17)

Jonah's escape plan did not work. God had determined his prophet would go to Nineveh, so he hurled a great storm against the ship on which Jonah was trying to escape. The sailors all feared for their lives, and in the end, Jonah confessed to them that he was responsible for their calamity. At his insistence, they threw him into the sea, so that at least their lives would be spared. The Lord prepared a great fish to swallow Jonah,[4] and Jonah ended up with three days in the fish's belly to think about what he had done.

Jonah's Desperation for God (Jonah 2)

A Cry to the Lord (Jonah 2:1–9)

Jonah's cry to the Lord from the belly of the fish was an amazing prayer indeed. Scholars have noted that Jonah quoted from or alluded to at least twenty different psalms. Ironically, one who knew the Scriptures so well still ran from God. At the end of his prayer, Jonah indicated he was now ready to serve God's purpose.

A Command from the Lord (Jonah 2:10)

Once the Lord heard Jonah's readiness, he spoke to the fish, which vomited Jonah up on the dry land. Jonah headed to Nineveh, though at the end of the book, we learn he still wasn't too thrilled to go.

---

4. Many people refer to the story of Jonah and the *whale*, but the text actually uses the Hebrew word for *fish*. Much speculation has ensued over the exact species of fish, but we cannot be certain; perhaps it was a fish created and prepared precisely for this purpose.

Jonah's Declaration about God (Jonah 3)

Nineveh Receives God's Message (Jonah 3:1-4)

Jonah arrived at Nineveh, and the city was so large it took three days to adequately proclaim the message throughout its limits. Jonah's message was simple: "Forty more days and Nineveh will be overthrown."

Nineveh Responds to Jonah's Message (Jonah 3:5-10)

Undoubtedly to Jonah's amazement, "the Ninevites believed God" (3:5). They proclaimed a fast and humbled themselves, and even the king issued a royal decree that everyone should humble himself before the God of Jonah.[5] God witnessed the Ninevites' repentance, and when he saw their changed hearts, he chose to spare the city from destruction.

Jonah's Depression before God (Jonah 4)

Jonah's Reaction to God (Jonah 4:1)

One might think a prophet who had traveled hundreds of miles to preach God's message of repentance would be thrilled that a city had turned to the Lord. Not Jonah! Rather, he was greatly displeased; in fact, he became furious.

Jonah's Reason before God (Jonah 4:2)

Jonah expressed his frustration to the Lord. He insisted that while he was still in his own country he had known that God might forgive them. Therefore, in order to forestall the whole thing, he had tried to flee to Tarshish. He knew God's mercy and compassion might shine through in a moment

---

5. Over the years, some have questioned the possibility that an entire city would repent at the presence of a small country prophet like Jonah. However, a city such as Nineveh that worshiped hundreds of gods would not necessarily know from where trouble was coming. Perhaps Jonah arrived at a time Nineveh was suffering from some form of trouble or hardship and sacrificing to the deities they knew had not worked. When Jonah came, speaking such a clear message, perhaps the Ninevites figured they had nothing to lose. At any rate, their response makes perfect sense in a society that worshiped many gods and thus couldn't know for sure which god was the source of their trouble.

of Ninevite repentance, and Jonah had not counted on that repentance, nor did he desire it.

Jonah's Request for God (Jonah 4:3)

Jonah requested that God take his life. Perhaps he feared people back home would think of him as a false prophet when he told them how his prophecy hadn't come true. Perhaps he felt he had come all that way for nothing, since God was not going to destroy the city. At any rate, he felt his life was over and begged to die.

Jonah's Response from God (Jonah 4:4–11)

The book of Jonah ends with a short dialogue between God and his struggling prophet. God created a fast-growing plant that provided shade for Jonah as he sat east of the city to see what might happen to Nineveh. But then God appointed a worm to attack the plant, and as the plant withered, the sun beat down on Jonah's head and he felt miserable. Again, he begged to die.

When God questioned him, Jonah's anger intensified. In response, God taught Jonah an important object lesson. Jonah was practically in tears over a plant he did not have anything to do with preparing or growing, yet he was not at all concerned that one hundred twenty thousand people might face the judgment of God. In fact, Jonah was disappointed in their repentance. The book ends with God's sober question "should I not have concern for the great city of Nineveh, in which there are more than a hundred and twenty thousand people?" (4:11).

Concluding Thoughts from Jonah

Ultimately, the Ninevites' repentance did not last, and the Assyrian Empire fell in 612 BC. Nonetheless, the Ninevites' repentance was highlighted by Jesus in Matthew 12:39–41. Jesus affirmed the historicity of the events in Jonah, drawing parallels to his own resurrection and the day of final judgment.

The book of Jonah also anticipates Jesus's coming through its powerful lesson that God cares deeply for all people. God's love for the whole world and not merely for the nation of Israel was not a message Jonah was ready to embrace, but it was a message God would bring through his Son the Lord Jesus.

Micah

The prophet Micah was a contemporary of the prophet Isaiah. His ministry occurred roughly from 750 to 700 BC. As such, he was part of the Divided Era (931–586 BC).[6]

As a contemporary of Isaiah, Micah was likewise a witness of the Assyrian victory over the Northern Kingdom of Israel. Micah confronted the sinful actions of both Israel and Judah, particularly their lack of concern for social justice and Judah's complacent attitude toward the things of God (3:11–12). Though Micah pronounced judgment, he also strongly stressed the hope of God's forgiveness and promised a glorious future for the people of God.

Introduction (Mic 1:1)

The book's introduction provides a lot of information. First of all, it tells us what the book is about: "the Word of the LORD . . . concerning Samaria and Jerusalem." Samaria was Israel's capital, and Jerusalem was Judah's capital.

Second, the first verse tells us from whom the book came. The word of the Lord "that came to Micah" thus came from the Lord to the prophet Micah and from him to his audience.

Third, the introduction tells us when all this happened. "During the reigns of Jotham, Ahaz and Hezekiah, kings of Judah" covers roughly the dates 750–700 BC. Of Judah's twenty kings, Jotham, Ahaz, and Hezekiah were the eleventh, twelfth, and thirteenth. Scripture records that Jotham and Hezekiah were good kings, while Ahaz was wicked.

6. Jones, *Puzzle of the Old Testament*, 113–35.

The Failings of God's People (Mic 1–3)

Their Rebellion (Mic 1)

Micah described a day when God would come and judge his people. Why would he do this? Micah 1:5 tells us: "All this is because of Jacob's transgression, because of the sins of the people of Israel. What is Jacob's transgression? Is it not Samaria? What is Judah's high place? Is it not Jerusalem?" The wicked activity in the northern and southern capitals was indicative of the wickedness that prevailed throughout the realm. God would tolerate it no longer.

Their Rulers (Micah 2–3)

Micah described four categories of people who took advantage of those they could. These categories included the privileged, the princes, the prophets, and the priests.

The Privileged (Mic 2)

Micah 2:1–2 described people of power and privilege who used their position for personal advantage. They plotted iniquity as they fell asleep and made sure they carried it out in the morning. Those who lacked power and privilege found themselves helpless before the onslaught of social injustice.

The Princes (Mic 3:1–4)

Micah called to the "leaders of Jacob and rulers of Israel . . . you who hate good and love evil" (3:1–2). They of all people should have known what justice was, so that they could model it and execute it in the land, but they did not. Micah described their wickedness as tantamount to chopping people up as meat for a kettle!

The Prophets (Mic 3:5–10)

Micah also had a word from God for "the prophets who lead my people astray" (3:5). These prophets were abusing their office, providing prophetic ministry only to those who could pay for it. To others, they announced God's judgment. God would judge them as well.

The Priests (Mic 3:11–12)

The priests likewise abused their office, being willing to "teach for a price" (3:11). Their thought was, "Is not the LORD among us? No disaster will come upon us." They had the attitude that no matter what they did, God's blessing would come. They would soon find out they were wrong.

The Future of God's People (Micah 4–5)

A Coming Reign (Mic 4:1–8)

God's coming reign featured three aspects: God's temple, God's people, and God's peace. First, Micah said that in the latter days, God would lift up Jerusalem and the temple to a place of prominence. The city would be exalted spiritually above everywhere else on earth. Second, Micah anticipated a day when people of all nations would come to Jerusalem to worship the Lord. At the same time, the word of the Lord would go forth to all of the nations. Third, Micah prophesied God's peace, God's *shalom*, life as it was meant to be. Every aspect of society would align with God's desire as the people laid down their weapons of war and embraced life as God intended.[7]

A Coming Rescue (Mic 4:9–13)

During Micah's days, Assyria was the major power in the ancient Near East. Somewhat surprisingly, then, Micah tells the people, "You will go to Babylon. There you will be rescued" (4:10). In the story God was writing, Babylon, not Assyria, would prove the ultimate enemy to Judah. The Assyrians would conquer Israel, but the Babylonians would conquer Judah. Micah proclaimed that the sooner the exile ended, the sooner the day of God's restoration could come.

---

7. Mic 4:1–3 closely parallels Isa 2:1–4. God privileged these two contemporaries to see the same great future day of restoration.

A Coming Ruler (Mic 5)

Micah announced a great day when a great ruler would come out of Bethlehem. The ruler would have a modest beginning, because Bethlehem was one of Judah's smallest cities. However, this ruler with humble beginnings would one day impact the nations. Micah's words clearly describe the coming of Jesus, who was born in Bethlehem. In the days of Jesus's birth, Jerusalem's religious leaders affirmed they understood Micah's words in this way (Matt 2:4–6).

This great ruler had a modest beginning, but a majestic ending. Micah prophesied that "his greatness will reach to the ends of the earth" (5:4). He would bring the people life as God intended it. Further, this peace would extend to the nations. All the earth would recognize the greatness of the ruler from Bethlehem.

The Forgiveness of God's People (Mic 6–7)

In the last two chapters of his book, Micah described the forgiveness that would come to God's people. These chapters cover three main areas: God's problem with his people, God's punishment of his people, and God's pardon for his people.

God's Problem with His People (Mic 6:1–9)

Micah brought God's case against God's people. He had done so much for them: brought them out of Egypt, redeemed them from slavery, led them through the wilderness, and given them the promised land. How had he wearied them? It made no sense that they would forsake him in view of his track record of faithfulness.

Micah responded with hypothetical questions of those who might hear. What could they possibly do to pay God back or to show their sincerity? Micah responded with a famous verse that is quite simple in its wording, yet often difficult to live out: "He has shown you, O mortal, what is good. And what does the LORD require of you? To act justly and to love mercy and to walk humbly with your God" (6:8). This verse described the people's proper but lacking response.

God's Punishment of His People (Mic 6:10—7:6)

Micah 6:10—7:6 described God's reaction. He would strike them down and bring desolation. As much as it pained him, he would give them over to destruction. Salvation one day would come, but judgment needed to come first.

Micah responded with his own personal feelings of woe (7:1–6). As he looked around society, he saw only people eager for their own gain taking advantage of others. Families broke down as trust crumbled even within what should have been the closest of relationships.

God's Pardon for His People (Mic 7:7-20)

Micah determined he would look to the Lord, because the Lord was indeed his only hope for salvation (7:7). He asked God to shepherd his people again, that they might live in security (7:14). He asked God to show his people his miracles again (7:15). He asked God to show them his uniqueness again, for no one was like him (7:18). Finally, Micah urged God to show them his compassion and forgiveness (7:19-20). One day, God would restore them and have compassion on them again. He would move in accordance with the promise he had made to Abraham and Jacob over a thousand years earlier. God is a God who keeps his promises.

Concluding Thoughts from Micah

Micah looked ahead to a day when all the nations would serve God. The prophet was privileged to foresee the grand culmination of history, when society would experience peace as God intended it. This peace naturally would come about under King Jesus, the King of kings.

Micah also predicted the birth of Jesus in Bethlehem (Mic 5). God would reach down into a small city in Judah and put his Messiah there. King David came from Bethlehem, and King David's descendant would one day rule as King of kings and Lord of lords.

Before we leave Micah, we must touch on a somber thought related to Micah 5. When the magi (important Persian officials) came to Jerusalem in the days of Jesus's birth, they asked where the king of the Jews was to be born. When evil King Herod consulted with his wise men and chief priests as to where the king of the Jews was to be born, his leaders immediately cited Micah 5: the king of the Jews, the Messiah, was to be born in Bethlehem.

Certainly these rulers saw the same star the magi did. Tragically, as far as we know, not one of them got on a donkey and rode south five miles to Bethlehem to see if maybe the Messiah had indeed come. The account in Matthew 2 illustrates for us the principle that we need to be on the alert to watch for what God is doing. What is the Lord doing right before your eyes, which you fail to see?

23

Nahum, Habakkuk, and Zephaniah

Nahum

THE PROPHET NAHUM MINISTERED during the Divided Era (931–586 BC).[1] He is called Nahum the Elkoshite, but we do not know which ancient site of Elkosh is intended.[2] The Northern Kingdom of Israel had long fallen to Assyria, but now Nahum prophesied Assyria's downfall. The prophet prophesied sometime around 660 BC or a bit later and announced the overthrow of Nineveh, Assyria's capital city. The city fell in 612 BC, effectively ending the Assyrian Empire.

The book of Nahum contains three chapters, and each chapter describes a feature of Nineveh's judgment: the comparison of Nineveh's judgment, the characteristics of Nineveh's judgment, and the certainty of Nineveh's judgment.

The Comparison of Nineveh's Judgment (Nah 1)

The prophet Nahum drew a sharp contrast between the punishment that would come to Nineveh and the peace that would come to Judah. The

---

1. Jones, *Puzzle of the Old Testament*, 113–35.

2. Arnold and Beyer, *Encountering the Old Testament*, 447, mention Galilee, Judah, and even the region of Nineveh as possibilities.

defeat of the Assyrian Empire would bring great joy to those the Assyrians had oppressed.

Punishment for Nineveh (Nah 1:1–14)

Nahum described the Lord as a "jealous and avenging God" (v. 2) who indeed would take revenge on his adversaries. He would make a complete devastation of Nineveh, and the city would not rise again (1:8–9). God would destroy Nineveh's city and Nineveh's gods (1:14).

Peace for Judah (Nah 1:15)

Nahum described the joy of the messengers who ran on the mountains to bring the news to Nineveh's destruction. Judah would celebrate its new-found freedom from the Assyrian oppressor.

The Characteristics of Nineveh's Judgment (Nah 2)

Nahum described the panic that ensued in Nineveh as Nineveh's enemies closed in. The chariots dashed madly in the streets, but dashing madly in the streets was not the purpose of chariots. They were to fight in the open country, but their enemies had hemmed them in. Historians tell us that a coalition of Medes, Babylonians, and others brought Nineveh down. All Nineveh had would be carried away.

Nahum described Nineveh's fall as an utter desolation. The people of Nineveh left their gold and treasures behind as they fled for their lives. Consequently, the city was open to looting by the invading armies. Ultimately, of course, it was the day of the Lord's judgment (Nah 2:13).

The Certainty of Nineveh's Judgment (Nah 3)

Nineveh's Judgment Announced (Nah 3:1–7)

Nahum described Nineveh as a "city of blood" (3:1). Nineveh was filled with oppression, but that oppression would come back on its own head. The Lord was against Nineveh and would humble the city and its empire.

The language of verse 7 implies that even though people were happy to see Nineveh fall, they recoiled at the magnitude of Nineveh's disgrace.

Nineveh's Judgment Assured (Nah 3:8–19)

Nahum compared Nineveh to the powerful Egyptian city of No-amon, also known as Thebes, which the Assyrians had conquered in 663 BC. Nahum assured the Ninevites they would fare no better than the people they had conquered.

Nahum closed his book with a taunt against the Assyrians: "Nothing can heal you; your wound is fatal. All who hear the news about you clap their hands at your fall, for who has not felt your endless cruelty?" (3:19). Nineveh's judgment was assured, and its fall would bring rejoicing to the world.

Concluding Thoughts from Nahum

Nineveh's fall and the destruction of the Assyrian Empire was the next step in the great story God was writing through human history. The Babylonian dynasty would follow, then the Persian dynasty, then the Greek dynasty, and finally the dynasty of Rome. During the days of Rome, God would send his Son as Savior of the world.

Habakkuk

Habakkuk prophesied near the end of the Divided Era (931–586 BC),[3] during a time of great sinfulness in Judah, the Southern Kingdom. The prophet wondered how much longer God would wait before bringing judgment upon his people. When God answered that he would soon use Babylon to discipline his people, Habakkuk was puzzled. How could God use a nation more sinful than Judah to carry out his purposes? In the end, Habakkuk learned it was best to trust God, no matter what.

---

3. Jones, *Puzzle of the Old Testament*, 113–35.

Habakkuk's Concern (Hab 1:1–11)

Habakkuk's Question (Hab 1:1–4)

Each of the book's first two chapters begins with Habakkuk's question, followed by God's answer. Here, Habakkuk began with a bold question; he likely spoke more boldly to God than we normally dare to do. Habakkuk asked, "How long, LORD, must I call for help, but you do not listen? Or cry out to you, 'Violence!' but you do not save?" (1:2). It just didn't make sense to Habakkuk that God would allow oppression and violence to run rampant in Judah. No one paid any attention to the law of Moses, and therefore, there was no justice in the land.

God's Answer (Hab 1:5–11)

God told Habakkuk he was doing something in Habakkuk's day that Habakkuk would find hard to believe (1:5). God planned to raise up the Chaldeans[4] as his instruments of judgment against Judah. God likened their ferocity to fierce birds who swooped down on many lands to devour them. They had no concern for smaller kings, for they ran over all they opposed.

Habakkuk's Confusion (Hab 1:12—2:20)

Habakkuk's Question (Hab 1:12—2:1)

God's answer was not the one Habakkuk expected. The prophet then retorted, "Your eyes are too pure to look on evil; you cannot tolerate wrongdoing. Why then do you tolerate the treacherous? Why are you silent while the wicked [Babylonians] swallow up those more righteous than themselves?" (1:13). Habakkuk went on to describe the Chaldeans' arrogance as they conquered other peoples and rejoiced in their own power. After airing his thoughts, Habakkuk awaited God's reply.

---

4. The term "Chaldeans" refers to the people also known as the Babylonians. "Chaldean" is the ethnic term that describes the group of people, whereas "Babylonian" describes the region the people controlled.

God's Answer (Hab 2:2-20)

God did not defend his answer to Habakkuk. Rather, he told him to record the vision and inscribe it on tablets as a testimony to what he would do. The vision would come at its appointed time, and it would not fail.

In verse 4, God laid out two possible choices for those who heard his prophetic message. First, they could become proud and refuse to believe God could work in this fashion. Second, they could choose to live by faith, trusting the Lord even in difficult times they did not understand. God's words here—"the righteous person will live by his faithfulness"—form the centerpiece of Paul's letter to the Romans (Rom 1:17).

The rest of God's answer to Habakkuk focused on five woes to Babylon. Babylon indeed would receive God's judgment, but Habakkuk and the other Judeans needed to trust God's plan.

Habakkuk's Cry (Hab 3:1–19)

The opening and closing words of chapter 3 set this chapter in a particular context. Verse 1 describes the chapter as the prophet's prayer. The Hebrew term *shigionoth* probably designates a highly emotional poem. The closing verse of the chapter dedicates the song (or psalm?) to the choir director for public worship. As the tough times came, Habakkuk wanted God's people to lean on his message for encouragement.

Habakkuk first expressed his desire for God in verses 1–2. He had heard God's report, and he was afraid. He asked for God to remember mercy as he judged his people.

Second, Habakkuk described God's splendor and majesty in many different ways in verses 3–15. In fact, the prophet referred to God thirty-three times in thirteen verses. He had the power to judge his people, but he also had the power to judge his people's enemies, and he would.

Third, Habakkuk expressed his dread before God in verse 16. He trembled within as he contemplated his circumstances—he must wait quietly for the day of judgment God would bring against Judah! He knew it was coming, and barring complete repentance by God's people, it would indeed come.

Fourth, Habakkuk expressed his dedication to God in verses 17–19. Though his circumstances were terrifying, he would choose to trust God, no matter what. God was his strength and would give him the grace to walk with confidence, like deer on mountain heights.

Concluding Thoughts from Habakkuk

Habakkuk ministered in Judah's last days. He cried out to God for justice, and when God told him how he planned to judge Judah, Habakkuk could not believe it. In the end, however, Habakkuk chose to trust in God, no matter what.

God sometimes calls believers today to do the same thing. We cannot wait until we fully understand God's plan to trust him. Instead, we must choose to believe him, to trust him, and to follow him, even when we don't understand how or where he is leading. Habakkuk 2:4 sums it up: "The righteous person will live by his faithfulness." That was life as it was meant to be for Habakkuk, and that is life as it is meant to be today for all who follow Jesus.

Zephaniah

The prophet Zephaniah prophesied during the reign of Josiah (640–609 BC), Judah's sixteenth king and Judah's last good king of the Divided Era.[5] Many Bible scholars believe the reference to Hezekiah in Zephaniah 1:1 refers to King Hezekiah, thus making Zephaniah at least a distant relative of Judah's king.[6] In his short book of three chapters, Zephaniah proclaimed retribution against all who opposed God but also promised a day of restoration when God would redeem his own.

Retribution Proclaimed (Zeph 1–2)

Against the Nation of Judah (Zeph 1:2—2:3)

God promised sweeping judgment against not only Judah but against the world. With respect to Judah, the princes, the priests, and the people would all face God's coming punishment. The princes and priests had tolerated or even encouraged idolatry and syncretism (the mixing of Yahweh worship

5. Jones, *Puzzle of the Old Testament*, 113–35.

6. Arnold and Beyer, *Encountering the Old Testament*, 451.

with worship of other gods), and among the general population a spirit of complacency loomed (1:12). Zephaniah announced a great day of the Lord was coming, and no one would escape (1:14–18). Only those who humbled themselves before the Lord and sought his ways could expect to survive (Zeph 2:3).

Against the Neighbors of Judah (Zeph 2:4–15)

Zephaniah announced God's judgment against Judah's neighbors as well. The Philistines, located along Judah's west coast, would face destruction. So would the Moabites and Ammonites, the descendants of Lot, Abraham's nephew (Gen 19:37–38). Their kingdoms lay along the east and northeast borders of Judah. Likewise, Cush would be slain with the sword of God's judgment, and Assyria, once the most powerful empire on earth, would soon fall (Zeph 2:13–15). Like many other prophets, Zephaniah stressed that God was not the God of Judah only, but he was God of the whole world.

Restoration Promised (Zeph 3)

Immediate Punishment (Zeph 3:1–7)

Zephaniah described Judah's terrible example. She was an oppressive, rebellious, and defiled city that heeded no instruction from the Lord or his prophets. Her princes, prophets, and priests abused their offices for their own personal gain, and they would face the consequences.

Ultimate Peace (Zeph 3:8–20)

Zephaniah 3:8 summarized God's prior words concerning his judgment of the nations. He would gather nations and kingdoms, and they would face his burning anger. Perhaps somewhat surprisingly, then, the rest of the book describes the ultimate peace God will bring, both to Judah and to the nations. People from all nations will call upon the Lord and serve him together (3:9). The people of God will sing for joy at all God has done for them (3:14–16), but even more amazingly, the Lord their God will rejoice over them (3:17).

Concluding Thoughts from Zephaniah

In the last verse, God promised to restore the fortunes of his people. To a limited extent, he fulfilled those words when he brought his people back from exile, introducing the Gathered Era (538 BC–Christ).[7] Ultimately, however, Zephaniah's words describe something much greater. As history as we know it comes to an end, God's saving hand will reach people from all nations, and they will worship him together (Rev. 7:9–17).

In the book of Zephaniah, we see God's character on display. On the one hand, his sense of justice demands that he judge the nations for their sin. He will even judge those who profess his name if they do not truly follow him. At the same time, God's grace stands ready to redeem, to forgive, to heal, and to restore. Zephaniah's words in 3:9–20 anticipate Jesus's Great Commission to his disciples to go make disciples of all nations (Matt 28:18–20).

---

7. Jones, *Puzzle of the Old Testament,* 163–85.

24

Haggai, Zechariah, and Malachi

Haggai

THE MINISTRY OF HAGGAI the prophet took place during the Gathered Era (538 BC–Christ).[1] In 538 BC, Zerubbabel, appointed governor of Judah, arrived in Jerusalem with the first group of almost fifty thousand Jews returning from their exile in Babylon. Rebuilding of the temple that Nebuchadnezzar had destroyed soon began, but within a short time, construction stopped due to local harassment from those unfriendly toward the Jews. For approximately fifteen years, the temple lay unfinished, until the prophet Haggai, accompanied by Zechariah, began a ministry of encouragement.

Haggai's book is a series of four short sermons both to Zerubbabel and the people, exhorting them to finish what they had started. The year was 520 BC; Ezra 4–6 gives the background of this powerful little book.

Message 1: To the People (Hag 1:1–15)

Haggai's first message to the people challenged them to consider their situation and to consider their ways. The prophet began by pointing out the people's sin: the temple lay desolate while they lived in their finely paneled houses. Clearly their priorities were out of order. Haggai corrected them by

1. Jones, *Puzzle of the Old Testament*, 165–85.

telling them to rebuild the temple. They had faced drought and plague as the consequences of their sin, but they had not accomplished God's work. The people responded in obedience and began working on the temple (1:12–15).

Message 2: To the Prince, Zerubbabel (Hag 2:1–9)

Haggai's second message had two parts. First, the prophet dealt with fears about the temple (2:1–5). He asked those who remained, who had seen the temple in its former glory, to compare it to the current temple's appearance; perhaps some of the elders of Judah could indeed remember. Many probably thought the rebuilt temple would never regain the splendor of Solomon's temple. However, Haggai encouraged them to build it again and not to fear, for God was with them.

Second, the prophet dealt with the future of the temple (2:6–9). He assured them God would bring glory to the house again, and the temple's glory would be even greater than it was before. Perhaps that was hard to imagine, but Haggai assured his hearers it would be so.

Message 3: To the People (Hag 2:10–19)

The Prophet's Rebuke of the People for Their Past (Hag 2:10–14)

Haggai asked the priests for a ruling. Can something clean make an unclean thing clean? The priests correctly answered it could not. Haggai then asked if something unclean could make something clean unclean. The priest answered that it could. Haggai's application was that God's people were rendering the temple area unclean by their unclean lives. Living by the temple grounds did not make them holy; rather, their uncleanness corrupted God's house of worship.

The Prophet's Revelation to the People about Their Future (Hag 2:15–19)

Haggai reminded the people that up to this point God had struck them with plagues and difficult times to get their attention (2:15–17). However, from that day on, God would bless them (2:18–19). He encouraged them to mark the day on their calendars, because the difference between cursing and blessing would be obvious.

Message 4: To Zerubbabel the Prince (Hag 2:20–23)

Haggai's last message focused especially on Zerubbabel, Judah's governor and descendant of King David. Haggai promised that one day as God did a great work among his people, he would take Zerubbabel and make him God's signet ring. The king's signet ring conveyed the king's authority, so calling Zerubbabel God's signet ring meant Zerubbabel would function as God's representative and accomplish God's purpose.

Concluding Thoughts from Haggai

The ministry of Haggai recorded in his book spanned about four months. We know from the book of Ezra (Ezra 6:15) that within a few years, the temple was completed. However, it did not have the glory of the former temple; perhaps the people lacked the faith to follow through fully on God's promise. At any rate, God's ultimate fulfillment of this prophecy would come in Jesus, who told his listeners, "Destroy this temple, and I will raise it again in three days" (John 2:19). Jesus was God's temple, God's perfect, ultimate dwelling place on earth. When Jesus's enemies crucified him, they thought they had destroyed him, but God raised him from the dead on the third day, fulfilling Jesus's words.

Zechariah

The book of Zechariah also dates to the Gathered Era (538 BC–Christ).[2] Zechariah was a contemporary of Haggai, so much of what we said at the introduction of the book of Haggai applies to Zechariah. Local adversity had caused construction on the temple to cease for approximately fifteen years until the year 520 BC. At that point, Zechariah and Haggai came along to encourage Zerubbabel and the people to resume construction (Ezra 5:1–2). The people finished rebuilding the temple in 516 BC (Ezra

---

2. Jones, *Puzzle of the Old Testament*, 165–85.

6:15). Zechariah divided his book into two parts: words of the Lord and burdens from the Lord.

Three Words of the Lord (Zech 1–8)

Return to God (Zech 1:1–6)

Zechariah encouraged the people to return to God. They had strayed from him, but they would find God willing to forgive if they returned to him. The Hebrew word translated "return" also can mean "repent," which here also fits the context.

Revelations from God (Zech 1:7—6:15)

Zechariah reported eight revelations he had received from God in the form of night visions. These revelations revealed what God was about to do in and through his people and those around them.

About the Reconstruction of the Temple (Zech 1:7–17)

The Lord sent messengers to control the earth, and the messengers reported the earth was quiet and ready for God's actions. God promised he would return to Jerusalem with compassion and rebuild his house (1:16).

About the Retaliation against Babylon (Zech 1:18–29)

Zechariah described the nations who had attacked Judah to scatter them. God's messengers would scatter those who tried to scatter Judah.

About the Restoration of Jerusalem (Zech 2)

Zechariah saw a man with a measuring line measuring Jerusalem as if surveying it. The angel of the Lord told Zechariah that Jerusalem would be inhabited again; indeed, God was reclaiming her as his own.

About the Reclothing of Joshua the Priest (Zech 3)

Joshua served as high priest of Judah under Zerubbabel's return. Many passages in the books of Haggai and Zechariah speak about Joshua.[3] Here, in Zechariah's vision, Joshua the priest removed his filthy garments and put on clean clothes, symbolizing the fact that God would restore and renew the priesthood again.

About the Recommissioning of Zerubbabel (Zech 4)

The people struggled to believe Zechariah's promise, but the prophet assured them the temple would not be completed by might or by power but by God's Spirit in their midst (4:6). God promised his people that "the hands of Zerubbabel have laid the foundation of this temple; his hands will also complete it" (4:9).

About the Recleansing of the Land (Zech 5:1–4)

God showed Zechariah an enormous flying scroll with curses and judgments written on both sides. God would cleanse the land of such evil.

About the Removal of Wickedness (Zech 5:5–11)

Zechariah's next vision showed a woman in a basket. The woman represented wickedness. Angels of the Lord threw her into the middle of the basket and carried her off to Shinar[4] (Mesopotamia), symbolizing the fact that God would remove Judah's evil far from them.

About the Retribution toward Babylon (Zech 6)

Zechariah assured God's people that Babylon would suffer retribution because of its wickedness against Judah. He also reaffirmed his commitment to the priesthood with a symbolic act that included Joshua the high priest (6:9–15). In some mysterious way, it seemed God was bringing together the

---

3. Hag 1:1, 12, 14; 2:2, 4; Zech 3:1–10; 6:9–15.

4. The locations of both the Tower of Babel and Babylon were on the plain of Shinar in what is now the territory of Iraq.

offices of king and priest into one person. This symbolic act ultimately is fulfilled in Jesus Christ, who is both King of kings and our great High Priest (Heb 7:1–3; 9:11–12).

Repentance before God (Zech 7–8)

God's Probing (Zech 7:1–7)

The people practiced all sorts of ceremonies that involved fasting and mourning as they commemorated sad moments in their past. God probed the issue at hand, challenging them as to the reasons for their fasting and mourning. Were they simply fasting and mourning for the sake of fasting and mourning, or were they actually trying to seek God and his mercy?[5]

God's Penalty (Zech 7:8–14)

Zechariah explained why God's penalty had fallen on other people. Their hearts had become hard, and they had not listened to the law of Moses and the words God had sent them through the prophets. Therefore, God's wrath had come upon them (7:12–14).

God's Pardon (Zech 8:1–17)

God announced a great pardon he would bring to the people. He would save them and bring them back to Jerusalem where they would live in its midst. He would establish a relationship with them again, and they would be his people and he would be their God (8:7–8).

God's Plan (Zech 8:18–23)

Zechariah described the awesome day that was coming when many people and mighty nations would come to seek the favor of the Lord in Jerusalem. In that day, Zechariah promised, people from foreign nations would recognize God's special grace to the Jewish people and beg them to instruct them in the word of God (8:22–23).

---

5. Most scholars believe the fasts commemorated the tragic events surrounding Jerusalem's fall (2 Kgs 25:8, 25).

Two Burdens from the Lord (Zech 9–14)

The Hebrew word translated "prophecy" (9:1) also can be translated "burden." It comes from the word meaning "to carry" and symbolically signifies the burden prophecy had become for prophets when they brought difficult words to people. Zechariah 9–14 breaks down into two basic sections. The first section focuses on the initial rejection of Christ (Zech 9–11), and the second section highlights the ultimate reign of Christ (Zech 12–14).

The Initial Rejection of Christ (Zech 9–11)

As Zechariah described the judgment of God against ancient nations, he also announced the coming of Jerusalem's king. Their king was coming to them, humble and mounted on a donkey (9:9). Matthew 21:2–5 describes how Jesus fulfilled these words as he rode down the Mount of Olives on Palm Sunday, as the people celebrated his coming.

Tragically, by the end of that week, many hearts had turned against Jesus, and Judas, one of the disciples, betrayed Jesus. Zechariah's words regarding thirty pieces of silver (11:12–13) were alluded to by the Gospel writer Matthew as he described Judas's betrayal of Jesus (Matt 26:15; 27:3–5).

The Ultimate Reign of Christ (Zech 12–14)

Zechariah 12–14 described a great coming day; in fact, the expression "in that day" occurs fifteen times in Zechariah 12–14. We will highlight three aspects of this ultimate reign of Christ.

God's People Recognize Their King (Zech 12:10–14)

Zechariah prophesied a day when God would pour out his Spirit upon his people. On that day, they would look upon the One they had pierced through and mourn for him as one might mourn the loss of an only son. The apostle John highlighted Zechariah's words as people looked at Jesus on the cross (John 19:37). However, we also anticipate a day when Jewish people will at last come to a saving knowledge of the Messiah, the Lord Jesus (Rom 11:15, 30–32).

Zechariah Prophesies Jesus's Arrest (Zech 13:7)

Zechariah foretold a day when the shepherd of the flock would be struck, and his sheep would be scattered. Jesus alluded to these words at the last supper when he prophesied that his disciples would forsake him and flee when he was arrested (Matt 26:31). Both Zechariah's and Jesus's words proved true; as Jesus was arrested, the disciples ran terrified into the night, unaware the dawn of the resurrection lay just around the corner.

Zechariah Predicts the Second Coming of Christ (Zech 14)

Zechariah foresaw a time when all nations would gather together to fight against Jerusalem. However, just as all seemed lost, the King of kings would return, and his feet would stand on the Mount of Olives. Human history as the nations knew it would come to an end, and peace would come under the King of kings and Lord of lords. Zechariah said that in that day, "the LORD will be king over the whole earth. On that day there will be one LORD, and his name the only name" (14:9).

Concluding Thoughts from Zechariah

Zechariah the prophet first spoke to his own generation about demonstrating their love for God by rebuilding his temple. However, his prophecies also looked into the distant future, not only when God would rebuild Jerusalem and its temple, but also when God's Messiah would bring ultimate salvation. Zechariah's prophecies/burdens from the Lord, especially chapters 9 and 12–14, highlight various aspects of Jesus's first and second comings.

Malachi

The prophet Malachi also prophesied during the Gathered Era (538 BC–Christ),[6] although his ministry was likely much later. Most scholars date his ministry to around 470–460 BC.[7] Malachi was probably a contemporary of Nehemiah or Esther, or slightly earlier. He prophesied to the people of Judah using a series of rhetorical questions and answers. Though he

6. Jones, *Puzzle of the Old Testament*, 165–85.

7. Arnold and Beyer, *Encountering the Old Testament*, 463.

begins with a denunciation of Judah's sins, he ends his book on a note of hope, as well as foreshadowing the coming of the Messiah by predicting the arrival of John the Baptist.[8]

Introduction (Mal 1:1)

Verse 1 tells us that we are reading a prophecy. As previously mentioned, the word translated "prophecy" also can mean "burden" and has the sense of a prophetic message the prophet may have found a burden to carry.[9] It came through Malachi, whose name means "my messenger." Indeed, Malachi served as God's messenger to bring this important message to God's people.

Denunciations from the Lord (Mal 1:2—3:15)

In each of the six denunciations Malachi proclaimed, he would bring a charge against God's people. He then anticipated their doubting response but assured them his charge was true.

They Doubted God's Love (Mal 1:2–5)

The people struggled to believe that God really loved them. Malachi reminded them that God had set his saving, covenant love on Jacob and let Esau go his own way. Esau and his descendants, the Edomites, would face God's judgment, but God had set his saving love on Jacob.

They Despised God's Name (Mal 1:6—2:13)

The despising of God's name first showed itself in the inadequacy of offerings people were bringing (1:6–14). They were bringing blind, lame, or sick animals for sacrifice. Malachi was furious and suggested they offer them to their governor to see if the governor would be pleased with such sacrifices! Of course, such sacrifices were no sacrifice at all; people were simply ridding themselves of weaker animals that were of limited use anyway.

8. Compare Mal 4:5 with Luke 1:17, 59–60.

9. See the discussion of Zech 9–14 earlier in this chapter.

The despising of God's name also manifested itself in the priests' insincerity (2:1-13). They were allowing the common people to dishonor God by their offerings, and as such, they were guilty as well. They were not taking to heart God's righteous decrees regarding the offerings.

They Disregarded God's Standard for Marriage (Mal 2:14-16)

Malachi testified against the people that they were divorcing the wives of their youth to marry other women, and God said he hated it. Today, divorce is not the unpardonable sin; yet, God's ideal is that husbands and wives live together for life in loving companionship.

They Disbelieved God's Justice (Mal 2:17—3:7)

First, Malachi's audience reflected a nonchalance about God's judgment (2:17). They didn't really think he was going to bring justice, since it seemed the evil people got away with their wickedness. If there was a God of justice, he didn't seem to be anywhere around.

Malachi assured them of God's coming judgment (3:1-2). He would send his messenger before him, and the Lord would suddenly come to his temple. Ironically, the people who doubted God's judgment would find themselves unable to endure that day.

Third, Malachi highlighted the causes of God's judgment (3:3-7). God's judgment would come upon evildoers of every kind. He would punish sorcerers, adulterers, liars, oppressors, and more. Malachi challenged them for disobeying God's statutes. They had strayed from the Lord, even though he had sought them and encouraged them to return to him.

They Discontinued God's Tithe (Mal 3:8-12)

Malachi accused the people of robbing God. How had they done so? By giving God less than their best with respect to tithes and offerings. Malachi challenged them to bring their whole tithes into the storehouses of Judah. If they would do that, God would demonstrate his faithfulness to them beyond measure.

They Disdained God's Majesty (Mal 3:13–18)

Malachi accused the people of speaking against God, yet the people did not believe it. They did not properly appreciate God's majesty, but he assured them he would demonstrate it in a mighty way. In response, the Lord told Malachi there would be a book of remembrance in which he would record the faithful acts of his faithful people. Certain judgment would come for those who opposed him and his ways.

Day of the Lord (Mal 4)

Promises about That Day (Mal 4:1–3)

The day of the Lord contained both negative and positive aspects. It would bring judgment against all the arrogant and every evildoer; all would experience God's wrath. However, there was also a positive promise: those who feared God's name would receive the great blessing of healing and righteousness.

Priority until That Day (Mal 4:4)

As Malachi began to conclude his book, he pointed the people back to the law of Moses. God had given Moses his commands at Mount Horeb (another name for Mount Sinai) and encouraged the people to live accordingly. Had the people done so, prophets such as Malachi would not have needed to prophesy! Interestingly, in some of the closing verses of the Old Testament, the prophet pointed his hearers back to the very beginnings of Scripture.

Predecessor to That Day (Mal 4:5–6)

God warned the people through Malachi that a great and terrible day of the Lord was about to come. He would send them Elijah the prophet to turn people back to him and to restore them to one another before the wrath of God swept them away. The New Testament heralds the fulfillment of Malachi's words in the ministry of John the Baptist (Matt 17:10–12; Luke 1:17, 59–60).

Concluding Thoughts from Malachi

More than anything else, Malachi challenged God's people to give him their best. He denounced the various areas of life in which they were failing to do so but encouraged them that if they did give him their best in these areas, he would bless them. In the end, he reminded them that the most important thing they could do was live out their faith in obedience to his commands. As they did, they would move God's great story closer to the day when God would first send John the Baptist as the forerunner to Jesus, and then Jesus himself.

Epilogue

"Brethren, What Shall We Do?"

THE NEW TESTAMENT BOOK of Acts records how on the Jewish festival Pentecost, Peter preached a message about Jesus's death and resurrection. When those present heard it, they experienced great conviction and asked Peter and the other apostles, "Brethren, what shall we do?" (Acts 2:37). After reading this book, you may wonder what your next steps are.

As we conclude our Old Testament study, we know you've read a lot of information, but we hope you've gained a lot more than that. We hope you've gained insights into the overall story God is writing through the Old Testament, preparing the world for the coming of his Messiah, his Anointed One.

We hope the next time you read your New Testament, you'll find the words you read sound a little more familiar to you, because the Old Testament is the field from which the New Testament harvests its ideas and concepts. The purpose of the New Testament writers is to show how all the pieces of God's story come together in Jesus Christ. You'll notice many similarities and will probably pick up a few differences, too, but you'll be surprised at the number of themes that carry over into the second part of God's revelation.

The Old Testament story lays a foundation for the New Testament story, and the New Testament comes along and says that all these wonderful things the prophets proclaimed have happened now! Remember all those things Moses highlighted in the Torah? They've happened now! Remember all those prophetic oracles? They've happened now! The New Testament declares that Jesus fulfills all to which the Old Testament story pointed.

Here's a quick summary of this incredible story God is writing: we have a deep spiritual need, and only God can meet that need. We've all fallen short through our failures and shortcomings. The Bible calls that failure sin, and sin separates us from God and demands restitution. Unfortunately, we can't pay the debt we owe, and we can't satisfy the spiritual need each of us has.

However, the New Testament announces that God paid our spiritual debt through his Son, the Lord Jesus Christ. Jesus died and rose again from the dead to secure the salvation of all who place their faith in him. There is no other way, no other plan to have reconciliation with God, save the one that God's incredible story presents to us.

We become reconciled to God when we admit our need (confession), express sorrow for our sin (repentance), and place our trust in the Lord Jesus Christ (faith). When we do this, we have the Bible's assurance that we become children of God. In fact, the Bible tells us that's when life really begins (2 Cor 5:17).

The most important decision we can ever make is to choose to follow the Lord Jesus Christ. Our relationship with Jesus is more than the most important thing in life; it is life itself (John 17:3). Everything we are, everything we do, flows from that supreme relationship. As we surrender our lives to the Lord and to his purpose, we find our highest fulfillment. We experience the joy of knowing we are stepping into our role in the great story he's writing. May God help us see his purpose and embrace it to the full.

Bibliography

Arnold, Bill T., and Bryan E. Beyer. *Encountering the Old Testament: A Christian Survey.* 3rd ed. Grand Rapids: Baker Academic, 2015.

Arnold, Bill T., and Bryan E. Beyer, eds. *Readings from the Ancient Near East: Primary Sources for Old Testament Study.* Grand Rapids: Baker Academic, 2002.

Beyer, Bryan E. *Encountering the Book of Isaiah: A Historical and Theological Survey.* Grand Rapids: Baker Academic, 2007.

Bullock, C. Hassell. *Encountering the Book of Psalms: A Literary and Theological Introduction.* Grand Rapids: Baker Academic, 2001.

Harrell, Daniel. "The Thirty-Day Leviticus Challenge." *Christianity Today,* July 25, 2008. https://www.christianitytoday.com/ct/2008/august/13.30.html.

Jones, Bill. *Putting Together the Puzzle of the Old Testament.* Atlanta: Authentic, 2007.

Powell, Terry D. *Wise Up: Smart Advice from the Book of Proverbs.* Wheaton, IL: Victor, 1990.

Walton, John H. *Chronological and Background Charts of the Old Testament.* Rev. ed. Grand Rapids: Zondervan, 1994.

Subject Index

Aaron, 44, 46
Abdon, 79
Abednego, 184n3, 185
Abel, 17, 153n2
Abijah (king), 117
Abimelech, 78
Abishai, nephew of David, 94
Abner, Saul's general, 94, 96
Abraham, 3, 7, 19–22, 182
Absalom, son of David, 99
abundant life, from knowing God, 9
accidental death, restitution for, 49
Achan, put to death, 69
Achish (king of Gath), 93, 94, 95
acrostic pattern, in Lamentations, 174
acrostics, in Hebrew poetry, 143
Acts, book of, 7
Adam, 111
Adam and Eve, 16–17
Adonijah, one of David's sons, 102
adultery, 191, 192–93
Aesop's Fables, 2
affection, of Solomon and his wife for
      each other, 159
agricultural cycle, 40
Agur, writer of Chapter 30 of Proverbs,
      149
Ahab (king), 105

Ahasuerus (king), 130
Ahaz (king), 117, 163, 207
Ahaziah, 117
Ai, victory over, 68–69
all, fall far short of God's expectation, 195
"all is vanity and striving after the wind,"
      154
alphabetic acrostic pattern, in
      Lamentations, 174
alphabetic poems, 143
Amalekites, 60, 91–92
Amaziah (king), 117
Ammonites, 79, 179, 219
Amnon (David's oldest son), 99
Amon (king), 117
Amos, book of, 198–200
Ancient of Days, 190
angel
    appeared to Daniel, 189
    appeared to Samson's mother, 80
anger
    of God, 175
    of Jonah, 206
animals
    Daniel's prophecy about two, 188
    people ridding themselves of weaker,
      229
Anointed One, Jesus as the ultimate, 7

anointing, of the priests, 37

Antiochus Epiphanes IV, persecution of the Jews, 188

antithetic parallelism, 143

Aramaic, similar to Hebrew, 127n4

ark (Noah's), 17, 18

ark of the covenant, 88, 96, 113

arrogance, 92

Artaxerxes, Persia's fifth king, 123, 125

Asa (king), 117

Asaph, writer of psalms, 142

Assyria
    conquered the Northern Kingdom, 101, 106, 183, 209
    defeat of bringing great joy, 214
    fall of, 219
    final word of woe against, 165
    hatred for motivated Jonah to resist God's call, 203
    as an instrument of judgment against Israel, 194
    Israel's defeat by, 109
    locust plague of, 196
    Nahum's taunt against, 215
    ruled through fear and intimidation, 194

Athaliah (queen), 117

Azariah (friend of Daniel), 184

Azariah (prophet), 117

Azariah/Uzziah (king), 117, 198

Baal, God's gifts credited to, 192

Baal worship, plague for, 47

Babylon
    captured Jerusalem and carried the people into exile, 101
    conquered Judah, 109, 209
    Isaiah anticipating Judah's exile to, 165
    Jeremiah prophesied that God would send, 169
    located on the plain of Shinar, 225n4
    Zechariah's revelation on retaliation against, 224
    Zechariah's revelation on retribution toward, 225–26

Babylonian names, of Daniel and his friends, 184n3

bad news, prophets bringing, 5

bad things, happening to good people, 135, 137, 139

Balaam, 47, 72

Balak, king of Moab, 47

Barak (military man), 77

barriers, between you and the Bible, 10

basket of fruit, signified harvest time, 200

Bathsheba, 97, 97n6, 98

battle instructions, for the battle of Jericho, 68

"begats," getting bogged down in, 4

Belshazzar, 186, 186n5

Belteshazzar, as Daniel's Babylonian name, 184n3

Benjamin, tribe of facing extinction, 82, 83

Bethel, victory over, 69

Bethlehem, 210, 211

Bezalel, 33

Bible, 3–10

biblical prophets, on God's sovereignty over the earth, 164

big picture, biblical writers often providing first, 18

Bildad (friend of Job), 137, 138, 139

birth of a Son, described by Isaiah, 164

blessing(s)
    accompanying the people's obedience or disobedience, 59
    immediate described by Joel, 197
    priestly given to Aaron by Moses, 44
    removing from Job's life, 136
    spoken by Moses, 61
    ultimate, 197

blood of a lamb, on the doorposts and lintels, 29–30

Boaz, 85, 86

body, Satan afflicting Job's, 136–37

boils, Satan struck Job with, 136

bond, existing between Solomon and his wife, 159

book of remembrance, 231

book of the Law of Moses, Ezra read from, 127

Book of the Twelve, Minor Prophets as, 191

branch image, of one coming from the stump of Jesse, 164

Branch of the Lord, 163

"Brethren, what shall we do?" asked of Peter and the other apostles, 233

bronze serpent, paralleling the cross of Jesus, 52

brothers of Joseph, not recognizing him, 26

building projects, of Solomon, 116

burdens, from the Lord in Zechariah, 227–28

burnt offering, offered to the Lord, 36

Cain, 17

calamity, of Job, 136–37

Caleb, 68n4, 70

call
of Jeremiah, 169
of Jonah, 203

Canaan
conquest of, 68–69
Moses seeing, 61

Canaanites, conquering the Hebrews spiritually, 74

capital punishment, sins leading to, 39

captain of the host of the Lord, 67–68

celebration, of marriage, 159

census 1, of the people, 43

census 2, of the people, 48

census of all Israel, by David, 114

central campaign, in the conquest of Canaan, 68–69

cereal offering. *See* grain offering

Chaldeans (Babylonians), 183, 216, 216n4

challenge, of Solomon to fear God and keep his commandments, 156

challenges, coming to all people, 140

character
of God, 220
of Job, 136

chief baker and butler, Joseph and, 25

children
of Hosea and Gomer, 192
needing to honor parents, 151
raising for Christ, 150

Chilion, 84

Chisholm, Thomas, 175

Christ. *See* Jesus Christ

Christian maturity, moving forward to, 45

Chronicler, on great things through David's line, 110–11, 116

1–2 Chronicles, 110–120

1 Chronicles, 111–15

2 Chronicles, 115–20

circumcision, reinstituting, 67

cities of refuge, establishing, 49, 57, 71

"city of blood," Nahum described Nineveh as, 214

civil laws, designed to guide Israel as a nation, 32

comforters, Job listening to his, 137–38

coming judgment, Malachi assured of God's, 230

coming rescue, described in Micah, 209

coming ruler, described in Micah, 210

commandments, 4, 31

commands
and guidelines for God's people, 37
from the Lord, 204

commission, of Ezekiel as the role of a watchman, 178

comparison, of Nineveh's judgment, 213–14

concubine, 82n6

condemnation, of the Edomites, 201–2

confession, expressing sorrow, 234

confusion, of Habakkuk, 216–17

conquests
of David, 113–14
of Joshua, 70

consecration, of the priests, 37, 44

consequences, of David's sin, 98–99

consolation, for the Israelites, 202–3

conspiracy, formed against Jeremiah, 170

consummation of human history section, of Isaiah, 168

continuous dynasty, in Judah, 105

coronation, of David over all Israel, 113

corruption, of Judah's governors and officials, 126

courtroom proceedings, maintaining fairness in, 57

covenant
God declaring his, 30–32
potential blessings and judgments, 40
recommitments to by the People,
59–60
relationship with the people, 53–54
renewing of by Ezra, 127–28
representative selected from the
people, 60–61
responsibility for the people, 54–59
creation, 16
creation of man, 3–4
cross of Jesus, looking to in faith, 52
crucifixion, David knew nothing about,
146
cry
of Habakkuk to God, 217–18
of Jonah to the Lord, 204
cupbearer, Nehemiah as, 126
curse, of Job, 137
Cush, slain with the sword of God's
judgment, 219
Cushan-Rishathaim, subdued by Othniel,
77
Cyrus, king of Persia, 119, 122, 166

Dagon, god of the Philistines, 81
Dan, tribe of, 81–82, 112
Daniel
deliverance of, 186–87
deportation and dedication of, 184
deported to Babylon by
Nebuchadnezzar, 183
entering into the Lord's rest at his
death, 189
exile of, 108
explained Nebuchadnezzar's dream,
184
saw the same vision as John in
Revelation, 190n15
serving God faithfully in his eighties,
190
thrown into the lions's den, 187
Daniel (book of), 131n7, 183–90
Darius (king), 122, 186, 186n7, 187
David
anointed as Israel's next king, 93

appointing Solomon as his successor,
102
author of most of the psalms, 142
begging the Lord for forgiveness in
Psalm 51, 144
bringing the ark to Jerusalem, 113
calling of, 92–93
came from Bethlehem, 211
children from prior to Solomon's
birth, 99n7
compromise of, 97–98
conquests of, 96–97, 113–14
consequences of sin, 98–99
death of, 102
defeated a lion and a bear, 93
helping make preparations for the
temple, 114
Israel's second king, 99
married Bathsheba, 98
as a military man, 103n2
preparing the spiritual aspects for his
son Solomon, 115
prospered by the Lord wherever he
went, 94
relationship with Absalom, 99
Ruth great-grandmother of, 86
serving Achish, king of Gath, 93
sin of, 97–98
struggles with Saul, 93–95
victory over Goliath, 93
David's line, 105, 119–20
day of atonement, Yom Kippur as, 38–39
day of redemption, highlighting, 165
day of the Lord, described in Malachi, 231
death, 39, 155
Deborah (prophetess), 77
dedication
of Daniel, 184
of Habakkuk to God, 217
of the people, 124
of the temple, 123
various acts of, 44
dedication of the foundation, of the
temple foundation, 122
dedicatory prayer, of Solomon, 115
Delilah, Samson's downfall with, 80–81
denunciations, from the Lord in Malachi,
229–31

deportations, of exiles, 177, 183, 184
depression, of Jonah before God, 205–6
destruction, by the locusts, 196
Deuteronomy, book of, 53–61
dialogues, series of in the book of Job, 137–39
diet, God's commands regarding, 56
Dinah, Jacob's daughter, 24
disappointments, remembering great, 55
disciples, ran terrified into the night as Jesus was arrested, 228
disobeying the voice of the Lord, as serious, 92
districts, Solomon divided the land into twelve, 103
Divided Era (931–586 BC), 101, 104–8, 109, 116–19
    Amos ministered during, 198
    book of Jonah falling in, 203
    Chronicles focusing primarily on, 110
    Habakkuk prophesied near the end of, 215
    Hosea ministered during, 191
    Isaiah prophesied during, 163
    Nahum ministered during, 213
divorce, 58
doom and destruction, Amos described for Israel's neighbors, 198–99
duties, of the Levites, 43

earth, God's final judgment of, 164
eastern tribes of Israel, established an altar only as a sign of unity, 71
Ebenezer, stone monument, 89
Ecclesiastes, book of, 153–56
economic balance, bringing people back toward, 40
Edomites, 24, 179, 201–2, 229
Eglon, king of Moab, killed by Ehud, 77
Egypt, 20, 172, 180
Egyptian deities, ten plagues focused on, 29
Ehud, killed Eglon, king of Moab, 77
Eli, 88, 89
Elihu, chastised Job's friends, 138
Elijah, 106, 231
Elimelech and Naomi, sons named Mahlon and Chilion, 84

Eliphaz (friend of Job), 137, 138, 139
Elisha, 106
Elkanah, with wives Peninnah and Hannah, 88
enemies of the faith, 183–87
Entering Era (1405–1043 BC), 65, 87
Ephraim, son of Joseph, 70n6
Epistles (Romans–Jude), Jesus's story in, 8
Esau, 22, 23, 24, 201, 229
Esther, 121, 129, 130, 131–32
Esther (book of), 123n2, 129–32
Eve, 16–17
every path of life, under the sun as meaningless, 156
everyone did as they saw fit, in those days, 83
evil, Adam and Eve knowing, 17
evil actions, facing the sad consequences of, 179
evil people, getting away with wickedness, 230
Evil-Merodach, 108, 173
exile
    Daniel recognizing the potential end of, 188
    returnees from, 112
exiles, deportations of, 183
Exodus, book of, 28–34
Ezekiel, book of, 177–82
Ezra
    desired to study the word of God, 9
    leadership of, 123–24
    man of principle, 129
    as the possible Chronicler, 110
    prefiguring Jesus, 125
    priest and scribe, led the second return, 121
Ezra, book of, 121–25

faith, 124, 217, 234
faithfulness
    God asking for, 22
    of God is great, 176
    Levites led all God's people in a vow of, 128
    righteous person living by, 218
    small acts of, 184
the Fall, of humanity into sin, 16–17

false prophets, in Babylon and in Jerusalem, 170

fasts, for events surrounding Jerusalem's fall, 226n5

fear of the Lord, 150, 151

Feast of Booths, 32. *See also* Feast of Tabernacles

Feast of Ingathering, 32

Feast of Purim, Mordecai declaring, 132

Feast of Tabernacles, 32, 127

Feast of the Harvest, 32

Feast of Unleavened Bread, 32

Feast of Weeks, 32

feasts, 32, 57

fellowship offering, 36

festivals, guidelines for, 39–40

fidelity, important to any marriage, 151

fiery furnace, Nebuchadnezzar ordered God's three faithful servants thrown into, 185

fiery serpents, of judgment, 47

fiftieth year, as a year of jubilee, 40

"fill-full-ment," of Isaiah's words, 163n2

final battle, of God's forces and forces of evil, 189

financial area, of human relationships, 58–59

fingers of a hand, writing words over Belshazzar's head, 186

fire, Amos's vision of, 199

first generation, transitioning to the second, 42, 49–51

firstborn, substitution of the Levites for, 43–44

firstborn from every family, death of as the final plague, 29

fish, swallowed Jonah, 204

Five Books of Moses. *See* Torah ("Instruction")

five visions, Amos proclaiming, 199–200

fleece, Gideon putting before the Lord, 78

the flood, 17–18

flying scroll, with curses and judgments written on both sides, 225

folly, experience of Solomon regarding, 154–55

food, commands concerning, 37

fools and sluggards, as a theme of Proverbs, 151–52

foreign nations, recognizing God's special grace to the Jewish people, 226

foreign pagans, the people's marriages to, 124

forgiveness, 98, 210–211

fortunes, restoration of Job's, 139

four beasts, Daniel's prophecy about, 187–88

friends of Job, believed that Job must have sinned, 137

fullness of life, Bible describing, 4

Gabriel, 97, 188

garden of Eden, responsibility to till, 16

Gathered Era (538 BC–Christ), 119–20, 220, 221, 223, 228

Gedaliah, governor over Judah, 172

genealogical interest, in First Chronicles 1–9, 111–12

genealogical records (family trees), of Ishmael and Isaac, 22

Genesis, book of, 4, 15–27, 201

Geshem, assault against the work of Nehemiah, 127

Gibeonites, 69

Gideon, 78

the glory of the LORD, filled the tabernacle, 33

God
allowing oppression and violence in Judah, 216

answer to Habakkuk, 216

appeared in a burning bush to Moses, 29

banished Adam and Eve from the garden of Eden, 17

becoming reconciled to, 234

blasphemed by Belshazzar, 186

blessed David in battle, 114

building David a house of people, 97

calling Israel, 193, 195, 196

caring deeply for people, 195, 200

coming and judging his people, 208

concern for the city of Nineveh, 206

counting Abraham's faith as righteousness, 21

created a fast-growing plant for Jonah, 206

declaring his covenant, 30–32

delivering his people, 29–30

designing his tabernacle, 32–34

displaying love for all people, 200

establishing a covenant with David forever, 113

establishing a relationship with his people again, 226

faithfulness to Solomon, 103

gave Saul's kingdom to David, 113

gifts of credited by Israel to Baal, 192

glory of, 34, 116

as God of the whole world, 219

great work of, 187

of history writing his story, 3

holding leaders accountable, 46

humbled Nebuchadnezzar, 185

importance of staying faithful to, 60

including us in his plan, 11

interacted with the writers of Scripture, 8

Jesus as son of, 146

Job learning from, 138–39

Jonah and, 203–6

judgment of, 179–80, 219, 230

justice of disbelieved by the people, 230

land as a blessing to his people, 197

laws on how to live life, 34

leading by a pillar of cloud by day and fire by night, 44

as Lord of all nations, 164

name of never appearing in the book of Esther, 132

not wanting David to build him a house, 96–97

opposing the proud but giving grace to the humble, 152

pardoning his people in Micah, 211

peace, God's *shalom*, Micah prophesied, 209

the people despised the name of, 229–30

placed his Son Jesus on a Roman cross, 22

plan of rejected at Kadesh-Barnea, 45–46

preparing Israel for David's reign, 92

preparing the world for the coming of Jesus, 109

prevailed through Samson, 81

problem with his people in Micah, 210

promise made to David, 96

promised to regather the people, 180–81

promising to restore the fortunes of his people, 220

punishment of his people in Micah, 211

putting unanswerable questions before Job, 138

Rahab confessed faith in Israel's, 66

raising the dead, 164

raising up the Chaldeans as instruments of judgment against Judah, 216

reaching people from all nations, 220

reasons for destruction of his people, 175

rebuke from, 170

rebuke of Job's friends, 139

reclaiming Jerusalem as his own, 224

reduction of the size of Gideon's army, 78

rejection of by Judah, 170

removing Judah's evil far from them, 225

restoration by, 170–71, 225

retribution of, 175

revealed himself to Jacob in a dream, 23

sent Nathan the prophet to David, 98

servant of having God's Spirit upon him, 166

setting covenant love on Jacob, 229

showed Ezekiel a vision of heaven, 177–78

sparing Nineveh from destruction, 205

stopped Abraham short of sacrificing Isaac, 22

God (*cont.*)

tested Abraham by asking him to take his son and offer him as a burnt offering, 21

tithes and offerings of the people, 230

turned Haman's evil intent into the salvation of the Jews, 132

using imperfect people, 18, 25

using lives of faithfulness, 86

victories to David, 96–97

wanting to include us in his plan, 52

warned Pharaoh of plagues, 29

way of as the right way, 152

wisdom coming from, 151

word of as life, 4

"God has heard," meaning of "Ishmael," 21

God's people. *See also* the people

failings of in Micah, 208–9

forgiveness of in Micah, 210–211

future of in Micah, 209–10

as his because of his gracious covenant, 55

not driving out the inhabitants of the land, 74

as often unfaithful, 60

recognizing their king, 227

rendering the temple area unclean, 222

golden calf, worshiping of, 33

Goliath, David's victory over, 93

Gomer, 191, 192–93

Gomorrah, 20

good people, bad things happening to, 135, 137, 139

Gospels, on Jesus, 7

grace, of God, 55, 73, 98, 220

grain offering, 36

graven images, Micah's mother making, 81

Great Commission, of Jesus, 168, 220

great day of God, 197

great future for God's people section, of Isaiah, 166–68

"Great Is Thy Faithfulness" hymn, 175

Greece, kingdom of, 188

guilt offering, 36–37

Habakkuk (prophet), 118, 216–17, 218

Habakkuk, book of, 215–18

Hagar, Sarah's maid-servant, 21

Haggai, 122, 221–22

Haggai, book of, 221–23

Haman, plot against the Jews, 130–32

hamas, denoting unjust violence, 202

Hanani (prophet), 117

Hananiah, friend of Daniel, 184

Hannah, dedicated her son to the Lord, 88

headings, of Psalms, 143

heart of love, obeying God from, 54–55

heaven, 168, 177–78, 182

Hebrew language, of the book of Job, 135n2

Hebrew poetry, described, 142–43

Hebrews, 29. *See also* God's people; Israelites; the people

Hebrews, book of, 45, 52, 152, 171

Hebron, Caleb asked for, 70

he-goat, representing the empire of Greece, 188

King Herod, 211

Hezekiah (king), 106, 117, 118, 163, 166, 207

high priest, Jesus as, 147

Hilkiah the priest, discovered a scroll, 107

Hiram, king of Tyre, Solomon's covenant with, 103

historical interlude section, of Isaiah, 165–66

history

coming to an end, 164, 228

fall of dynasties during, 215

as linear in the Bible, 3

Micah privileged to foresee, 211

holiness, 35, 39

Holy Spirit

in the early church, 197

guided the writing of the Bible, 8

homeland, Abraham left his, 19

honesty, in business dealings, 39

Hophni, 88, 89

Mount Horeb, as another name for Mount Sinai, 231

Hosea, book of, 191–95

human relationships, areas of, 58–59

humility, Job responded in, 139

husband and wife, 150, 159. *See also* marriage

hymns, as psalms of praise and thanksgiving, 144

Ibzan, God's purposes continued through, 79

identity, of the four kingdoms, 187–88

idol worshiper, Ahab as, 105

idolatry, mandates on, 56

Ilon, God's purposes continued through, 79

Immanuel, birth of described by Isaiah, 163

immediate blessing, from God described by Joel, 197

immorality, kinds of, 39

imprecatory psalms, calling for God's judgment, 145

"in that day," in Zechariah 12–14, 227

"In the Wilderness," Book of Numbers called, 42

individuals, God's work in the lives of, 183–87

initial rejection, of Christ, 227

inscription, on Belshazzar's kingdom coming to an end, 186

internal threats, faced by Nehemiah, 126

intertestamental period, between Malachi and Matthew, 189

Isaac, 21–22

Isaiah (prophet), 117, 122, 163–68, 166n5

Ishbosheth, death of, 96

Ishmael, birth of, 21

Israel

  Assyria's conquest of, 106

  consecrating, 67–68

  David becoming king over all, 96

  disobeying by serving other nations spiritually, 75–76

  disobeying God, 75

  as an empire, 97

  failings of, 192–94

  genealogy of the twelve tribes of, 112

  God's call to, 195

  as guilty of social injustice, 199

  history of, 3

  as the new name for Jacob, 24

  Northern Kingdom of, 104–5

  strayed from God, 191

Israel and Judah, compared to two wicked sisters in Ezekiel, 179

Israelite army, arose and chased the Philistines, 93

Israelites. *See also* God's people; the people

  consolation for, 202–3

  generation of dying in the wilderness, 45

  not controling the entire promised land, 70

  took the ark of the covenant into battle, 89

  treaty with the Gibeonites, 69

  worshiping God, 33

Israel's hymns and songs, book of Psalms comprising, 141

Jabesh-Gilead, 82

Jabin, king of Hazor, 77, 77n2

Jacob

  covenant love on, 229

  deceived by Laban, 23n4

  as father of the Israelites, 201

  favored Joseph and gave him a nice coat, 24–25

  horrified by news of Joseph's death, 25

  let Benjamin go along with his brothers, 26

  revealed to Rebekah as primary, 22

  story of, 23–24

  violence to by Edom, 202

Jacob's family, 26, 27

Jael, killed Sisera, Jabin's general, 77

Jair, served God's purpose, 79

James, the Lord's half-brother, 200

Jehoahaz (king), 107, 117

Jehoiachin (king), 107, 108, 118, 119, 171, 173

Jehoiakim (king), 107, 108, 118, 119, 171, 184

Jehoram (king), 117

Jehoshaphat (king), 117, 118

Jephthah, 79, 79n4

Jeremiah (prophet), 117, 118
    as author of Lamentations, 174
    called on the Lord to look upon his
        suffering people and pleaded with
        God, 175–76
    encouraged Zedekiah to surrender,
        172
    foretold returnees from exile, 112
    on the people's unwillingness to free
        slaves, 171
    prophecy of a wonderful day of
        restoration, 170
    prophesied Cyrus's decree, 122
    sermons of, 172–73
    taken as prisoner to Egypt, 172
    warned the people of impending
        disaster, 108
    as writer of the book of Kings, 101
Jeremiah, book of, 169–73
Jericho, 66, 68
Jeroboam II (king), 198
Jerusalem
    destruction of, 172
    as Judah's capital, 207
    lifting to a place of prominence, 209
    nations coming to seeking favor of
        the Lord, 226
    reforming of, 128–29
    ruin of, 174
    siege of, 171–72, 179
    sin of, 179
    slaughter of, 178–79
    wall of, 125–27, 128
    Zechariah on the coming of the king
        of, 227
    Zechariah on the restoration of, 224
Jesse, father of David, 86
Jesus Christ
    alluded to words of Zechariah at the
        last supper, 228
    announced Jeremiah's new covenant
        had come, 171
    Bible telling us about, 4
    book of Daniel pointing to, 190
    book of Jonah anticipating, 206
    came from Abraham's line, 20
    choosing to follow, 234

    coming of presented in the Gospels, 7
    connecting the feasts with, 32
    as crucified in Psalm 22, 146–47
    crushing the serpent's head, 20
    Daniel seeing a vision of the risen, 189
    as David's Lord, 147
    David's ultimate descendant and
        Messiah King, 114
    descendant of Judah, son of
        Abraham, and Son of God, 27
    encouraged us to pray for our
        enemies, 145
    Ezra modeled the work of, 125
    fulfilled Isaiah's words, 166, 167–68
    as God's son in Psalm 2, 146
    God's story coming together in, 233
    as God's temple, 223
    on the historicity of the events in
        Jonah, 206
    John the Baptist as forerunner to, 232
    as the King in Psalm 45 and 110, 147
    as King of kings and as our great
        High Priest, 181
    as King of kings and our great High
        Priest, 226
    from the line of David fulfilling God's
        promise, 97
    Micah clearly describing, 210
    as our great high priest, 125, 181, 226
    parables of, 2
    Passover meal and, 32
    Perez an ancestor of, 25
    prophecy of, 182
    rejection and ultimate reign of, 227–28
    as risen, 146
    secured eternal redemption, 39
    as the son of David and Son of God,
        100
    suffering of, 167
    Zechariah prophesying the arrest of,
        228
Jethro, father-in-law of Moses, 29, 30
Jewish dietary laws, from the law of
    Moses, 184
Jewish people, coming to a knowledge of
    the Messiah, the Lord Jesus, 227

Jewish refugees, expansion into Edom accommodating, 202
Jews, defending themselves in Esther, 132
Jezebel, 105, 106
Jezreel, valley of, 192
Joab, 97, 99
Joash (king), 117
Job, book of, 135–40
Job's friends, God's rebuke of, 139
Job's wife, suggested he curse God and die, 136–37
Joel, book of, 195–98
John
    highlighting Zechariah's words, 227
    imagery from Ezekiel in Revelation, 182
John the Baptist, 229, 231, 232
Jonah, book of, 203–7
Jonathan, Saul's son, 94
Jordan, crossing, 66–67
Joseph, story of, 24–27
Joseph and Mary, lesser wealth of, 38
Joshua
    called for the sun to stand still, 69
    calling the people to choose God, 72–73
    commissioning of, 65–66
    death and burial of, 73
    Moses selecting, 60
    parting the waters of the Jordan River, 66–67
    requested land within the tribe of Ephraim, 71
    succeeding Moses, 48
    took the entire land, 70
Joshua, book of, 65–73
Joshua and Caleb, believed God's promise, 45
Joshua the Priest, reclothing of, 225
Josiah (king), 107, 117, 118–19, 169, 218
Jotham (king), 117, 163, 207
jubilee year, 40
Judah
    characteristics of the Kingdom of, 105
    complacent attitude toward the things of God, 207

David becomes king over, 96
deportation to Babylon taking place in stages, 177
Ezekiel's prophecies against the nation of, 178–79
judgment against the nation of, 218–19
kings of, 107, 117–18
leadership of failed their people and led them into ruin, 175
peace for, 214
prophets of, 117–18
sin of, 170–71
Judah (son of Jacob), 26
Judah (tribe of), as the tribe of David, 112
Judas, betrayed Jesus, 227
judges, 57, 76–81, 83, 87
Judges, book of, 74–83
judgment
    bringing a personal knowledge of the Lord, 178
    certainty of Nineveh's, 214–15
    God bringinv on the whole world, 165
    of God coming upon all nations, 164
    of God upon evildoers of every kind, 230
    reasons for God's, 199–200
    roar of God's, 198–99
judgment and salvation section, of Isaiah, 165
justice, of God, 220

Kadesh, 44–46
Kadesh-Barnea, ultimate failure at, 51–52
king and priest, bringing offices of into one person, 226
king and Shulamite woman, exchanging loving descriptions of each other, 158
King of kings, return of, 228
king of the north, representing the Seleucids, 189
king of the south, referring to Egypt, 189
kingdom of God, overcoming all earthly kingdoms, 188
kingdom of priests and a holy nation, Israel intended to be, 30

kingdoms
  comparing Israel and Judah, 104–5
  kingdom of God surpassing all, 187
1–2 Kings, books of, 101–9
kings, responsibilities of, 57, 90
kingship, 90, 147
Korah and his family, wanted the
    priesthood, 46

Laban, Jacob and, 23n4, 23
labor, Solomon on, 155
lament, of David fulfilled in Jesus, 147
lament psalms, of sorrow and lament, 144
Lamentations, book of, 174–76
land
  allowing to rest, 40, 56
  for the nine and one-half tribes and
    Joshua, 71
  renovation of by God, 181–82
  for special groups, 71
  for the two and one-half tribes and
    Caleb, 70
  Zechariah on the recleansing of, 225
land of Gilead, 79n3
languages, God confusing, 18–19
the Law. *See* Torah ("Instruction")
law of Moses
  discovery of the book of, 118
  Malachi pointed the people back to,
    231
  much of foreign to us, 5
  on a widow marrying a near relative,
    85
laws, 37, 54
leaders, hating good and loving evil, 208
leadership, 91, 125
legacy
  of Joshua, 73
  of Solomon, 156
Lemuel, writer of Proverbs 31, 149
lessons, Job learning from God, 138–39
Levi (tribe of), 39
Leviathan (Satan), God destroying, 165
levirate marriage, 58
Levite, Micah making into his own
    personal priest, 81
Levite and his concubine, example of, 82

Levites, 43–44, 46, 115
Levitical cities, allotted by Joshua, 71
Leviticus, 5, 35–41
life
  Jonah requested that God take his, 206
  lived above the sun giving life
    meaning, 156
  lived with the Son (Jesus), 156
  Moses encouraging the people to
    choose, 60
  temporary aspect of, 153
line of David, as continuous in Judah, 105
lions' mouths, shut by God, 187
little apocalypse section, of Isaiah,
    164–65
lives, stories impacting, 2
living God, serving fully, 55
living water, 181
Lo-ammi ("not my people"), indicated
    God's separation from his people,
    192
locusts, 196, 198, 199
Lord
  allowing Samuel to appear before
    Saul, 95
  led Abraham to send his servant to
    secure a wife for Isaac, 22
  response of, 196–97
  told Samuel he would raise up a true
    leader and bring the house of Eli
    to ruin, 88
"The LORD is there," as the name of the
    city, 182
Loruhamah ("not pitied'), highlighting
    the end of God's compassion for
    Israel, 192
Lot, 20, 219
love, of God for the whole world, 206–7

magi (Persian officials), asked where the
    king of the Jews was to be born,
    211
Mahlon, married Ruth, 84
majesty, of God, 138, 139, 231
Malachi, 7, 228, 229, 232
Malachi, book of, 228–32
man, creation of, 3–4

man and woman, creation of, 16

Manasseh (king), 117, 118

Manasseh (son of Joseph), 70n6

Manasseh (tribe of), received territory west of the Jordan, 71

mandates, Moses proclaiming many specific, 55–57

manna, 30, 67, 67n3

marriage, 58, 159, 160, 230

marriage and family, as a theme in Proverbs, 150–51

Mary (mother of Jesus), 38

meal offering. *See* grain offering

meaninglessness, of everything, 153

"mediator," priest as, 37

Melchizedek, a high priest, 20

Meshach, 184n3, 185

Messiah, 6–7, 111–12, 163

Messianic hope section, of Isaiah, 163–64

messianic psalms, 145–47

Micah (idolator), example of, 81–82

Micah (prophet), 81n5, 117, 207, 208–9, 211

Micah, book of, 207–12

Middle East, ownership of land in, 197

Midianites, 48

"might makes right," principle of, 104

military conquests, of David, 97, 114

millennial kingdom, with a restored temple, 182

ministry, 33, 43

Minor Prophets, 191

miracles, of Elisha connected with Jesus, 106

Miriam and Aaron, criticized Moses, 44

Mishael, friend of Daniel, 184

mishkan, meaning "dwelling place," 32–33

mixed marriages, difficulty with, 124

Moab, Elimelech's family settled in, 84

Moabites, 172, 179, 219

monogamy, Proverbs assuming as the norm, 150

Mordecai, 130, 131, 132

Moses

  called the people to renew the covenant, 59, 60

  commissioning Joshua, 48

  death of, 61

  erected a bronze serpent for people to look upon and live, 47

  exhorted the people to ratify the covenant, 59

  frustration of, 46

  killed an Egyptian and fled to the land of Midian, 29

  lesson on leadership from Jethro, 30

  priestly blessing given to Aaron, 44

  proclaimed many specific mandates, 55–57

  raised in Pharaoh's court, 29

  reminded the people of the covenant, 53

  responsible for the composition of the Torah, 15

  sang a song, 60

  saw Canaan, 61

  selected Joshua, 60

  sent twelve spies, 45

  spoke a blessing, 61

  writer of Psalm 90, 142

Moses and Aaron, disobeyed God's command, 46

motherhood, commands concerning, 38

musicians, from the Levites received assignments, 115

Nabonidus, appointed Belshazzar as co-regent, 186n5

Nadab and Abihu, sinful actions of, 37

Nahash, king of the Ammonites, 90

Nahum (prophet), 117, 213

Nahum, book of, 213–15

names, as hard to pronounce, 5–6

Naomi, 84

Nathan, 98–99, 102

nations

  experiencing God's judgment for their wickedness, 202

  foreign, 226

  gathering together to fight against Jerusalem, 228

  God's heart for, 18

  God's words concerning his judgment of, 219

nations (*cont.*)
    Isaiah's oracles against other, 164
    Israel's repeated failure to drive out
        other, 75
    people of all, 209, 219
    prophecies of Jeremiah concerning
        other, 172
Nazirite status, of Samson, 80
Mount Nebo, Moses saw the promised
    land from, 61
Nebuchadnezzar (king of Babylon), 108,
    171, 183, 184–85
Nehemiah, book of, 125–29
neighbors of Judah, God's judgment
    against, 219
new covenant, of God with his people,
    170–71
new heaven and a new earth, God
    creating, 168
new Jerusalem, Ezekiel describing, 181,
    182
New Testament
    fulfillment of Malachi's words in the
        ministry of John the Baptist, 231
    as fulfillment of the Old Testament, 6
    highlighting how Jesus lived by God's
        commands, 31
    impacted by Isaiah, 168
    Proverbs cited a few places in, 152
    on wonderful things the prophets
        proclaimed, 233–34
    words of psalmists finding fulfillment
        in Jesus, 146
night visions, received from God by
    Zechariah, 224–26
Nineveh, Assyria's capital city, 203, 205,
    213–15
Ninevites, 205, 205n5, 206
Noah, 17, 18
No-amon (Thebes), Nahum compared
    Nineveh to, 215
northern campaign, in the conquest of
    Canaan, 69–70
Northern Kingdom (Israel), 101, 104,
    105, 106, 200
northern tribes, revolted against
    Rehoboam, 104

Numbers, book of, 42–52

Obadiah (prophet), 118, 201
Obadiah, book of, 201–3
Obed, son of Boaz and Ruth and father of
    Jesse, 86
obeying, as better than sacrifice, 92
offerings, 36–37, 114, 229
Og, king of Bashan, 47
Oholiab, 33
Old Testament, 6, 10–11, 233
one God, creation of the world by, 16
one great story, Bible as, 8–9
one man, two kings, and the time of the
    end, Daniel's prophecy about,
    188–89
oracles, against the nations in Isaiah, 164
Ornan, 114
Orpah, 84
Othniel, subdued Cushan-Rishathaim, 77

pagan spouses, the people separating
    from, 124
pagan worship, Solomon's involvement
    of, 104
pain, of Hosea in his sad marriage to
    Gomer, 195
panic, in Nineveh as Nineveh's enemies
    closed in, 214
parables, of Jesus, 2
parallelism, in Hebrew poetry, 142–43
pardon
    of God, 226
    of Israel's unfaithfulness, 194–95
parents, as a team, 151
partitioning, settling, 70–71
Passover, 30, 67
Passover Lamb, 30
past failures, Satan's strategy to remind
    us of, 55
patriarchal period, 15, 19–27
patriarchs, meaning "founding fathers," 19
Paul, 20, 21, 44, 152, 166
peace, 68–70, 182, 210, 214, 228
peace offering. *See* fellowship offering
penalties, for breaking the covenant, 40
penalty, of God, 226

Peninnah, 88
penitential psalms, focusing on sorrow
    for one's sin, 144
the Pentateuch ("five scrolls"), 15. *See also*
    Torah ("Instruction")
Pentecost, Holy Spirit fell on the early
    church, 32
the people. *See also* God's people
    affirmed allegiance to the Lord, 73
    dedication of, 124
    failed to follow God's commands, 81
    God's work in the lives of individuals,
        183–87
    organizing to construct the wall of
        Jerusalem, 126
    recommitment of, 128
    singing for joy, 219
    sinned against the LORD their God,
        106
    wanted a king, 89
people groups, big picture of the
    development of, 18
people of all nations
    calling upon the Lord and serving
        him together, 219
    coming to Jerusalem to worship the
        Lord, 209
Perez, 25
Persian customs, 131
Persian king Xerxes. *See* Ahasuerus
    (king)
Persians, conquered the city of Babylon,
    173
Peter, 11, 30, 146, 152, 233
Pharaoh, 25, 26
Philistine leaders, not trusting David to
    fight alongside them, 94–95
Philistine woman (Delilah), Samson's
    relationship with, 80–81
Philistines
    attacked Israel, 89
    captured Samson, 80
    captured the ark of the covenant, 89
    David joining, 94–95
    experiencing God's judgment, 172
    facing destruction, 219
    origins of, 179

put forward Goliath to fight against
    an Israelite, 93
rejoiced while Israel mourned, 95
Phinehas, 88, 89
physical adultery, in Hosea's life, 191
pillar of cloud and fire, God as, 34
place names, hard to pronounce, 5–6
plagues of Egypt, revealed God's purpose,
    29
plan, of God, 226
pleasure, experience of Solomon
    regarding, 154
plumb line, Amos's vision of, 199
political victories, of David, 96, 113
Potiphar and his wife, 25
power
    of story tellers, 2–3
    transition of from David to Solomon,
        114–15
priesthood, 46, 225
priests
    began temple service at age thirty,
        177
    consecration of, 37
    described in Micah, 209
    Ezekiel describing the future role of,
        181
    God's requirements for, 39, 46
    insincerity of, 230
    responsibilities of, 57
    on something clean making an
        unclean thing clean, 222
    willing to "teach for a price," 209
Primeval History (Gen 1–11), 15, 16–19
princes
    described in Micah, 208
    Ezekiel describing the future role of,
        181
princes and priests, tolerating or
    encouraging idolatry and
    syncretism, 218–19
private observations, of Solomon, 155
the privileged, described in Micah, 208
problems, faced by Nehemiah, 126
proclamation
    of Israel's unfaithfulness, 193
    sounding in Joshua, 72–73

prologue, to the book of Job, 135–37
"a promiscuous woman," Gomer called, 192
promised land, 48–49, 67
promises
    of God of a Savior, 17
    of God to Abraham, 19–20
    of God to David, 96
    of God to regather the people, 180–81
    Joshua and Caleb believed God's, 45
    of restoration from Ezekiel, 180–82
prophecies
    of Daniel, 187
    of Zechariah, 228
"prophecy," translating as "burden," 227, 229
prophets, 5, 7, 57, 108, 208–9, 227
protectors of justice, responsibilities of, 57
Proverbs, book of, 149–52
proverbs, describing powerful truths, 149–50
providing for others, God wanting us to know the joy of, 59
prudent wife, as a gift from the Lord, 150
Psalm 51, David expressing sorrow over his sin, 98
Psalm 119, extolled the virtues of God's word, 9
psalm types, seven different, 144–47
psalmists, committing their cause to God, 145
Psalms, book of, 141–48
punishment
    of Israel's unfaithfulness, 194
    for Nineveh, 214
purim, literally meaning "lots," 132
purity, 58, 128
purpose, living for a, 152

Qohelet ("the teacher"), in Ecclesiastes, 153
queen of Sheba, visit of, 103–4, 116
question, of Habakkuk, 216

Rachel, death of, 24
Rahab, 66, 68
rainbow, as a sign, 18

rainfall, normal in Israel, 91n4
ram and a he-goat, vision of, 188
reasons, for God's judgment, 199–200
Rebekah, wife of Isaac, 22
Rebekah and Jacob, acting deceitfully, 23
rebellion, 92, 171, 208
rebuke, from God, 139, 170
recollection, of Jeremiah, 175
recommitment, Levites led the people in a time of, 128
reconstruction of the temple, Zechariah's on, 224
"redeemer," as a reference to Jesus, 138
reforming, of Jerusalem, 128–29
regulations, God articulating, 35
Rehoboam (King), 104, 117
relationship
    between Absalom and David, 99
    areas of human, 58–59
    commandments focusing on, 31
    establishing with God, 226
    with God as a theme in Proverbs, 150
    of God with his people, 55
    with Jesus as life itself, 234
    of the people with the covenant, 53–54
    of Samson and the Philistine woman (Delilah), 80–81
religion mandates, 56–57
religious conquests, of David, 114
repentance, 206, 226
rescue of Israel, by God from Egypt, 194
respect, for one's elders, 39
restoration
    Amos pointed ahead to a great day of, 200
    Ezekiel's promises of, 180–82
    by God, 170–71, 197
    promised by Zephaniah, 219
retribution
    Babylon suffering, 225
    Ezekiel's prophecies of, 178–80
    of God, 175
    proclaimed by Zephaniah, 218–19
return to God, Zechariah encouraged the people to, 224
returnees, from exile, 112

revelation
of Haggai to the people, 222–23
of Zechariah from God, 224–26
Revelation, book of, 8, 182
revivals, during Israel's spiritual decline,
76–81
righteous kingdom, coming one day, 165
righteous person, living by faithfulness,
217, 218
rivalry, between Jacob and Esau, 23
roar, of God's judgment, 198–99
Romans, book of, 156
royal psalms, speaking of Israel's king,
145
ruin
of Jerusalem, 174
from the Lord, 196
rulers, 57, 208–9, 210
Ruth, book of, 83–86, 124

Sabbath violations, Nehemiah stopping,
128–29
sabbath year, celebrating a "sabbath rest,"
56
sacrifice, as worship of God, 36–37
sadness, God's people facing, 175
sailors, threw Jonah into the sea, 204
Samaria, as Israel's capital, 207
Samson, 80–81
Samuel
associating stature with competence,
92–93
birth of, 87, 88
caution of, on having a king, 89
confronted Saul disobedience, 91–92
consecration of, 88
crying to the Lord, 88–89
forecasting Saul would die the next
day in battle, 95
heard a voice and asked what Eli
needed, 88
as the last judge, anointed Saul, 87
led the Israelites in a time of
rededication of the Lord, 89
sending rain on Israel's wheat harvest,
91
sons of not following in his ways, 89

stepping aside as Israel's leader, 90
as writer of the book of Judges, 74
1 Samuel, book of, 87–95
1–2 Samuel, books of, 87–100
Sanballat, assault against the work of
Nehemiah, 127
sanctification, as walking with God,
37–41
Sarah, 3, 21
Sarai, 19
Satan, 136–37, 136n3
Saul
as a common threat to David and the
Philistines, 94n5
consulting a medium, 95
crowning of, 90–91
death on Mount Gilboa, 95
disobeying God's command
regarding the Amalekites, 91–92
followed by David, the former
shepherd, 87
jealousy of David, 94
lost his life in battle with the
Philistines, 113
rallied Israel and defeated the
Ammonites, 90
reconfirmation as Israel's king, 90
remained king throughout the end of
the book of 1 Samuel, 92
selection of as wrong, 90n3
Savior, God promised, 17
"Sayings of the Wise," in Proverbs, 149
scapegoat, 38
Scattered Era (605–538 BC), 101, 107–8,
119–20, 174, 177
scattering, of the people to the winds, 178
scoundrels, who lived a long life, 155
scripture, 10, 127
seal of the covenant, circumcision as, 67
Second Coming of Christ, Zechariah
predicting, 228
"second law," word Deuteronomy
meaning, 53
self-righteousness, Elihu charged Job
with, 138
Sennacherib, Assyria's king, 106, 118, 165

sermons
   of Haggai, 221
   of Jeremiah, 172–73
serpent, 16, 17
servant, suffering greatly, 167
servant passages or songs, of Isaiah, 166
Seth, birth of, 17
seven years, cycles of, 40
seventy elders, anointed to help Moses, 44
seventy weeks, Daniel's prophecy about,
   188
sexual area, of human relationships, 58
sexual love in marriage, exalting the joy
   of, 157
sexual relations, of David and Bathsheba,
   98
sexuality, not to be used as an expression
   of worship, 58
Shadrach, 184n3, 185
Shamgar, victory over the Philistines, 77
Sheba, queen of, 103–4, 116
Shechem, 20, 72
Shema, challenging God's people, 54
Shemaiah (prophet), 117
shigionoth, designating a highly
   emotional poem, 217
"Shulamite," meaning of, 157n3
Sidon, judgment of God upon, 180
siege, of Jerusalem, 171–72, 179
signet ring, conveyed the king's authority,
   223
signs and wonders, Joel referring to, 197
Sihon, king of the Amorites, 47
silent four hundred years. *See*
   intertestamental period
Simeon, held hostage by Joseph, 26
Simeon and Levi, led an attack upon
   Shechem, 24
sin
   cycle of, 74–76, 83–84
   God judging, 164
   of Jerusalem, 179
   of Judah, 170–71
   leading to death, 17
   national confession of, 128
   separating us from God, 234
sin offering, 36, 38

Mount Sinai, 42, 44, 54
Sisera, Jabin's general, 77
six days of creation, interpretations of, 16
sleep, loving too much, 151
sling, stone from David's struck Goliath's
   skull, 93
sluggard, 151
social injustice, 200, 208
social justice, Amos focusing on, 198
Sodom and Gomorrah, 20
Solomon
   accommodation of the worship of his
      wives, 104
   asked God for wisdom ("a listening
      heart"), 102
   as author of Ecclesiastes, 153
   as author of Proverbs, 149
   as author of "Song of Songs," 157
   born to Bathsheba and David, 98
   conclusions of, 155–56
   courtship of the Shulamite woman,
      158
   David's charge to, 102
   David's commissioning to build the
      temple, 115
   as the economic man, 103n2
   on his bride as "altogether beautiful,"
      158, 159
   as Israel's third king, 87
   on life's ultimate meaning, 154–55
   love for his Shulamite bride, 157
   reign of, 102–4, 115–16
   warning to, 103
   wealth of, 103–4
   wisdom of, 102
   wives of, 104
   work of, 102–3
Something Era (2090–1445 BC), 135
song, Moses singing, 60
Song of Solomon, 157–60
sons of Korah, psalms credited to, 142
southern campaign, in the conquest of
   Canaan, 69
Southern Kingdom, called Judah, 101, 104
sovereignty, Job presenting lessons on
   God's, 139

speaking against God, Malachi accused the people of, 231
special groups, land for, 71
speeches, Joshua delivered to the people, 72
Spirit of God, showing a harvest of people, 32
spiritual adultery of Israel, 192–93
spiritual condition, Chronicles stressing Judah's, 110
spiritual conquests, of David, 113–14
spiritual decline, 76–81, 83
spiritual defeat, reasons for Israel's, 75–76
spiritual departure, results of Israel's in Judges, 81–83
spiritual harlotry, charge of, 193
spiritual hypocrisy, charge of, 193–94
spiritual maturity, pressing ahead into, 52
spiritual one-upmanship, having no place in God's story, 45
spiritual outpouring, Joel described, 197
spiritual shallowness, of Judah, 165
spiritual victories, of David, 96–97
spirituality, of the people, 165
"stand still" book, Leviticus as, 35
statue of gold, erected by Nebuchadnezzar, 185
stories
    Bible containing, 8–9
    power of, 1–3
strength, of Samson, 80
struggles, of David with Saul, 93–95
suffering
    the Lord sending on Israel, 75
    Satan inflicted upon Job, 135
sukkot, marking the fall harvest, 127n5
summer fruit, God showed Amos a basket of, 200
supplication, of the people crying out to God, 75
synonymous parallelism, 143

tabernacle, 32–34, 56
Tamar (daughter of David), 99
Tamar (Judah's daughter-in-law), 25
Tarshish, Jonah fleeing to, 204
Temanites, descendants of Esau, 135n2

temple
    built on the model of the tabernacle, 103
    dedication of, 123
    dedication of the foundation, 122
    God's glory filled, 116
    Haggai on the future of, 222
    Josiah cleaning up, 118
    laying desolate, 221
    not having the glory of the former temple, 223
    rebuilding of, 181
temptations, leadership bringing, 97
Ten Commandments, 31, 54
tent of meeting, 33
Terah, sons Abram, Nahor, and Haran, 19
Thebes, Nahum compared Nineveh to, 215
thirty pieces of silver, Zechariah's words regarding, 227
Tiglath-Pileser III, reign of in Assyria, 106
Tigris, Daniel's vision of a man standing on the banks of, 188–89
times of plenty and of want, pointing us to God, 55
tithing, 59, 230
Tobiah, assault against the work of Nehemiah, 127
Tola, served God's purpose, 79
Torah ("Instruction"), 13, 15
Tower of Babel, 18–19, 225n4
trade routes, Solomon's control of, 103
tree of the knowledge of good and evil, 16
tribes
    division of the land by, 70, 182
    of Israel, genealogy of, 112
    of Israel turned from the Lord, 74
    of Reuben, Gad, and half tribe of Manasseh, 48, 66, 70
trust, in the Lord, 150
truths, applying to lives, 149
Tyre, 180

ultimate blessing, Joel describing, 197
ultimate peace, to Judah and to the nations, 219
ultimate reign, of Christ, 227–28

unbelieving generation, dying in the
wilderness, 46
uncleanness, corrupting God's house of
worship, 222
unfaithfulness
of Israel, 192–93
pardon of Israel's, 194–95
punishment of Israel's, 194
unhealthy conditions, commands
concerning, 38
uniqueness, of the Bible, 6–9
United Era (1043–931 BC), 87, 90, 101,
102–4, 108–9, 110, 112–15
Uriah, 97, 98
Uz, land of, 135n2
Uzziah/Azariah (king), 117, 163, 198

Vashti (queen), 130
vengeance, 145
victories, 47, 68, 93, 96–97, 113, 203
violence, 202
virtuous woman, 150
vows, guidelines regarding, 40–41

wall, of Jerusalem, 125–27, 128
warning
to all who would serve God faithfully,
92
of Solomon by the Lord, 116
water
during the flood, 17
Moses providing by striking a rock, 46
of the sea parted by God, 30
weaknesses, of Abraham, 20
wealth, of Solomon, 103–4, 116
wealthy, exploiting the poor by charging
interest, 126
wedding, of King Solomon and the
Shulamite woman, 158–59
whale, Jonah and, 204n4
wickedness, 208, 225

widows, security of, 58
wilderness, wandering in, 46, 48
wisdom
in Proverbs, 151
of Solomon, 102, 115, 154
wisdom psalms, 144
wives, of Solomon, 104
woe, Micah's personal feelings of, 211
woman, desire for her husband, 158
woman in a basket, vision of representing
wickedness, 225
women, not to be passed around as
sexual playthings, 58
word of God
Bible as, 8
going forth, 163, 209
on Israel's spiritual crookedness, 199
in Zechariah, 224–26
work, of Solomon, 102–3, 115–16
wrestling match, between Jacob and the
angel, 24

Xerxes, Persia's fourth king, 123n2

"Yahweh is God," as the meaning of Joel's
name, 196
"year of sabbath rest," for the land, 40
yom kippur, day of atonement, 38–39

Zebulun, 112
Zechariah, 122, 223, 228
Zechariah, book of, 223–28
Zedekiah (king), 107, 108, 118, 119,
171–72
Zelophehad's daughters, inheritance of, 49
Zephaniah (prophet), 117, 218
Zephaniah, book of, 218–20
Zerubbabel, 121, 122–23, 221, 222, 223,
225
Zipporah (wife of Moses), 29
Zophar (friend of Job), 137, 139

Scripture Index

OLD TESTAMENT

Genesis   7, 15–27, 28, 201

1	16, 17, 18
1:1	18
1:1—2:4	16
1–2	15, 16
1–11	15, 16–19, 27
1:28	18
2	16, 18
3	16
3–5	15, 16–17
3:6	16
3:15	111
3:16	17, 20
3:22	17
5	17, 19
5:5	17
5:8	17
5:11	17
6	17
6–9	15, 17–18
7	17
7:11	17
8	17
8:15–22	18
9	18
9:1, 7	18
9:7	18
9:11–17	18
9:20–29	18
10	18
10–11	15, 18–19
11	19
11:1–9	18
11:26–30	19
11:32	19
12:1	19
12:1–3	27, 182
12:2–3	111
12:3	19, 20
12:4—14:24	20
12:6–7	20, 72
12–25	19–22
12–50	15, 19–27
13:5–17	20
14:18–20	20
15:4	21
15:5	20
15:6	21
15–24	20
16:16	21

Genesis (*cont.*)

17	67
17:1	21
17:17	21
18:12–15	21
19:36–38	179
19:37–38	219
22:1–2	21
22:8	21
24	22
24:12–19	22
25	23
25:1–11	22
25:12–18	22
25:19–34	22, 23
25:22–23	22
25:23	23
25–26	22
25:30	179
26	22
26:3–4	22
27	23
27:33	23
27–36	23–24
27:41	23
28:2	23
28:10–22	23
28:15	24
28–31	23
29:15–27	23n4
29–30	23
32	23
32:26	24
32:44–55	23
33:1–17	24
33–34	23, 24
34:24–29	24
35	24
35:1	24
35:9–15	24
35–36	23, 24
36	24
36:1	179
36:9–11	135n2
37	24
37:3–4	25
37:35–36	25
37–38	24
37–50	24–27
38	25
39	24, 25
39:21	25
40	24
40:20–23	25
41:37–40	26
41–50	24
41:50–52	70n6
42:1–2	26
42:24	26
43:1–2	26
44:18–34	26
45:4–8	27
49:10	111

Exodus

	15, 28–34
1:5	43
1:8–14	180
1:18	29
1–18	29–30, 28
2:1–10	29
3:2–5	29
3:5	68
3:10	29
5:1	29
5–12	29
7:5	29
7:17	29
8:10, 22	29
8:22	29
9:14–16, 29	29
9:29	29
10:2	29
12	29, 67
12:7, 13	29
12:12–13	44
12:13	29
12:40	180
13–18	30
14	66–67
14:21–31	30
16	67n3
16:13–35	30
17	60

18:13–26	30	15	38
19:1	33	16–17	38–39
19:5–6	30	18	39
19–24	28, 30–32	18–20	39
20	31	19	39
20:1–17	54	19:2	37–41
20:2	31	20	39
20:8–11	129	21–22	39
20–23	31, 54	23	39–40
21–22	32	23:33–43	127n5
23	32	25	40, 56
24	32	25:4	40
24:3	32	25:10–17	40
25:8	32	26	40, 59
25:9	33	26:1–13	40
25–31	33, 36, 56	26:14–39	40
25–40	28, 32–34, 88	26:40–46	40
26:33	33	27	40–41
27:9	33		
28:1	39	**Numbers**	15, 42–52
31	33	1	49
31:1–6	33	1:1	49
32:11–14	33	1–2	43, 48
32–34	33	1–21	42, 43–47
35–39	33	2	49
40	33	2:32	43
40:2	33	3	50
40:34	33	3–4	43
40:36–38	44	3–9	43–44
		4	50
Leviticus	15, 35–41, 53	5	50
1	36	5–9	44
1–7	36–37	5:11–31	44
1–10	36–37	6	50
4	36	6:1–21	44, 80
5:14–19	36	6:22–27	44
8	37	7	44, 50
8–10	37	7:1–89	44
9	37	8	44, 50
10	37	8:5–26	44
11	37, 56	9	50
11–27	36, 37–41	9:15–23	44
12	38	10	50
13	38	10:11–12	50
13–15	38	10–12	44–45
14	38	11	50

Numbers (*cont.*)

11:1–9	44
11:10–14	44
11:16–30	44
12	50
12:1–16	44
13	45, 50, 68n4
13:1–16	45
13–14	45–46, 51, 52, 54, 60, 77
13:26	50
13:30	45, 70
14	50
14:6–9	45, 70
14:10–38	45
14:22–25	50
15	50
15:1	50
15–21	46
15:23	50
16	50, 142
16–17	46
16–19	46
17	50
17:1–11	46
18	50
18–19	46
19	50
20	46, 50
20:12	46
20:22–29	46
20:28	50
21	47, 51, 52
21:4–9	47
21:12	51
21:21–35	47
22	51
22:1	51
22–24	72
22–25	47
22–36	42, 47–49
23	51
24	51
25	51
26	48, 51
27	51
27:18–23	48
27–32	48
28	51
29	51
29–30	48
30	51
31	51
31:1–18	48
31:16	47
32	47, 48, 51, 66, 70
33	48, 51
33:38	50
34	51
34:1–15	49
34:16–29	49
34–36	48–49
35	49, 51, 71
36	49, 51

Deuteronomy — 15, 53–61, 65

1:2	54
1–3	53
1–4	53–54
2:14	51
4	53
4:5–8	54
5	54
5:26	54–59
6:4–9	54
6–11	54–55
7:7–8	55
8	55
9	55, 60
10–11	55
12	56
12–16	56–57
12–26	55–57
13	56
14	56
15	56
16	57
17	57, 90n3
17–21	56, 57
18	57
19–21	57
22–23	58
22–26	56, 58–59

24–25	58	13–22	70–71
26	58–59	14	70
27	59	14:6–14	77
27–28	59	14:7, 10	68n4
28	59	14:10	68n4
29	59	14–19	71
29–30	59–60	15–19	71
30	60	18:1–10	170n2
30:19–20	60	19:47–48	81
31	60	19:49–50	71
31:7–13	60	20	71
31–34	60–61	20:1–9	49
32	60	20–22	71
32:47	4	21	71
33	61	23	72
34	61	23–24	72–73
34:1–6	65	24	72–73
		24:5–7	72
Joshua	61, 65–73, 74	24:8–10	72
1	65–66	24:9–10	72
1:1	65	24:13	73
1–5	65–68	24:13–15	83
1:5	66	24:14–15	73
2	66	24:15	73
2:8–11	66	24:31	73
3–4	66–67		
5	67–68	**Judges**	74–83
5:1–9	67	1	75
5:10–12	67	1:1	74
5:15	68	1–2	75
6	68	1:21	75
6–9	68–69	2	75–76
6–12	68–70	3:7	76
6:23–25	68	3:8	76
7–8	68–69	3:9	76
8:30–35	72	3:12	76
9	69	3:13	76
10	69	3:15	76
11	69–70	3–16	76–81
11:1	77n2	3:31	77
11–12	68	4:1	76
11:23	70	4:2	76
12	70	4:3	76
13	70	4:4–5	77
13–14	70	4–5	77
13–15	67–68	4:6	76

Judges (*cont.*)

4:6–8	77
5	77
6:1	76
6:7	76
6–8	78
6:12	76
6:36–40	78
7	78
8:22–23	78
9	78
9:22	78
10	79
10:1–5	79
10:6	76
10:7	76
10:10	76
11–12	79
11:29	76
12	79
13	80
13:1	76
13:5	76
13–16	80–81
14	80
14–15	80
15:9–20	80
16	80
17	81
17:6	81, 83
17–18	81
17–21	81–83
18	81
19	82
19–20	82
21	82–83
21:25	83

Ruth

	83–86, 124
1	84–85
1:1	84
1:16–17	85
2:3	85
2:20	85
3	85–86

3:11	86
4	86
4:17	86

1 Samuel

	87–95, 113
1–2	88
1:3—3:21	170n2
1–8	87–89
3	88
3:10	88
4–7	88–89
6	89
7:12	89
8	87–89
8:5	89
9	87
9–10	90
9–15	90–92
10:1	90
10:25	87
11–12	90–91
12:23	91
13	91
13:3–5	179
13–15	91–92
14:1–23	179
14:47–52	91
15	91
15:22–23	92
16	92–93
16—2 Samuel 24	92–99
17	93
17:1–52	179
18–23	94
18–27	93–95
24	94
25:1	87
26	94
27	94–95
28	95
28–31	95
29	95
29–30	95
31	95
31:1–10	179

2 Samuel

1–4	96, 113
1–5	96
1–10	96–97
3:2–5	99n7
5	96
6	96
6–7	96–97
7	96, 100, 102, 105, 113
7:4–7	103
7:12–13	112
8–10	97
11	97–98
11–12	97–98
11:27	98
12	98, 102, 143
12:10	98
13	99
13–14	99
13–24	98–99
15–18	143
15–19	99
19:41–43	99
20–24	99
24:18	114n3

1 Kings | 87, 110

1–2	92, 102, 114
1–11	101, 102–4
3	102, 104
3–11	102–4
3:16–28	102
4–8	102–3
4:29–34	103
6–7	103
9	102, 103
10	102, 103–4, 116
10:21	104
11	102, 104
11:1–3	160n4
11:41	101
12	104
12—2 Kings 23	101, 104–8
16–22	105
96–99	
16:33	105
17:1	106
18:19–40	106
21:25–26	105

2 Kings | 110

8:1	194
8:14	194
9	105
10:14–15	194
17	106
17:7	106
17:7–41	106, 194
18–20	106
22–23	107
24:1–6	171
24:1–7	108
24:8–16	108
24:10–17	177
24:17—25:17	108
24–25	101, 107
25	173
25:1–21	177
25:8, 25	226n5
25:25	226n5
25:27–30	108

1 Chronicles | 111–15

1:1–4	111
1–3	111–12
1–9	111–12
1:24–27	111
1:34	111
2:1	111
2:3–5	111
2:9–15	111
3:1–5	112
3:10–19	112
4–8	111, 112
9	112
10	113
10—2 Chronicles 9	112–15
11–12	113
11–22	113–14

1 Chronicles (*cont.*)

11–29	113–15
13–17	113
16:4–5	142
17	113
18–20	114
21–22	114
21:26	114
22	114
23–26	115
23–29	114–15
27	115
28	115
29:29	87

2 Chronicles — 111, 115–20

1	115
1:3–6	102
1–9	115–16
2:1—7:10	115–16
7:1	103
7:1–2	116
7:11–22	116
8:3	107
8–9	116
9	116
10–12	117
10–35	116–19
13	117
14–16	117
15:9	112n2, 195
17–20	117, 118
21	117
22	117
22–23	117
23–24	117
25	117
26	117
27	117
28	117
29–32	117, 118
30:1–11	195
30:1–22	112n2
33	117
34–35	117, 118–19
36	117, 118

36:5–21	119
36:22	119
36:22–23	119–20, 166

Ezra — 121–24

1:1	166
1–2	122
1–6	122–23
2	125n3
2:64–65	119
3	122
3–6	122–23
4–5	122
5:1–2	223
6	123, 129, 132
6:15	123, 223–24
7	129, 132
7:1	123
7–8	123
7–10	123
7:10	123, 125
8	123
9	124
9:1	124
9–10	124
10	124

Nehemiah — 125–29

1–2	125–26
1–7	125–27
3	126
3–5	126
4–5	126
6–7	127
6:15	127
7	125n3
8:1–12	127
8:8	127n4
8:10	127
8–10	127–28
8:13–18	127
9–10	128
11	128
11–13	128–29
12	128
13	128–29

Esther	123n2, 129–32
1	130
1–2	130
2	130
3	130–31
3–8	130–32
4	131
4:14	131
5–8	131
9:1–19	132
9–10	132
9:20—10:3	132

Job	135–40
1:1	135n2
1:1–5	136
1–3	135–37
1:6—2:10	136–37
1:6–22	136
2:1–10	136–37
2:11–13	137
3	137
3:1	137
4:1—42:6	137–39
4–37	137–38
15–21	137
19:25–26	138
23–31	138
32–37	138
38	138
38:1—40:5	138
38:1—42:6	138–39
38:3	138
39	138
40:4	138
40:6—42:6	139
40:8	139
42:7–9	139
42:7–17	139
42:10–17	139

Psalms	141–48, 149
1	144
1:2	142, 148
1:3	148
1:6	142

2	145, 146
2:7	146
3	143, 144
4–9, 16, 74	143
8	144
14	144
16	143, 146
16:8–11	146
22	144, 146
22:1	146, 147
22:7–8	147
22:12–13	146
22:14–18	147
22:16–17	146
22:18	146
35:4–6	145
45	147
45:6–7	147
51	98, 143, 144
51:10–13	98
73	144
74	143
90	142
93	145
97	145
99	145
100	144
110	147
110:1	147
110:4	147
119	9
136	144
137:8–9	145
150	144

Proverbs	149–52
1:1—22:16	149
1:7	150, 151
1:8	151
2:1–5	151
2:6	150, 151
3:5–6	150
3:11–12	152
3:34	152
6:9–10	151
7:4–5	151

Proverbs (*cont.*)

7:6–27	151
8	151
9:10	150, 151
10:1	151
11:31	152
15:21	151
18:22	150
19:14	150
22:6	150
22:13	151
22:17—24:34	149
24:30–34	151
25:21–22	152
25–29	149
30	149
31	149
31:10–31	150

Ecclesiastes — 153–56

1:1–11	153
1:2–3	153
1:12—2:26	154–55
1:12—12:8	154–55
1:12–14	154
1:12–18	154
1:17	154
2:1–11	154
2:11	154
2:12–17	154–55
2:17	155
2:18–26	155
2:26	155
3:1—12:8	155
3:10	155n3
3:16	155n3
3:22	155n3
4:1	155n3
4:4	155n3
4:7	155n3
4:15	155n3
6:1	155n3
7:15	155n3
8:9	155n3
8:10	155n3
8:17	155n3

9:11	155n3
9:13	155n3
10:5	155n3
10:7	155n3
12:8	155
12:9–12	156
12:9–14	155–56
12:13	156
12:13–14	156
12:14	156

Song of Solomon — 157–60

1:1—3:5	158
1:1–4	158
1:5—2:17	158
1:5–15	158
1:16—2:17	158
3:1	158
3:1–5	158
3:6—5:1	158–59
3:6–7	158
3:6–11	158
4:1—5:1	158–59
4:7	159
5:2—6:3	159
5:2—7:8	159
5:2—8:14	159
5:10	159
6:4—7:8	159
6:5	159
7:9—8:14	159
7:11–13	159
8:6–7	159

Isaiah — 163–68

1–12	163–64
1–35	166
2:1–4	163, 209n7
4:2–6	163
9:6–7	164
11:1–10	164
13–23	164, 172n3
24	164
24–27	164–65
25:6–8	164
26:19–20	164

27:1	165	26:4–6	170
27:12–13	165	28:1–4	170
28:9–13	165	28:4–6	170
28–33	165	29	188n9
29:11–14	165	29:10	170
30–31	165	29:10–14	169
32	165	29:11	170
33	165	30–33	170–71
34	165	31:31–34	170, 173
34–35	165	33:15–17	173
35	165	34:8–11	171
36	165	34–35	171
36–39	165–66	34–44	171–72
37	165	36:1–18	171
38	165	36:21–26	171
38–39	165	37–38	171
39	165	37–39	171–72
40–66	166–68, 166n5	38:17–20	172
42:1–4	166	39	172, 173
49:1–6	166–67	40–44	172
49:3	166	41:1–3	172
50:4–11	166, 167	42:1–6	172
52:13—53:12	166, 167, 167n6	42:7–12	172
53:2	167	43:1–4	172
53:4–6	167	43:6	172
53:7–9	167	44:15–19	172
53:10	167	45–51	172–73
53:11–12	167	46:13–24	172
61:1–3	166, 167–68	47:1–4	172
65:17–25	168	48:1–7	172
65–66	168	49:1–39	172
66:19–20	168	50–51	173
		52	173
Jeremiah	169–73	52:31–34	173
1	169		
1:4–5	169	**Lamentations**	119n4, 174–76
1:6–10, 17–21	169	1	174
1:17–21	169	1:1–11	174
2–24	170	1:3	174
2–33	170–71	1:7	174
7:3–7	170	1:9	174
11:18–23	170	1:12–22	174
23:5–6	173	2	174, 175
25	188n9	3	175
25:11–12	112, 170	3:1	175
25–29	170	3:1–3	174n7

Lamentations (*cont.*)

3:4–6	174n7
3:21–22	175
3:21–23	175, 176
4	174, 175
4:6	175
4:13–15	175
4:22	135n2
5	174, 175–76
5:1	175
5:21	176
5:22	176

Ezekiel

Ezekiel	177–82
1:1	177
1:1–3	177
1–3	177–78
1:4—2:10	177
1:5–10	182n4
1:13	182n4
1:28	178
2:1–10	178
3	178
3:11	178
3:17–21	178
4–7	178
4–24	178–79
4–32	178–80
5:2, 10, 12	178
5:10	178
5:12	178
6	178
6:7	178n2
6:8	178
7	178
7:4	178n2
7:9	178n2
7:27	178n2
8–19	178
9:6	178
10:10	178n2
10:13	178n2
10:14	178n2
20:4	179
20–23	179
22:2	179
23	179
23:36	179
24	179
24:2	179
25	179
25–32	172n3, 179–80
26–28	180
29–32	180
33	180
33:21	180
33–39	180–81
33–48	180–82
34:12–16	180
36:9–11	180
36:19–28	180
37:11–14	180
37:24–25	182
39:17–20	182n4
39:23–29	180
40:1	181
40–43	181
40–46	181
40–48	182
44	181
45–46	181
47:1–12	181
47:13–23	181
47:22–23	181
47–48	181–82
48:1–9	182
48:10–20	182
48:21–22	182
48:23–29	182
48:30–35	182, 182n4
48:35	182

Daniel

Daniel	183–90
1	184
1:1–2	108, 177
1–6	183–87
1:7	184n3
2	184–85
2:4–11	184
2:38	185
3	184n3, 185n4
3:1—4:3	185

4	185
4:4–47	185
5	186
5:7	186n5
5:30–31	173
6	186–87
6:7–9	131n7
6:12	131n7
6:15	131n7
7	187–88
7:9–14	190, 190n15
7–12	183, 187–89
8	188
9	188
10:4–21	188
10:5–6	189n11
10–12	183n2, 188–89
11–12	189, 189n12
11:36	189n14
11:40	189n14
12:1	189n14
12:1–3	189

Hosea — 191–95

1:1	192
1:2	192
1–2	192–93
1:2–9	192
1–3	192–93
1:10—2:23	192–93
2:1–6	192
2:8	192
2:14	193
2:14–23	192
3	193
4:1	193
4–5	193
4–7	193–94
4:10	193
4:11	193
4:12	193
4:13	193
4:14	193
4:15	193
4:18	193
5:3, 4	193

5:4	193
6:1	193
6–7	193–94
7:10	194
7:14	194
8–10	194
8:13	194
9:9	194
11:8	194
11–14	194–95
13:4–6	195
14	195
14:1–4	195
14:8–9	195

Joel — 195–98

1:1—2:11	196
1:1–7	196
1:8—2:11	196
1:14	196
1:15	196
2:12	196
2:12–17	196
2:15–17	196
2:18—3:21	196–97
2:18–27	196, 197
2:25	197
2:27	197
2:28—3:21	197
2:28–32	197
3	197

Amos — 198–200

1:1	198
1–2	172n3
1:2	198
1–2	198–99
2:6–16	199
3	199
3:2	199
3–6	199
3–9	199–200
4	199
4:6	199
4:8–11	199
5:4	199

Amos (*cont.*)

5–6	199
5:6	199
5:14	199
7:1–3	199
7:1—9:10	199–200
7:4–6	199
7:7–9	199
8:1–3	200
9:1–10	200
9:11–15	200

Obadiah

	201–3
1:1	202
1:3	202
1:4	202
1–9	202
1–16	201–2
10:10	202
10:11	202
10:15–16	202
10–16	202
17:17	202
17:18–20	202
17–20	202
17–21	202–3
21	203

Jonah

	203–7
1	203–4
1:1–2	203
1:3	204
1:4–17	204
2	204
2:1–9	204
2:10	204
3	205
3:1–4	205
3:5	205
3:5–10	205
4	205–6
4:1	205
4:2	205–6
4:3	206
4:4–11	206
4:11	206

Micah

	207–12
1	208
1:1	207
1–3	208–9
1:5	208
2	208
2:1–2	208
2–3	208
3:1–2	208
3:1–4	208
3:5	208
3:5–10	208–9
3:11	209
3:11–12	207, 209
4:1–3	209n7
4:1–8	209
4–5	209
4:9–13	209
4:10	209
5	210, 211
5:4	210
6:1–9	210
6–7	210–11
6:8	210
6:10—7:6	211
7:1–6	211
7:7	211
7:7–20	211
7:14	211
7:15	211
7:18	211
7:19–20	211

Nahum

	213–15
1	213–14
1:1–14	214
1:2	214
1:8–9	214
1:14	214
1:15	214
2	214
2:13	214
3	214–15
3:1	214
3:1–7	214–15
3:7	215
3:8–19	215

3:19	215
Habakkuk	215–18
1:1–4	216
1:1–11	216
1:2	216
1:5	216
1:5–11	216
1:12—2:1	216
1:12—2:20	216–17
1:13	216
2:2–20	217
2:4	217, 218
3	217
3:1	217
3:1–2	217
3:1–19	217–18
3:3–15	217
3:17–19	217
3:19	217
Zephaniah	218–20
1:1	218
1–2	172n3, 218–19
1:2—2:3	218–19
1:12	219
1:14–18	219
2:3	219
2:4–15	219
2:13–15	219
3	219
3:1–7	219
3:8	219
3:8–20	219
3:9	219
3:9–20	220
3:14–16	219
3:17	219
Haggai	221–23, 225
1:1, 12, 14	225n3
1:1–15	221–22
1:12	225n3
1:12–15	222
1:14	225n3
2:1–5	222

2:1–9	222
2:2	225n3
2:4	225n3
2:6–9	222
2:10–14	222
2:10–19	222–23
2:15–17	222
2:15–19	222–23
2:18–19	223
2:20–23	223
Zechariah	223–28
1:1–6	224
1:7—6:15	224–26
1:7–17	224
1–8	224–26
1:16	224
1:18–29	224
2	224
3	225
3:1–10	225n3
4	225
4:6	225
4:9	225
5:1–4	225
5:5–11	225
6	225
6:9–15	225, 225n3
7:1–7	226
7–8	226
7:8–14	226
7:12–14	226
8:1–17	226
8:7–8	226
8:18–23	226
8:22–23	226
9	228
9:1	227
9:9	227
9–11	227
9–14	227–28, 229n9
11:12–13	227
12:10–14	227
12–14	227–28
13:7	228
14	228
14:9	228

Malachi   189, 228–32

1:1	229
1:2—3:15	229
1:2–5	229
1:6—2:13	229–30
1:6–14	229
2:1–13	230
2:14–16	230
2:17	230
2:17—3:7	230
3:1–2	230
3:3–7	230
3:8–12	230
3:13–18	231
4	231
4:1–3	231
4:4	231
4:5	229n8
4:5–6	231

NEW TESTAMENT

Matthew   7, 189

1	111, 163n2
1:3	25
1:5	68, 86
1:22–23	163
2	212
2:4–6	210
5:33–37	41
5:44	145
12:18–21	166
12:39–41	206
17:10–12	231
17:35	147
21:2–5	227
22:41–45	147
26:15	227
26:31	228
27:3–5	227
27:41–43	147
27:45	197
27:46	147
28:18–20	168, 220

Mark   7

Luke   7

1:17, 59–60	229n8, 231
1:32–33	97
1:59–60	229n8, 231
2:22–24	38
4:16–30	168
22:19–20	32
22:20	171, 173

John   7

2:14–15	47
2:19	223
3:14–15	52
7:37–38	32
17:3	150, 234
19:37	227

Acts   7, 233

2	197
2:25–32	146
2:37	233
2:41	32
13:32–33	146
13:36	71
13:47	166
15	200

Romans   156

1:17	217
3:23	195
4:3, 16–22	21
4:5	195
4:16–22	21
8:29	140
11:15, 30–32	227
11:30–32	227
12:18–19	145
12:20	152

1 Corinthians

5:7	30
7	124
10:31	56
12:31	44
15:9–10	55

Scripture Index

2 Corinthians

5:17	234

Galatians

3:8	20

Ephesians

5:21–33	160

Philippians
191

Colossians
191

Hebrews

1:8–9	147
3:12–19	45
5:11—6:2	52
6:1–2	45
6:20	147
7:1–3	147, 226
7–10	125
7:25	39
8:8–12	171
9:11–12	226
9:14	39

11:4	154n2
12:5–6	152

James

4:6	152

1 Peter

2:9	30, 46
4:18	152
5:5	152

2 Peter

1:3	11

Revelation
8, 164

1:13–16	189n11
4:5	182n4
4–5	190n15
4:6–7	182n4
7:9–17	220
12:9	165n3
19:17–18	182n4
20:2	165n3
21:12–13	182n4

CPSIA information can be obtained
at www.ICGtesting.com
Printed in the USA
BVHW060729090222
628125BV00007B/9

9 781666 702453